Praise for Previous Edition

"It provides an excellent overview of bullying research in general, paying proper attention to research from around the world, and a good overview of the cyberbullying research, much of which the authors have been directly involved in conducting."

Research Papers in Education

"*Cyber Bullying* provides the most current and essential information on the nature and prevalence of this epidemic, providing educators, parents, psychologists and policy-makers with critical prevention techniques and strategies for effectively addressing electronic bullying."

The Parent Report

"Champions and critics of the [cyberbullying] laws agree that preventive education is a more powerful deterrent to cyberbullying than discipline. That notion is supported by Patricia Agatston, co-author of *Cyber Bullying: Bullying in the Digital Age* and a counselor at Cobb County School District's Prevention-Intervention Center in Georgia."

Washington Post

"A must-read for anyone who has access to technology, and it is particularly relevant for any parent and educator who works with youth. *Cyber Bullying* provides eye-opening and helpful suggestions for helping parents and educators monitor and track students' use of technology. Provides a very useful roadmap for educators and parents about this phenomenon."

PsycCritiques

"A very helpful guide to the cyber world for parents, teachers, school counselors and parent educators."

NASAP Family Newsletter

"Much needed addition ... Mandatory reading for parents of adolescents and school personnel, administrators and teachers ... Now is the time to read this book."

Metapsychology

"A useful introduction to the growing problem of electronic harassment among children. The chapters providing advice to parents and educators are quite helpful."

American Journal of Psychology

"This book provides an eloquent mix of research theories and findings, together with actual experiences, in the important area of cyberbullying. It is especially strong in well-developed and comprehensive chapters about what parents and educators can do, to reduce both the likelihood of cyberbullying happening, and its negative consequences."

Peter K. Smith, Goldsmiths,
University of London

About the Authors

Robin M. Kowalski, Ph.D., is Professor of Psychology at Clemson University. She is the author or coauthor of several books including *Complaining, Teasing, and Other Annoying Behaviors* (2003), *Social Anxiety* (1997), *Aversive Interpersonal Behaviors (1997)*, *Behaving Badly* (2001), and *The Social Psychology of Emotional and Behavioral Problems* (2000).

Susan P. Limber, Ph.D., is the Dan Olweus Professor at the Institute on Family and Neighborhood Life and Professor of Psychology at Clemson University. She has published numerous articles on the topic of bullying. In 2004 she received the American Psychological Association's Early Career Award for Psychology in the Public Interest.

Patricia W. Agatston, Ph.D., is a Licensed Professional Counselor and Prevention Specialist with the Cobb County School District's Prevention/ Intervention Center in Marietta, Georgia. She was a participant in the CDC's Expert Panel on Electronic Media and Youth Violence, and has presented nationally and internationally on cyberbullying.

CYBERBULLYING
BULLYING IN THE DIGITAL AGE

SECOND EDITION

ROBIN M. KOWALSKI PH.D.
SUSAN P. LIMBER PH.D.
PATRICIA W. AGATSTON PH.D.

A John Wiley & Sons, Ltd., Publication

This second edition first published 2012
© 2012 Robin M. Kowalski, Susan P. Limber, Patricia W. Agatston

Edition History: Blackwell Publishing Ltd (1e, 2008)

Blackwell Publishing was acquired by John Wiley & Sons in February 2007. Blackwell's publishing program has been merged with Wiley's global Scientific, Technical, and Medical business to form Wiley-Blackwell.

Registered Office
John Wiley & Sons Ltd, The Atrium, Southern Gate, Chichester, West Sussex, PO19 8SQ, UK

Editorial Offices
350 Main Street, Malden, MA 02148-5020, USA
9600 Garsington Road, Oxford, OX4 2DQ, UK
The Atrium, Southern Gate, Chichester, West Sussex, PO19 8SQ, UK

For details of our global editorial offices, for customer services, and for information about how to apply for permission to reuse the copyright material in this book please see our website at www.wiley.com/wiley-blackwell.

The right of Robin M. Kowalski, Susan P. Limber, and Patricia W. Agatston to be identified as the authors of this has been asserted in accordance with the UK Copyright, Designs and Patents Act 1988.

Library of Congress Cataloging-in-Publication Data

Kowalski, Robin M.
Cyberbullying : bullying in the digital age / Robin M. Kowalski, Susan P. Limber, Patricia W. Agatston. – 2nd ed.
    p.   cm.
  Includes bibliographical references and index.
  ISBN 978-1-4443-3480-7 (hardback) – ISBN 978-1-4443-3481-4 (paperback)
 1. Cyberbullying. 2. Bullying. I. Limber, Sue. II. Agatston, Patricia W. III. Title.
 HV6773.K69 2012
 302.34'3–dc23
                                                      2011046026

A catalogue record for this book is available from the British Library.

Set in 10.5/13pt Minion by SPi Publisher Services, Pondicherry, India
Printed in Singapore by Ho Printing Singapore Pte Ltd

1   2012

CONTENTS

FOREWORD

October 7, 2003, will always be the day that divides my life. Before that day, my son Ryan was alive. A sweet, gentle, and lanky 13-year-old fumbling his way through early adolescence and trying to establish his place in the often confusing and difficult social world of middle school. After that day, my son would be gone forever. A death by suicide. Some would call it bullycide or even cyberbullycide. I just call it a huge hole in my heart that will never heal.

Ryan's young teen life included swimming, camping, skateboarding, biking, snowboarding, playing computer games and instant messaging. A typical array of "healthy" and "normal" teen activities ... or so it seemed. My son loved being online, staying connected with his friends after the school day and throughout the summer. But, during the summer of 2003, significantly more time was spent online, mainly instant messaging. I was concerned and felt compelled to remind him of our internet safety rules.

No IMing/chatting with strangers
No giving any personal information (name/address/phone) to strangers
No sending pictures to strangers
No secret passwords

Our last rule was a safety one. I told my two older children that they had to use the password I gave them for any accounts they signed up. I promised I would not read personal messages or spy on them but, "God forbid you don't follow the first few rules and you just disappear one day. I will want instant access to all of your activities online." Never in a million years did I imagine this rule would someday end up becoming the key to unlocking the mystery of why my son took his own life.

A few days after his funeral, I logged on to his AOL IM account because that was the one place he spent most of his time during the last few months.

I logged on to see if there were any clues to his final action. It was in that safe world of being somewhat anonymous that several of his classmates told me of the bullying and cyberbullying that took place during the months leading up to his suicide. One boy had bullied Ryan since 5th grade, and briefly befriended him after Ryan stood up to him in an after school brawl. My son the comedian shared an embarrassing and humorous moment with his new friend. The "friend" twisted this information into a rumor that Ryan had something done to him and, therefore, Ryan must be gay. The rumor and taunting continued beyond that school day … well into the night and throughout the summer of 2003. My son approached a pretty, "popular" girl from his school online and worked on establishing a relationship with her, I'm sure as a surefire way to squash the "gay" rumor.

When the 8th grade school year started up again, Ryan approached his new girlfriend in person. I'm sure he was never prepared to handle what happened next. In front of her friends, she told him he was just a loser and that she did not want anything to do with him. She said she had been only joking online. He found out that she and her friends thought it would be funny to make him think she liked him and to get him to say a lot of personal, embarrassing things. She copied and pasted their private IM exchanges into ones with her friends. They all had a good laugh at Ryan's expense.

Now certainly my son was not the first boy in history to be bullied and have his heart crushed by a pretty girl's rejection. But when I discovered a folder filled with IM exchanges and further interviewed his classmates, I realized that technology was being utilized as a weapon far more effective and far reaching than the simple tools we had as kids.

It's one thing to be bullied and humiliated in front of a few kids. It's one thing to feel rejection and have your heart crushed by a girl. But it must be a totally different experience, compared to a generation ago, to have these hurts and humiliation witnessed by a far larger, online adolescent audience. I believe my son would have survived these incidents of bullying and humiliation if they had taken place before the advent of computers and the internet. But I believe there are few of us who would have had the resiliency and stamina to sustain such a nuclear level attack on our feelings and reputation as a young teen in the midst of rapid physical and emotional changes and raging hormones. I believe bullying through technology has the effect of accelerating and amplifying the hurt to levels that will probably result in a rise in teen suicide rates. Recent statistics indicate that, indeed, teen suicide is on the rise again after many years of declining rates.

My son was an early casualty and his death an early warning to our society that we'd better pay close attention to how our children use technology. We need to study this new societal problem with a sense of urgency and great diligence. We must also be swift and deliberate in our law-making and social policy development when it comes to protecting our youth from the misuse of technology against them and amongst them.

This book will prove to be an invaluable resource. It will level set the reader about what bullying is and its harmful effects. Then it will explore the increasing ways technology is utilized to extend bullying behavior well into cyberspace. It brings us up to speed on the latest research findings and maps out very concrete preventative and responsive actions for both parents and educators.

John Halligan, Ryan's Dad
www.RyanPatrickHalligan.org

PREFACE

We originally decided to write about cyberbullying after working together on various bullying prevention efforts and collaborating on research on cyberbullying. One day we came face to face with an extreme example of cyberbullying that occurred in a suburban school district. Patti Agatston can still remember calling Sue Limber and saying, "You need to look at this Web site targeting a student. The mother has asked me to help her find out who did it and get it removed, and I cannot believe what I am seeing!" From that initial conversation, we began carving out the steps necessary to intervene in an actual severe cyberbullying episode, with much help from the Center for Safe and Responsible Internet Use's online documents authored by Nancy Willard. After that trial-by-fire experience, we met and discussed how useful it would be to personally interview students and parents, via focus groups and individual interviews, to better understand their experiences and perspectives. We noted that the paper and pencil surveys were insufficient to capture the emotional impact of this new form of bullying on parents and children. A broader idea emerged: writing a book describing our findings that would include actual interviews from students and parents. The first edition of this book appeared in 2008. In just the few years since that time, the percentage of teens involved with technology has continued to increase, and the venues by which children (and adults) can engage in cyberbullying have also expanded. For example, sexting has become a mode of cyberbullying others that carries with it a host of legal complications for those involved.

One purpose of this book is to educate parents, educators, and community organizations about the growing problem of cyberbullying. But another is to empower the adults in the community to prevent this new form of bullying from becoming a regular experience for youth navigating the internet and other technological tools. Many adults and educators have found themselves in our position, learning about cyberbullying at the moment when intervention is necessary. We hope that this book will help adults gain the knowledge and tools necessary to be true resources to young people in preventing and addressing cyberbullying episodes, rather than being viewed as hindrances, which unfortunately is frequently a perception of young people, as we will discuss.

Robin Kowalski and Sue Limber, psychologists and faculty members at Clemson University in South Carolina, have been researching cyberbullying through a variety of methods for several years, and some of their innovative research is published in this book, including new research focusing on cyberbullying among children with ADHD and/or Asperger Syndrome. In addition, Patti Agatston, a psychologist and counselor, collaborated with Robin and Sue to develop individual and group questionnaires to use while interviewing parents and students regarding cyberbullying. Patti teamed up with her colleague Michael Carpenter to conduct focus groups during the spring and fall of 2006. Michael Carpenter was one of the first nationally certified trainers for the Olweus Bullying Prevention Program and one of the founders of the Prevention/Intervention Center, the Cobb County Georgia School District's nationally recognized student assistance program, where Patti Agatston also works. Patti conducted the female focus groups on cyberbullying, while Michael led the male focus groups. In addition, Patti conducted a variety of individual interviews with parents and students from various middle and high schools in the district who were willing to be interviewed regarding their experiences with cyberbullying. The reader will have an opportunity to hear first hand from some of the parents and students who were interviewed for this book.

We will share some suggestions and recommendations as a result of the research and interviews that we and others have conducted. We hope that the reader will find it more meaningful to know that these recommendations are being made based on research that has involved parents and youth in actual dialogue, in addition to survey methods. We also realize that new technologies with new potentials for bullying will emerge that require continued dialogue with parents and youth to understand the experiences they are having. The challenge is to incorporate these new technologies in a way that enhances rather than detracts from our daily life.

There are many people who contributed to the writing of this book, and the conducting of the research, to whom we offer our heartfelt gratitude. First, we want to thank a number of principals of the Cobb County School District who made it possible to conduct focus groups and individual interviews, including Linda Clark, William D. Griggers, Susan Gunderman, Denise Magee, Janet Peeler, Geraldine Ray, Ivia Redmond, Grant Rivera, and James Snell. Special thanks are given to the following school counselors for going above and beyond the call of duty to facilitate our work: Yvonne Young, Colleen Brown, and Susan Strickland, as well as health teacher Eric Homansky. Thanks also go to the staff of the Prevention/Intervention Center – Jeff Inman, Jeff Dess, Luisa Resendiz, Joyce Hutchings, Janice Mosher, and Michael Carpenter – who provided encouragement, support, and a place to lock up sensitive data. Weijun Wang and Natura Agani at Clemson University provided invaluable assistance with research on cyber-bullying policies. Many students at Clemson University invested considerable time and energy collecting, inputting, and analyzing data: Lindsey Sporrer, Erin Hunter, Richard Reams, Karissa Chorbajian, Kristy Kelso, Natalie Irby, Angela Gorney, Amy Scheck, Ryan Cook, Melissa Redfearn, Jessica Allen, Kelly Simpson, Ann-Mac Calloway, Melinda Keith, Stephanie Kerr, Laura Singer, Jana Spearman, Lance Tripp, Jessica Farris, Kelly Finnegan, Laura Vernon, Rebecca Fulmer, Alison Richman, Liz Johnson, Stephanie Freeman, Sarah Louderback, Micah Lattanner, and Gary Giumetti. We are grateful for their help.

We would also like to thank Nicole Benevenia at Wiley-Blackwell for her support of this project and for her encouragement throughout the process. We are indebted to her and the staff at Wiley-Blackwell for their support.

Thanks to the many work colleagues, friends, and relatives who supported us by offering encouragement, suggestions, and by reading and responding to our work, including Andrew Agatston, Robert Agatston, Teresa Hubbard, Rachel Galli, Frank and Kathy Walton, and Randolph and Frances Kowalski.

Finally, we thank our children, Austin, Jack, Mary, Noah, and Jordan, who inspire us to believe that all children have the right to feel safe from bullying, in both the real and the virtual worlds.

1

INTRODUCTION

What makes cyber bullying so dangerous ... is that anyone can practice it without having to confront the victim. You don't have to be strong or fast, simply equipped with a cell phone or computer and a willingness to terrorize.

(King, 2006)

Bullying creates memories that often last a lifetime. Simply hearing the name of a person who bullied them, even years or decades after the bullying occurred, may be enough to send chills up the backs of many people. When most adults think of bullying, they conjure up the image of a big thug who terrorized kids on the playground at school. Usually a male, he was someone to be feared. As horrible as encounters with this bully[1] may have been, though, the end of the school day often brought a reprieve as the victim left school and went home.

Cyberbullying, however, is a bit different. In spite of recent media attention devoted to the topic, many people are still not familiar with the term. But, for those who are and who have experienced it, the memories, like those of traditional bullying, may also last a lifetime. Cyberbullying, also known as electronic bullying or online social cruelty, is defined as bullying through e-mail, instant messaging (IM), in a chat room, on a Web site, on an online gaming site, or through digital messages or images sent to a cellular phone. Although sharing certain features in common with traditional bullying (see Chapter 3 for a more detailed discussion of this), cyberbullying represents a somewhat unique phenomenon that has been receiving

Cyberbullying: Bullying in the Digital Age, Second Edition. Robin M. Kowalski, Susan P. Limber, and Patricia W. Agatston.
© 2012 Robin M. Kowalski, Susan P. Limber, and Patricia W. Agatston.
Published 2012 by Blackwell Publishing Ltd.

increasing attention in recent years in both the popular press and in academic circles. Cyberbullying not only looks and feels a bit different than traditional bullying, but, as will be discussed later in this book, it presents some unique challenges in dealing with it, especially for parents, educators, and other adults who interact with children. In discussing the relationship between traditional bullying and cyberbullying, a reporter for MSNBC stated: "Kids can be cruel. And kids with technology can be cruel on a world-wide scale" (Sullivan, 2006). As is clear from its definition, cyberbullying is a method of bullying made possible because of technological advances over the past 15–20 years. Two of the most notable of these advances are the Internet and the cellular phone.

One of the interesting questions that is often raised in connection with the Internet is: To what degree has it changed the lives of the adolescents who are using it? We believe that this is really the wrong question. Although the Internet may have changed the lives of the parents of these adolescents, for the adolescents themselves the existence of the Internet is all they have ever known. It simply *is* part of their life. The fact that parents of many of these children did not grow up with cellular phones and in-room computers, whereas these technologies are prevalent in the lives of the adolescents, accounts, in part, for the gap between parents and children in understanding both the uses and risks of the Internet (Kowalski & Fedina, 2011).

Parents, at least initially, tend to view the Internet as a helpful tool to aid their children with homework. Similarly, in parents' eyes, cellular phones are a means for kids to call home in emergencies. Children and youth, on the other hand, perceive the Internet, cellular phones, and related technologies as critical tools for their social life. For most parents, this technology is relatively new and somewhat foreign and, therefore, something about which their children need to be cautious. For children and youth, on the other hand, these communication technologies have always existed, so they have a comfort level with technology that is foreign to many of their parents. Many parents candidly admit that their children are the ones who have taught them most of what they know about the Internet and related technologies. For example, in a focus group interview about cyberbullying, one teenager stated that she had taught her father how to access her brother's computer search history. In another study (Kowalski & Fedina, 2011), just over 27% of the parents perceived that their technology skills were equal to or worse than those of their children.

Importantly, though, what children are doing today isn't all that different from what their parents did when they were growing up – it is just that the vehicle through which they are doing it differs. For example, Lindsay Notwell referred to text messaging as "the note-passing of the new millennium … the Game Boy of wireless communications, for people who think with their thumbs" (Carpenter, 2003). Researchers with the Media Awareness Network (Wing, 2005), in discussing the extent to which the Internet affords adolescents the opportunity to try on new roles and identities, pointed out that kids have been playing "dress up" for centuries. The technological mediums used today, however, present some unique challenges that didn't confront children two or three decades ago. Traditionally, notes were passed between two individuals, often in class, and hidden from the view of the teacher and most other students in the class. Today, "notes" are passed via instant messaging and e-mail for a much wider audience to see. Hand-held electronic devices, such as Game Boys, that might, only a few years ago, have been played while a child watched television in the living room have been replaced by X-Box Live that is played with multiple other people on a computer that most likely resides in the child's room.

For better or for worse, technology is here to stay, and it is a staple in the lives of adolescents today. *Time* magazine's 2006 selection of "You" as the person of the year attests to this (Grossman, 2006). In trying to select a person who helped to shape the course of history, writers at *Time* realized that the story of 2006 was "a story about community and collaboration … It's about the cosmic compendium of knowledge Wikipedia and the million-channel people's network YouTube and the online metropolis MySpace" (Grossman, 2006). In focus groups conducted with Canadian children in grades 4 through 11, researchers found that children and adolescents view the Internet as "an opportunity to explore the adult world without supervision" (Wing, 2005). This preference is in keeping with their need to test their wings outside the family. A majority of children (57%) also use the Net to explore topics that interest them on an average school day, and a significant proportion use it to express themselves on their own Web sites (28%) or in online diaries and Web logs (15%; Wing, 2005).

Children and the Internet

So many kids use the Internet and its many communication venues that it has been referred to as the "digital communication backbone of teens' daily lives" (Lenhart, Madden, & Hitlin, 2005, p. iii). Want to punish a teenager? Simply threaten to take their computer or cell phone away. To a teenager, that may seem to be a punishment worse than death (or, at least, a punishment that is the equivalent of a social death).

Several large-scale surveys have given us a picture of the prevalence of the use of technology among teenagers today and some of the potential dangers faced by teens. According to *The 2010 Digital Future Report* (Center for the Digital Future, 2010), released annually over the last decade, Internet use among Americans has continued to increase, as has overall time spent online. In 2005, 79% of Americans spent time online, averaging 13.3 hours a week, a significant increase over the previous four years. In 2009, 82% of Americans spent time online, averaging 19 hours a week. In the 2005 report, among all Americans e-mail was the most frequent online activity, with instant messaging appearing ninth in the list. In 2009, instant messaging was the most common method of communicating online. Social networking sites are increasing as a communication tool of choice with 58% of individuals using social network sites at least once a week, an increase of 14% from the previous year. Notably, 100% of individuals surveyed under the age of 24 spend time online. This high rate of Internet activity among children and young adults has led people such as Bill Belsey, President of Bullying.org Canada, to refer to teenagers today as the "always on generation."

The 2010 Pew Internet & American Life Project report indicated that 93% of the 800 teens between the ages of 12 and 17 surveyed spend time online. Over half of these teens (63%) reported that they spent time each day online (Lenhart, 2010). Thirty-six percent of these go online several times a day. Three fourths (75%) of the adolescents had their own cell phones, compared to 45% in 2005 and 18% in 2004; notably, 58% of 12-year-olds had a cell phone. Just under three-fourths of all teens send text messages, translating to 88% of all teens with cell phones (Lenhart, 2010). The average teen sends/receives 50 text messages a day, although one-third send/receive approximately 100 texts a day or 3,000 a month (Lenhart, 2010). Given these statistics, it is hardly surprising that texting has now surpassed instant messaging as the most common mode of communication among teens. Eight percent of the teens in this survey visited virtual worlds, such as Second Life. The use of virtual worlds was more popular among younger teens than older teens, and more popular among teens than adults. Highlighting the "wired" nature of today's youth, the survey found that the average youth has 3.5 gadgets out of 5 surveyed: cell phones, MP3 players, computers, game consoles, and portable gaming devices (Lenhart, 2010).

The biggest leap in online activity occurs between the 6th and 7th grades, according to the Pew report (Lenhart, 2010). Whereas 83% of 6th graders indicated that they used the Internet, 92% of 7th graders reported online activity. In a demonstration of technology trends, the 2005 Pew report noted that boys (particularly 6th grade boys) were much less active in their use of the Internet than girls. Whereas only 44% of the 6th grade boys reported going online, 79% of 6th grade girls reported using the Internet. Girls also were more likely than boys to use instant messaging. Seventy-eight percent of girls and 71% of boys said that they had tried instant messaging. Girls also tried instant messaging at an earlier age than boys. In the 2010 report, however, Lenhart found that boys and girls were equally likely to go online. Seventy-three percent of teens between the ages of 12 and 17 use social network sites, an increase of 18% since 2006 (Lenhart, 2010). Girls and boys were equally likely to use social networking sites. Only 8% of teens 12–17 reported using Twitter. Older teens were more likely than younger teens to use this social networking service, and, among older teens, girls reported being more likely to tweet than boys (Lenhart, 2010).

In 2000 and again in 2003, the Media Awareness Network (Wing, 2005) launched a series of research studies examining the online behavior of Canadian children and adolescents. In 2003, the organization conducted a series of focus groups with both parents and adolescents. Two years later, they administered a survey to 5,272 children in grades 4 to 11 to examine their online activities. Among other things, the study found that 23% of the children and youth had their own cellular phone. Twenty-two percent of school-aged children had Web cams. By the time they reached 11th grade, 31% had personal Web cams. Internet use tends to decline slightly once kids reach high school in part because most are driving or have friends who drive. Once they have the ability to see one another in person, they rely less on technology to keep in touch with one another. In addition, they are connecting with their friends differently, using cell phones more than computers at home. Eighty-nine percent of the respondents in grade 4 reported playing games online. As the ages of the children increased, the percentage that played games decreased and the percentage who used instant messaging increased. Across all age groups, instant messaging was ranked as the first choice of online activity by 62% of the girls and 43% of the boys. Of concern, only 16% of the respondents reported talking about their online activities with their parents.

The Canadian survey revealed some disturbing information about the kinds of sites that adolescents like to visit. Of the 50 favorite Web sites listed, nearly one-third included violent or sexual information. In Quebec, the most popular site among girls in grades 8 to 11 is Doyoulookgood.com. "On this Montreal-based site, users post photos, videos and information about themselves so others can vote on their looks. Members can search for people by age, starting as young as 13" (Wing, 2005).

The use of social networking sites, such as Facebook, MySpace, Xanga, LiveJournal, Formspring, and Nexopia has increased markedly in the last few years. Facebook is currently the most popular social networking site worldwide, with over 800 million active users. An active user is defined as someone who has logged into their Facebook account at least once within the previous month. Half of these active users log into their accounts daily. Across all users, people spend in excess of 700 billion minutes a month on Facebook (Facebook statistics, 2011)! Nexopia, the Canadian equivalent of Facebook and the largest social network site for youth in Canada, has a user base of approximately 1.2 million. Bebo (Blog early, blog often), similar to MySpace except affiliated more with schools and universities, and more likely to be used by teens, has seen similar rates of growth. Within its first year, Bebo acquired 25 million users ("Focus: Brave new world," 2006). Currently, Bebo is the largest social networking site in the United Kingdom ("What is Bebo," 2010). Formspring, which launched in November, 2009, uses a question and answer style format for users to network with one another. Askers can choose to remain anonymous as they ask questions that are then responded to by the user to whom they are directed. The questions and answers are then posted on the user's profile. Users' profiles can be linked to other social networking sites, such as Facebook and Twitter. Ernie Allen, President of the National Center for Missing and Exploited Children, said, in reference to adolescents posting personal information on social networking sites: "What they're doing [when they post information about themselves online] is opening a window to people who may not have the best intentions" (Olsen, 2006b).

A survey conducted by the National Center for Missing and Exploited Children (NCMEC) and Cox Communications oriented toward online and wireless safety examined the online experiences of 655 children between the ages of 13 and 17. The survey responses showed that 72% of 13–17-year-old children have a personal profile on a social network site ("Teen online," 2006, 2009). Sixty-two percent had posted photos of themselves on a blog or their social networking profile. Ninety-one percent listed a personal e-mail address, and 60% had a screen name that they used for instant messaging. Nineteen percent had engaged in sexting. Nine percent had sent a sext, 17% had received a sext, and 3% had forwarded a sext. One in ten of the individuals who had sent sexts had sent them to someone that they didn't know. A similar survey conducted two years earlier with 1070 teens in the same age range found that 8% had had a face-to-face interaction with someone they had met over the Internet (a decrease from 14% in 2006). Sixteen percent said they were considering a face-to-face meeting with someone they had met online, a decrease from 30% in 2006. Sixty-nine percent had received a personal message from someone they didn't know ("Cox Communications," 2007; "Take charge," 2006).

In a desire to examine the online presence of even younger children, the National Center for Missing and Exploited Children and Cox Communication's Take Charge program subsequently administered a similar survey to 1,015 tweens ages 12–15, all of whom had access to the Internet. The findings reinforced the wired culture in which our youth live. The presence of children online more than doubled between the 8–10 and 11–12 age ranges. Girls showed more of an online presence than boys. Fifty percent of tweens ages 11–12 reported having a cell phone and 34% of tweens in the same age range had a profile on a social network site. Twenty-eight percent reported that they had been contacted via the Internet by someone that they did not know. Almost 20% did not tell anyone about messages that they had received from strangers ("Tweens and Internet," 2011).

Not surprisingly, given that children and adolescents communicate with all sorts of people on the Internet, some of whom are friends and others of whom are strangers, experiences with the Internet and related technologies may be positive or negative. Profiles of children and youth on the Internet, and data on the types of information to which they are exposed while surfing the Internet, change rapidly. For example, in comparing data from the first Youth Internet Survey (YISS-1; Ybarra & Mitchell, 2004), and the second Youth Internet Safety Survey (YISS-2; Wolak, Mitchell, & Finkelhor, 2006), which were conducted approximately five years apart, researchers reported that the percentage of children and youth who reported receiving online sexual solicitations had decreased from YISS-1 to YISS-2, but the proportion who reported online harassment and unsolicited exposure to sexual images had increased. A disturbing note to this reported increase in the number of children experiencing online exposure to sexual material is the fact that an increased number of parents (55%) in YISS-2 reported the use of computer blockers, filters, and keystroke software programs, compared to YISS-1 (33%). So, despite these increased parental controls, the number of children and youth who reported unwanted exposure to sexual material continued to increase. Also disturbing, according to YISS-2 (Wolak et al., 2006) an increasing number of perpetrators of online harassment are friends or acquaintances of the victim: 46% in the YISS-2 survey compared to 28% in YISS-1. Furthermore, the proportion of respondents in YISS-2 (14%) who said that the individuals making online sexual solicitations were offline friends or acquaintances increased from YISS-1, by 3%.

Effects of Internet Use on Children and Youth

There is debate regarding the extent to which high levels of Internet use interfere with psychological functioning, particularly among children and adolescents. On the one hand, Internet use allows for the possible development of new relationships, and for the easy maintenance of existing friendships and relationships. Russell and his colleagues (2003) found that frequent Internet use broadened people's social networks, particularly for people who were shy and socially anxious (see also, Gross, Juvonen, & Gable, 2002; Mazalin & Klein, 2008; McKenna & Bargh, 2000). Related research by Roberts, Smith, and Pollock (2000) found that socially anxious individuals were more confident communicating electronically than face-to-face. With time, however, this confidence carried over into face-to-face interactions. Socially anxious individuals are also more likely than nonsocially anxious people to communicate electronically with strangers or acquaintances (Gross et al., 2002). Using Thibaut and Kelley's (1959) analogy, Bargh and his colleagues (2002) compared the Internet to talking to "strangers on a train": people often freely disclose to strangers sitting next to them on a train aspects of themselves that they would not reveal to others. The Internet affords people the opportunity to disclose aspects of their "true self" that they would not reveal in face-to-face interactions.

Thus, the Internet has the potential to increase students' social interaction and enhance collaborative learning experiences (Beran & Li, 2005). At the same time, however, Robert Mahaffey, a criminal investigator for the Mississippi Attorney General's cyber crime unit, stated that: "The Internet is the wild, wild West of the 21st century, and it should be viewed that way" ("FBI: Blogging can be dangerous," 2005). Just like the wild, wild West, the Internet is full of excitement and adventure, but it is also full of danger and often unknown "bandits." Using a similar analogy, Franek (2005/2006) stated that "we need to be vigilant sheriffs in this new Wild West – a cyberworld buzzing with kids just a few keystrokes away from harming other people, often for no other reason than that the sheriffs are sleeping. As any-one who has ever been the victim of bullying and harassment will tell you, the bullets may not be real, but they can hurt" (p. 40).

On the positive side, the anonymity afforded by the Internet allows peo-ple to try on multiple roles and experiment with different "selves" without fear of negative evaluation or social sanctions that might follow such exper-imentation in face-to-face encounters. Significant numbers of adolescents (24%) in the 2005 Pew Internet & American Life survey admitted to pre-tending to be different people online (Lenhart et al., 2005). Fifty-six percent had more than one e-mail address or screen name. Users can pretend to be older or younger, male or female, African American or Caucasian, liberal or conservative, homosexual or heterosexual. The list of possible roles they can play and identities they can assume is endless. On the one hand, this can be beneficial to a teenager who is searching to discover who he or she is.

On the other hand, pretending to be someone they are not may lead chil-dren and adolescents to "meet" people online and, perhaps, subsequently in the real world, who also are not who they say they are. Indeed, 39% of the respondents in the 2001 Pew report (Lenhart, Rainie, & Lewis, 2001) admit-ted to playing a trick on someone or pretending to be somebody different when using instant messaging. Sixty percent of the teens reported that they had received e-mails or IMs from a stranger and 50% exchanged e-mails or IMs with a stranger. Seventeen percent of respondents in the Young Canadians in a Wired World Survey (Wing, 2005) reported that they "had pretended to be someone else so 'I can act mean to people and not get into trouble.'" In addition, 59% of the respondents admitted to pretending to be someone that they weren't online. Of these, 52% pretended to be a different age, 26% assumed different personality characteristics, 24% pretended to have abilities they didn't have, and 23% claimed an appearance that was different from their actual appearance. Eighteen percent of the respondents to the NCMEC/COX Communications Survey ("Teen Online," 2009) indi-cated that they had posted a fake age on a public blog or a social networking site. Over 60% of the respondents to the NCMEC/COX Communications Survey ("Take charge," 2006) indicated that they had friends who had lied about their age over the Internet; another third stated that they had friends who had discovered that the person with whom they were communicating online was a different gender or age than they had originally claimed.

Opportunities for self-affirmation and self-expression provided by the Internet can quickly become vehicles for denigration and cyberbullying. For example, as noted earlier one site, doyoulookgood.com, allows users to set up personal accounts whereby they post pictures of and personal information about themselves. Site visitors can then pull up a person's profile and vote on the individual's attractiveness as well as send messages to the person. Ironically, although billed as a "social dating community" for individuals age 18 to 34 on its Web site, doyoulookgood.com was rated as the most popular site among Canadian girls in grades 8 to 11 (Wing, 2005), At the time of writing, 115,205 new photos had been posted this week and just under two million messages had been sent today. Of the almost 1,000 members currently online, 60% were men and 40% were women. Although the individual who receives positive ratings has the potential to have his or her self-esteem raised, the opposite scenario is probably more likely – negative ratings or negative comments that serve to denigrate the individual whose photo is posted on the Web site. Such negative postings represent only the tip of the iceberg of cyberbullying.

Perhaps not surprisingly, some evidence suggests that increased Internet use is associated with adverse psychological effects. In one of the first large-scale studies examining the psychological effects of Internet use, Kraut et al. (1998) found higher levels of Internet use to be associated with higher levels of depression and loneliness (see also Moody, 2001; Sum, Matthews, Hughes, & Campbell, 2008). Indeed, some experts are increasingly talking about the need for youth to "disconnect" or take digital sabbaticals. They are encouraging parents to look at helping the "always on" generation find opportunities to disconnect, reflect, and meditate. Other researchers suggest, however, that the Internet increases social and communication skills and can actually decrease loneliness by providing quality online relationships (Ong, Chang, & Wang, 2011).

In a nationwide survey of more than 63,000 children in 5th through 8th grade conducted by i-SAFE America, 30% said they had said mean or hurtful things to another person online, with 3% saying they did so often. Conversely, from a pool of approximately 20,700 students, 37% of the respondents said that someone had said mean hurtful things to them online. Four percent reported that it happened quite often. Nine percent had felt worried or threatened in the past year because someone was bothering or harassing them online (i-SAFE, 2006–2007). Thirty-four percent of the respondents in the Young Canadians in a Wired World survey reported having been bullied, with 74% of these being bullied at school and 27% being bullied over the Internet (Wing, 2005). Another 12% reported having been sexually harassed, with 70% of these being sexually harassed over the Internet.

How prevalent has cyberbullying become? Pretty prevalent. It used to be that kids could go off to summer camp to make new friends, gain some independence, learn new skills, and quite simply have an enjoyable way to spend part of their summer.[2] Long before the days of cellular phones, palm pilots, and laptops, campers might take a camera with them so that they could remember some of the cool things they saw at camp and so that they could have pictures of their new friends. Now, however, summer camp is a bit of a different experience. Kids might walk around camp listening to their iPod or talking on their Droid or Blackberry. Back at the lodge, they might be found tied to a computer, IMing their friends or posting information on their own or another person's Facebook site – until recently, anyway. Cyberbullying has become so worrisome for some adults that some summer camps have decided to ban digital cameras from the camp premises (Belluck, 2006). The fear? That not-so-well-meaning campers will take inappropriate pictures of other campers or doctor "normal" pictures and then post these images on the Web, such as on social networking sites, like Facebook or MySpace (Belluck, 2006). In some instances, camps are trademarking their names and logos so that they have legal recourse if such images are posted (Belluck, 2006).

Prototypes of Cyberbullying

In recent years, countless examples of cyberbullying have been reported in the media, a few of which will be briefly recounted here as prototypes of cyberbullying. As will become apparent, cyberbullying includes a range of experiences, some legal, some illegal. Many of these examples highlight some of the worst examples of cyberbullying. Yet, they help illustrate how issues such as the speed of distribution, anonymity, 24/7 accessibility, and permanence come into play with cyberbullying, issues that we will return to later in the book.

In perhaps one of the first and best-known illustrations of cyberbullying, Ghyslain Raza created a video of himself on November 4, 2002, acting out a scene from the movie *Star Wars*, using a golf-ball retriever as his light saber. Unfortunately, classmates then posted the video online without his permission or knowledge, where it was seen by millions. Eventually, in 2004, a Web site was created that contained original and modified clips from the video, along with special effects, and music from the *Star Wars* movie. The site received over 76 million hits (Lampert, 2006). In addition, other Web sites contained clips from the video spliced into action movies. Some speculated that Ghyslain's image was the most downloaded image of 2004. Labeled the "Star Wars Kid," Ghyslain was forced to change schools and received psychiatric help. On April 7, 2006, Raza's parents, who had filed a lawsuit against the classmates who had placed the video on the Internet, settled out of court with the families of these students. Ghyslain is currently a law student at McGill University and the President of a non-profit organization designed to preserve the cultural heritage of town called Trois-Rivères (Axon, 2010).

A young man, angry over the fact that his girlfriend broke up with him, used photo-editing tools to paste her head onto a pornographic picture and sent it to everyone in his e-mail address book (Paulson, 2003).

In March, 2011, a group of high school students in Westchester, New York created a list known as the SMUT List. About 100 girls were rank-ordered on the list based on their sexual activity. The list first circulated via text messaging, but was later posted on a Facebook group page. Within 24 hours, over 7000 people had "liked" the page (Stamoulis, 2011).

Taylor Wynn and McKenzie Baker, 15- and 16-year-old teenagers in Florida, created a fake profile of a classmate. On the profile, they superimposed her head on the nude body of someone else. Additionally, they juxtaposed a doctored photo of the classmate with her mouth agape next to an erect penis. After being forced to remove the first profile, the girls created a second. After being arrested and charged with aggravated cyberstalking, the girls expressed no remorse, saying that it was "all in good fun" and that "no one liked" the classmate (Kenny, 2011; Mandell, 2011).

15-year-old Jodi Plumb discovered a Web site devoted entirely to insulting her. Included on the Web site were comments about her weight as well as a date for her death. She discovered the Web site when a classmate used a digital camera to take a picture of Jodi for the Web site. Jodi said "I was really hurt because I did not know who'd done it" ("Cyber bullies target girl," 2006).

Phoebe Pluckrose-Oliver, 10 years old, received abusive text messages and phone calls from girls at her school. According to Phoebe, "They started phoning me and saying that I was in the cow club and that I should phone the loser line and stuff" ("Girl tormented by phone bullies," 2001).

Kylie Kenney was a victim of cyberbullying though multiple modalities. First, a Web site was created calling for her to die, the "Kill Kylie Incorporated" Web site. This was accompanied by countless harassing e-mails and phone calls. Furthermore, rumors spread that Kylie was a lesbian, and messages were sent ostensibly from her own instant messaging account asking other girls out on a date. In a news conference on cyberbullying, Kylie described how she was forced to change schools twice and how she had to be home-schooled for one semester because the cyberbullying was so bad. In the news conference, Kylie said "I was scared, hurt, and confused. I didn't know why it was happening to me. I had nowhere to turn except to my Mom" (Gehrke, 2006).

A 15-year-old female from Rhode Island was charged with cyberstalking for creating a fake profile of a 9th grade student. Included on the profile, in addition to the freshman's name and birth date, was a picture of a "severed bloody foot," an attempt to poke fun at the fact that the student had been born missing part of one of her feet. The title of the facebook profile: Halfafoot (Mulvaney, 2011).

A 14-year-old girl who had survived cancer and the loss of a limb when she was 10 years old was cyberbullied via text messaging for several months. Although the perpetrator's identity remained unknown for some time, it turned out to be the victim's best friend. The perpetrator would talk to the target on Skype while she was sending cyberbullying text messages so that she could witness the target's reactions to the bullying (Kennedy, 2011).

Two Toledo, Ohio, teenagers, aged 16 and 17, were arrested for posting death threats on MySpace against a 15-year-old classmate. They threatened to slit her throat, bash her head in, and discussed going to jail together if they were caught ("Ohio girls sentenced for MySpace threats," 2006).

A young boy posted sexually explicit pictures of himself online when he was 12 or 13 years old. A few years later, a young man named Matthew Bean became aware of the photos and forwarded them to the victim's school (Dale, 2011). Although Bean posed as a concerned parent, the school discovered his identity and pressed charges against him. An online group including Bean indicated that they wanted to drive the victim to kill himself (Dale, 2011). Bean was convicted and sentenced to time in prison.

An 8th grader in Pennsylvania was charged for posting a depiction of "his algebra teacher's severed head dripping with blood, an animation of her face morphing into Adolph Hitler and a solicitation for $20 contributions 'to help pay for the hitman'" (Poulsen, 2006).

A Facebook page called the "Stonewall Hoes" was created by a 16-year-old girl at Stonewall Jackson High School in Manasssas, Virginia, to highlight who she perceived to be the "hoes" in her class. Included on the page were photos of the girls along with degrading comments about the girls.

The teen has been charged with cyberbullying and faces up to 1 year in prison (Thompson, 2011).

In February 2006, five students at Kirkwood High School posted a "hot or not" list of junior girls on Facebook. Once the site was discovered, each of the five boys was given a 10-day suspension from school (Beder, 2006).

A male student at Oak Park River Forest High School in Chicago created a list of the "Top 50" female students at his school, including his commentary of these women (e.g., racial slurs and notes about their anatomy). In addition to posting the list on Facebook, he distributed copies by hand throughout the school (Sobotka, 2011). The student has been suspended, and faces possible expulsion and criminal charges.

16-year-old Jade Prest became a prisoner in her own home and even contemplated suicide in reaction to the relentless cyberbullying she experienced by peers at school. Beginning as a disagreement over a boy at school, the cyberbullying included "midnight prank phone calls, an internet chatroom whispering campaign, abusive text messages, threats, intimidation and the silent treatment" (Crisp, 2006).

A Facebook page was created with threatening posts directed at an 11-year-old girl from Orlando, Florida, who had appeared in a music video. In spite of multiple attempts to have the page removed, it remained for sometime under the premise that, by appearing in a music video, the girl was now a public figure and, according to Facebook's terms of use, public figures can be criticized on the social networking site. It was only when a *New York Times* reporter contacted Facebook that the site was removed (Helft, 2010).

In New Zealand, a 14-year-old girl's name and cell phone number were posted on Bebo along with offers of sex with no strings attached. The girl was unaware that the message and personal information about her had been posted ("Schools face new cyber bullying menace," 2006).

In the fall of 2005, two students at Oregon City High School were suspended for comments they posted on MySpace about 32 other girls at the school. Included among the comments was the following about one of the students: "Every time you speak all I can think about is where is the closest body of water, so I can tie a brick to your ankle and throw you in. Which would be good exercise because it's hard to pick up fat people" (Pardington, 2005).

Mary Ellen Handy's ordeal started because another student, named Gretchen, liked the same boy as Mary Ellen Handy. Gretchen verbally abused Mary Ellen, and then sent her harassing e-mails. Taking it a step further, she then communicated using IM as if she were Mary Ellen, sending embarrassing and threatening communications to which, not surprisingly, she received insulting responses back. The result for Mary Ellen – she developed an ulcer from the stress. At least two of her friends who were harassed because of their relationship with Mary Ellen switched schools (Levine, 2006).

Ryan Patrick Halligan died by suicide at the age of 13 as a result of being persistently bullied and humiliated by peers at school. The bullying began at school and continued online. Toward the end of 7th grade, it was rumored at school and in IM conversations that he was gay. His father discovered after Ryan's death IMs saved on his computer demonstrating he was cyberbullied in regard to this rumor. His father also discovered that Ryan approached one of the pretty popular girls in his class online during the summer in between 7th and 8th grade, supposedly as a way of combating the gay rumor. Ryan learned on the first day of the school year that the girl only pretended to like him and that she had forwarded their private conversations to others to humiliate him. Two weeks before his death and only four weeks into the school year, Ryan wrote in an IM to a friend: "Tonight's the night, I think I'm going to do it. You'll read about it in the paper tomorrow." The "friend" replied, "It's about f . ˙ time!" (J. Halligan, personal communication, January 17, 2007)

A female respondent in one of our focus groups described the following: "An ex-boyfriend got kind of crazy once. He started e-mailing me and saying that he was gonna come to my house and kill me and stuff like he was watching [my] sister. I knew he wouldn't do anything but I went ahead and told my mom because he was like a freak. So, it was getting kind of scary. Yeah, he would say stuff to my friends online too so I kind of freaked out."

Overview of the Book

It would be difficult to discuss and understand cyberbullying without a clear understanding of traditional or school-yard bullying. Chapter 2 will provide an overview of traditional bullying – how it is defined, who the victims and perpetrators are, and the effects of traditional bullying on both sources and targets. Chapter 3 will delve into the world of cyberbullying. After defining cyberbullying, we will examine the methods by which people cyberbully, who perpetrates cyberbullying and who is victimized by cyberbullying, and how cyberbullying is similar to and different from traditional bullying. The chapter will include a discussion of one of the key variables distinguishing electronic and traditional bullying – anonymity and the disinhibition that often results.

Although research on cyberbullying is still in its early developmental stages, Chapter 4 will provide an overview of what extant research says about the topic, including assessments of the prevalence of cyberbullying, methods for studying cyberbullying, and a discussion of gender differences observed with cyberbullying. In particular, we will draw from our own research on cyberbullying with over 3700 middle school children throughout the country, and from focus groups that we held with middle school students. An examination of the psychological effects of cyberbullying will close out the chapter. Chapters 5 and 6 take an applied look at what parents (Chapter 5) and educators and other adults who work with youth (Chapter 6) can do to deal with cyberbullying. Strategies for dealing with cyberbullying once it has already occurred, as well as prevention methods to deter incidents of electronic violence from beginning at all, are discussed. In Chapter 7 legal and public policy concerns related to cyberbullying will be discussed. In the United States, policy-makers and school personnel have been somewhat slower than those in Canada or the United Kingdom to address cyberbullying in statutes and in school policies (Osmond, 2006). In Chapter 8 we will draw some conclusions and provide some suggestions for future research and policy decisions.

A danger in writing a book on cyberbullying is that we will leave the reader with the impression that technological advances are bad and that children and youth would be better off if they did not have access to the Internet, cellular phones, etc. This is not the message we intend to convey. Indeed, technology is a good thing. The Internet provides a window to the world for many children and youth. Not only does it open up sources of knowledge to people (adolescents in particular) that might otherwise be too difficult to access, but technology also affords adolescents and adults an easy means of establishing and maintaining social contacts. For some socially anxious individuals, this may be their social saving grace. And, most children and youth when asked about their experiences with the Internet and related technologies rate their experiences positively. One of our former students getting ready to attend graduate school told us how she had already become friends with two or three individuals who would be in her program. Knowing that she could not have met these people in person, we asked her how she had already become friends with them. Her answer: Facebook (A. Scheck, personal communication, August 2, 2006). We couldn't help but think at that moment what a "leg up" these students would all have in moving to a new location and starting a new program simply because they had used a social network site to get acquainted with one another beforehand.

The Internet also provides a venue for youth to engage in creative enterprises, such as creating content (e.g., blogging, creating and sharing music), and to mobilize for social change on various political and environmental causes.

Nevertheless, cyberbullying is real, it is occurring with increasing frequency, and the psychological effects may prove to be as devastating, if not more so, than traditional bullying. We also want to emphasize that adults will never be able to completely shelter youth online. So, the solution cannot be just increasing adult supervision. Digital citizenship becomes increasingly important *because* there are fewer adults present. Taking time to focus on digital rights and responsibilities with youth is critical. We need to rely on partnerships (e.g., between parents and children, parents and educators, schools and community leaders) and empowerment of youth to take appropriate action.

Notes

1. Where possible in this book, we have tried to avoid referring to a child as a "bully" or a "victim." We believe that it is critical not to label children as "bullies" or as "victims" or in any way to imply that bullying others or being bullied are indelible traits (which in turn can be quite damaging to children). Instead, we try to refer to "a child who bullies" or "a child who is bullied" and to focus on the bullying behavior of children rather than their status. Where this language becomes unwieldy, we have on occasion used the terms "bully" and "victim." We hope that in these instances, the reader will understand our intent.
2. We do not mean to imply that children have never been bullied while at summer camp. Certainly there are many children who can tell traumatic stories about times when they were mercilessly bullied while away at camp.

2
CHILDREN'S EXPERIENCES WITH TRADITIONAL FORMS OF BULLYING

with Weijun Wang

"Unless you've been bullied, you really can't understand what it's like and how hard it is to forget. It really leaves a scar that even time can't heal."
(15-year-old focus group participant)

Although the advent of cyber technologies has provided new arenas in which children and youth can bully each other, the phenomenon of bullying is hardly new. In order to better understand cyberbullying, it is important to be familiar with the various dynamics at work in traditional forms of bullying as well as what "best practices" are available for preventing and intervening with traditional bullying.

What Is Bullying?

Bullying is aggressive behavior that is intentional and that involves an imbalance of power or strength (Nansel, Overpeck, Pilla, Ruan, Simmons-Morton, & Schmidt, 2001; Olweus, 1993a, 2010; Olweus & Limber, 2010a). Sometimes this imbalance involves differences in physical strength between children, but often it is characterized by differences in social power or status. Because of this imbalance of power or strength, a child who is being bullied has a difficult time defending himself or herself. Typically, bullying does not occur just once or twice, but is repeated over time. Admittedly, sometimes it is quite difficult for adults to know whether behavior between children has

Cyberbullying: Bullying in the Digital Age, Second Edition. Robin M. Kowalski, Susan P. Limber, and Patricia W. Agatston.
© 2012 Robin M. Kowalski, Susan P. Limber, and Patricia W. Agatston.
Published 2012 by Blackwell Publishing Ltd.

occurred repeatedly, as children are often good at hiding bullying and reluctant to report bullying that they experience or witness. However, it is important to understand whether a behavior is a one-time occurrence or whether it is part of a pattern of ongoing behavior. Although adults should intervene whenever they observe inappropriate aggressive behavior (even if it appears to be an isolated occurrence), *how* adults respond to bullying as opposed to other aggressive behavior may be different.

What Does Bullying Look Like?

Jack was small and somewhat immature for his age. For the past 2 years (since 2nd grade), Jack had been the target of jokes about his size. Most of the boys in his class called him "shrimp." He usually tried to laugh off the name-calling, but lately it seemed to be getting even worse. During the past week, several boys had been getting physically rough with him – tripping him on the school bus, and shoving him on the playground when the teachers weren't looking. When he mentioned to his parents that he was being picked on, his father lectured him about ways he could "stick up for himself," so he hadn't brought it up again.

Tara had been attending Grove Street Middle school for only 1 month, but she was having trouble fitting in with her fellow 7th graders. Her family was new in town, and Tara didn't know a single student when she walked in the front door on the first day of school. Although the kids at school weren't exactly friendly for the first couple of days, the bullying didn't start until the second week, during English class. After Tara answered a question from the teacher, a popular girl called her a nasty name under her breath, and all the students sitting near them laughed. Before long, several popular boys had started taunting her in the hallways. Each day, when she tried to find a seat in the cafeteria, her fellow classmates made animal noises or blocked open seats with their books. Tara had never experienced bullying at her other middle school, and she was at a loss to know what to do. She missed a lot of school, complaining of stomach aches and nausea. When her parents insisted on a trip to the doctor, Tara finally broke down and told them what she'd been experiencing. "I hate this school! Please don't make me go back – I'd rather die!"

As these stories (composites of real-life children) suggest, traditional forms of bullying include direct behavior, such as hitting, kicking, having money or other things taken or damaged, taunting, malicious teasing or name-calling. However, they also involve indirect (and often less obvious) behavior, such as rumor-spreading, social exclusion or shunning, and manipulation of friendships ("If you're her friend, you can't be *our* friend"). Other types of bullying involve sexual comments and gestures, threats, and taunts based on race or ethnicity. Researchers also use other terms to describe bullying, such as relational and social bullying. Relational and social bullying behavior is intended to damage a child's reputation or social standing with peers, or use the threat of loss of the relationship to manipulate others. Most common forms of bullying (for both boys and girls) involve the use of words, such as name-calling, malicious teasing, or verbal taunts about one's looks or speech (Nansel et al., 2001; Olweus & Limber, 2010c).

How Common Is Bullying?

Although bullying is an age-old phenomenon, it has only been in the past 30 years that researchers have tried to measure bullying systematically. The earliest studies of bullying were conducted by Dan Olweus with children in Norway and Sweden in the 1980s (Olweus, 1993a). In an anonymous survey with over 150,000 children and youth, Olweus found that approximately 15% of the students in elementary and lower secondary schools (roughly corresponding to ages 8–16) had been involved in problems with bullying with some regularity (Olweus, 1993a). Nine percent had been bullied by peers, 7% had bullied others, and 2% had been bullied *and* had bullied others.

Studies of children and youth in the United States were not conducted until a decade after Olweus' early studies and typically found significantly higher rates of bullying (Limber, Nation, Tracy, Melton, & Flerx, 2004; Melton, Limber, Cunningham, Osgood, Chambers, Flerx, Henggeler, & Nation, 1998; Nansel et al., 2001). The first study of bullying in the US to use a nationally representative sample was conducted with more than 15,000 students in grades 6 through 10 and published in 2001 (Nansel et al., 2001). Using an anonymous self-report questionnaire, Nansel and her fellow researchers found that, within a single school term, 17% of children and youth said they had been bullied "sometimes" or more often, 19% had bullied others "sometimes" or more frequently, and 6% said they had been bullied *and* had bullied others "sometimes" or more often. Students were asked about the frequency with which they had experienced five specific types of bullying – being "belittled about religion or race," being "belittled about looks or speech," being "hit, slapped, or pushed," being "subjects of rumors," and being "subjects of sexual comments or gestures" – and found that being belittled about one's looks or speech was the most common.

More recently, in the 2007 School Crime Supplement to the National Crime Victimization Survey, Robers, Zhang, Truman, and Snyder (2010) reported that 32% of students (ages 12–18) reported having been bullied at school during the school year. More specifically, 21% of students said that they had experienced bullying that consisted of being made fun of; 18% reported having been the subject of rumors; 11% reported having been pushed, shoved, tripped, or spit on; 6% reported having been threatened with harm; 5% said they had been excluded from activities on purpose; and 4% of students reported others had tried to make them do things they did not want to do or that their property had been destroyed on purpose. Of those students who had been bullied, 63% reported that it had happened once or twice during the year, 21% said that it happened once or twice a month, 10% said it had happened once or twice a week, and almost 7% reported that they had been bullied daily. The Centers for Disease Control and Prevention (2010), using the 2009 national school-based Youth Risk Behavior Survey (YRBS) data, reported that nationwide, 20% of students had been bullied on school property one or more times during the past 12 months.

Olweus and Limber (2010c) collected data from 524,054 students from 1,593 schools (94% public) in 45 states plus the District of Columbia and the US Virgin Islands who had completed the anonymous Olweus Bullying Questionnaire. They found that 17% of students from grades 3–12 had been bullied by their peers two to three times per month or more often and 10% had bullied others two to three times per month or more often. To get an estimate of the total volume of bullying problems experienced by students, Olweus and Limber (2010c) separated students according to their bullying status. In total, 25% of boys and 20% of girls had been involved in bullying two to three times per month or more often – as a "bully only" (8% of boys and 4% of girls), as a "victim only" (13% of boys and 14% of girls), or as both (4% of boys and 3% of girls). Considering that there are approximately 50 million public school students in the United States, Olweus and Limber estimated that approximately 11 million students are involved in bullying on a regular basis.

Craig and her fellow researchers (Craig, Harel-Fisch, Fogel-Grinvald, Dastaler, Hetland, Simons-Morten, et al., 2009) compared the prevalence of bullying and victimization among boys and girls from nationally representative samples of 11-, 13-, and 15-year-old school children in 40 countries. The researchers found, in their sub-sample of 3,775 American school children, that 22% of boys and 17% of girls had been involved in bullying either as a bully, a victim, or as both a bully and a victim at school in the past 2 months according to student self-report surveys.

How do rates of bullying vary among children in different countries? The most comprehensive cross-national study of bullying and other health behaviors was the Health Behaviour in School-Aged Children (HBSC) study, which was conducted among 11-, 13-, and 15-year-olds in 40 countries (Craig et al., 2009; Currie et al., 2004; see also Žaborskis, Cirtautienè, & Žemaitienè, 2005). Craig and colleagues (2009) reported that exposure to bullying two or more times a month varied across countries, with estimates ranging from 9% (in Sweden) to 45% (in Lithuania) among boys, and from 5% (in Sweden) to 36% (in Lithuania) among girls. Adolescents in Baltic countries reported higher rates of bullying and victimization, whereas northern European countries reported the lowest prevalence (Craig et al., 2009). Many other studies have also documented the prevalence of bullying behavior a wide variety of countries and cultures (see, e.g., Morita, Soeda, Soeda, & Taki's 1999 study of Japanese elementary school children; Hokoda, Lu, & Angeles' 2006 study of junior high school students in Taiwan; Cheng, Newman, Qu, Chai, Chen, & Shell's 2010 study of middle school students in China; Rigby and Slee's 1999 study of elementary school students in Australia; Cluver, Bowes, and Gardner's 2010 research with 10–19-year-olds in South Africa). Differences in prevalence rates across countries likely reflect social and cultural differences in bullying itself (or the interpretation of the term) and in the implementation of policies and programs to address bullying (Craig et al., 2009; Olweus & Limber, 2010a).

Has the Amount of Bullying Increased in Recent Years?

There is no denying that there is much more awareness about bullying today (on the part of media, educators, researchers, and policy-makers) than in years past. The massacre at Columbine High School in 1999 seems to have been a pivotal event in focusing attention on bullying in the United States. Although the specific motivations for this (or other school shootings) may never be fully understood, retrospective accounts in the popular press and in the research literature pointed to bullying as a contributing factor in many of these crimes (Dinkes, Kemp, & Baum, 2009; Fein, Vossekuil, Pollack, Borum, Modzeleski, & Reddy, 2002; Limber, 2006b). The suicide in January 2010 of a 15-year-old girl (Phoebe Prince) in

Massachusetts brought additional international attention to the problem of bullying in US schools.

To see just how much attention to school bullying has changed in recent years in the United States, we conducted a combined search of the Lexis/Nexis database, using the search terms "bullying" and "school" (see Figure 2.1). In 1998, the year prior to the Columbine shootings, school bullying was in the headlines of major US Newspapers & Wires 86 times. The number of news stories on school bullying doubled in 2000, and, in 2001, shot to more than 630. In 2010, there were 1,930 headlines on school bullying.

Not only has attention to bullying increased remarkably in the popular press since the late 1990s, but there also has been a significant increase in attention to bullying among researchers since that time. To gauge just how much the research focus has changed in recent years, we conducted a search of the PsycINFO database (an online social science database of journal articles, books, and other academic publications owned by the American Psychological Association) using "bully" or "bullying" or "bullied" as search terms. As Figure 2.2 illustrates, we found only five publications in 1990. By 2000 (one year post-Columbine) the number increased to 104, and in 2004 there were 268 such publications. There were 472 publications in 2010. Presumably this trend will continue.

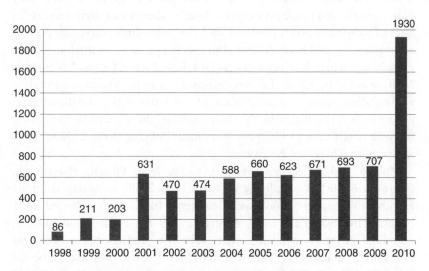

Figure 2.1   The number of Lexis/Nexis citations in which "bullying" and "school" appeared in the headlines of U.S. newspapers and wires.

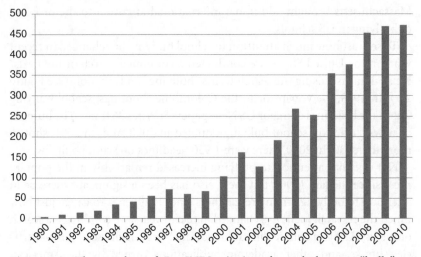

Figure 2.2   The number of PsycINFO citations located that use "bully" or "bullying" or "bullied."

Does the recent attention reflect a dramatic increase in bullying in recent years? According to the supplement to the National Crime Victimization Survey (DeVoe, Peter, Noonan, Snyder, & Baum, 2005), which asked students if they had been bullied (e.g., picked on or made to do things they didn't want to do) in the previous six months, there was a slight increase in rates of bullying between 1999 and 2001 (by about three percentage points) among American school children, but no change between 2001 and 2003. Finkelhor and his fellow researchers (Finkelhor, Turner, Ormrod, & Hamby, 2010) assessed trends in children's exposure to abuse, violence, and crime victimization based on a comparison of two cross-sectional national telephone surveys conducted in 2003 and 2008. Significant declines in physical bullying (from 22% to 15%) and emotional bullying (from 25% to 22%) were reported between these years.

Molcho and colleagues (Molcho, Craig, Due, Pickett, Harel-Fisch, Overpeck, & the HBSC Bullying Writing Group, 2009), using data from the Health Behaviour in School-Aged Children (HBSC) study collected in 21 countries in 1993/94 and in 27 countries in 1997/98, 2001/02 and 2005/06, examined the trends in the occurrence of bullying and associated victimization among adolescents (11–15 years old) in North American and European countries. They observed overall decreases in reported rates of bullying and victimization in the majority of the 27 participating countries. However, it is difficult to find a clear pattern in this regard. For example, with regard to the prevalence of chronic bullying (bullying others two or more times this term), the largest decrease was reported in Denmark, with a 75% decrease for boys and an 83% decrease for girls between 1993/1994 and 2005/2006. But obvious increases in the prevalence of bullying were reported in other countries, such as Greece, which saw a 99% relative increase in bullying among boys and a 121% increase among girls between 1997/1998 and 2005/06. The United States saw a 16% decrease among boys (from 48% to 40%) and a 4% decrease among girls (from 32% to 30%) from 1997/98 to 2005/06. Although these data are promising for the US, at best they represent modest reductions for boys only. Therefore, much of the recent attention in the US likely reflects increased interest in (or concern about) the topic of bullying (particularly post-Columbine), rather than a radical change in the likelihood that children are bullied.

Age Differences and Bullying

At what ages are children most likely to be involved in traditional forms of bullying? The answer to this question depends upon whether one is asking about children's experiences of *bullying others* or *being bullied*. Children also may be involved in different forms of traditional bullying behavior at different developmental stages depending on their verbal and cognitive development (Dodge, Coie, & Lynam, 2006; Rubin, Cheah, & Menzer, 2010). Most studies find that children are most likely to be *bullied by others* during elementary grades. They are somewhat less likely to be bullied in middle school, and less likely still to be bullied in high school. For example, in their study of children and youth aged 2–17, Finkelhor and colleagues (Finkelhor, Ormrod, Turner, & Hamby, 2005) found that children aged 6–12 experienced the highest rates of physical bullying. Preschoolers experienced the second-highest rates of physical bullying, and teenagers (13–17-year-olds) experienced the least physical bullying. Children aged 6–12 also experienced the most teasing or emotional bullying of all three groups. Similar results were found by Nansel and her colleagues in their national study of 6th through 10th graders in the US (Nansel et al., 2001). Although 24% of 6th graders said that they had been bullied sometimes or more often, only 16% of 8th graders and 9% of 10th graders reported that they had been bullied. Dinkes, Kemp, and Baum's (2009) national data on school crime and student safety in US schools during the 2007–08 school year showed that a higher percentage of middle schools than high schools reported daily or weekly occurrences of student victimization from bullying. Rigby (2002) also found decreases in rates of victimization among Australian children in grades 4 through 12, with an important exception. There was a temporary increase in rates of victimization during the year that students first entered secondary school.

Olweus and Limber's survey of 524,054 students in the United States (Olweus & Limber, 2010c) showed a steady decrease in being bullied (two to three times per month or more) for girls from grades 3 through 12. For example, 25% of 3rd graders, 18% of 6th graders, and 8% of 12th graders reported that they had been bullied. There was also a steady decrease for boys from grades 3 to 11. For example, 24% of the 3rd graders, 20% of 6th graders, and 12% of 11th and 12th graders reported that they had been bullied by their peers.

The picture looks quite different, however, when focusing on children's rates of *bullying others*. Most researchers have found that children are most likely to bully each other (according to anonymous, self-report measures of traditional forms of bullying) during early to mid-adolescence (Eisenberg & Aalsma, 2005; Espelage & Swearer, 2004; Nansel et al., 2001; Olweus & Limber, 2010c). For example, in their study of 6th through 10th graders, Nansel and her colleagues (2001) found the highest rates of bullying others in 8th grade (24%, compared with 19% in 6th grade and 16% in 10th grade). Olweus and Limber's (2010c) findings revealed somewhat different age trends for boys and girls with respect to children's rates of bullying others. For girls, bullying behavior peaked in 8th grade (where 10% admitted bullying others) and then decreased through 12th grade. For boys, bullying behavior appeared to level off around 8th grade and remained high through high school. What accounts for the difference in age trends for bullying others versus being bullied? One likely explanation is that children and youth typically bully peers their same age or they bully *younger* children and youth.

Gender Similarities and Differences in Traditional Forms of Bullying

Although both boys and girls are frequently involved in bullying, there has been debate among researchers about which gender is more likely to engage in and experience bullying. Studies that have used anonymous, self-report measures typically have found that boys are more likely than girls to bully (Cook, Williams, Guerra, Kim, & Sadek, 2010; Craig et al., 2009; Currie et al., 2004; Centers for Disease Control and Prevention, 2010; Nansel et al., 2001; Olweus, 1993a, 2010; Olweus & Limber, 2010c), and a recent meta-analysis of 153 studies since 1970 concluded that boys were more likely than girls to be "bullies" and "bully victims" (Cook et al., 2010). However, findings are less consistent when looking at gender differences in experiences of being bullied. Some studies have found that boys report higher rates of victimization than girls, whereas others have found no gender differences or only slight differences between boys and girls (see Olweus, 2010). In their meta-analysis, Cook and colleagues (2010) found that boys were more likely than girls to be bullied, although the effect size was weak.

Probably more important than comparisons in rates of bullying between boys and girls are comparisons between the *types of bullying* in which boys and girls engage. Research has shown that boys are more likely to be physically bullied by their peers (Finkelhor et al., 2005; Nansel et al., 2001; Olweus, 1993a; Olweus & Limber, 2010c; Rigby, 2002) and girls are more likely to be bullied through rumor-spreading or through sexual comments or gestures (Nansel et al., 2001; Olweus & Limber, 2010c). Olweus and Limber (2010c) also found that boys are more likely to be bullied than girls by having money or other things taken or damaged, being threatened or forced to do things, and being bullied about their race or color. It also is important to note that, although boys are typically bullied by other boys (and rarely girls), girls are bullied by both boys and girls (Finkelhor et al., 2005; Nansel et al., 2001; Olweus, 1993a; Olweus & Limber, 2010c).

Racial and Ethnic Issues in Traditional Forms of Bullying

Although race and ethnicity clearly play a role in some instances of bullying, there has been relatively little focus on this topic by bullying researchers (Larochette, Murphy, & Craig, 2010; Peskin, Tortolero, & Markham, 2006; Spriggs, Iannotti, Nansel, & Haynie, 2007). Nansel and her colleagues (2001) found that, among 6th through 10th graders who had been bullied, one-quarter said that they had been belittled about their race or religion at least once during the current school semester, and 8% had experienced such bullying once a week or more often. Olweus and Limber (2010c) found, in a sample of 524,054 students from 3rd through 12th grades, that 9% of boys and 6% of girls reported having been bullied with mean names or comments about their race or color.

Some studies have examined similarities and differences in rates of bullying among children of different races in the United States. For example, Spriggs and colleagues (2007) found that, in a nationally-representative sample of 11,033 adolescents in grades 6 to 10 in the 2001 Health Behaviour in School-Aged Children (HBSC) survey, African American adolescents (6%) were less likely to be bullied than white (9%) and Hispanic students (9%). White adolescents (9%) were less likely to bully their peers than Hispanic students (11%) and African American students (10%). However, there were no differences in terms of bully-victims (3%) across race/ethnicity.

A more recent analysis of the HBSC data involving 7,182 US students in grades 6–10 (Wang, Iannotti, & Nansel, 2009) found that African American adolescents were more involved in bullying perpetration (physical, verbal, and cyber), but less involved in victimization (verbal and relational). Hispanic American adolescents were more likely to be physical bullies or cyberbully-victims than white adolescents. Adolescents in "other" race/ethnicity category (e.g., Asian Americans) were less likely to be relational bullies or verbal bully-victims, but more likely to be the targets of cyberbullying than white adolescents. Socioeconomic status has been found to influence bullying involvement in racial minority youth. For example, Peskin et al. (2006) found that African American students of low socioeconomic status were at a higher risk of involvement in bullying and victimization than were Hispanic American students.

What has research found in other countries in terms of racial bullying? Fandrem and colleagues (Fandrem, Strohmeier, & Roland, 2009) compared bullying experiences among 2,938 native Norwegians and 189 immigrant adolescents (13–15 years old). Immigrant adolescents (especially boys) were at higher risk of bullying others. In the Netherlands, Vervoort and Scholte (2010) found that, among 2,386 adolescents, ethnic minority adolescents were less likely to be bullied than the ethnic majority group members. There was no difference between the groups in rates of bullying others. They found that victimization was more prevalent in ethnically diverse classes in the Netherlands. In a study using the 2001/2002 Health Behaviour in School-Aged Children Survey (HBSC) (involving 3,684 students from 116 schools across Canada), Larochette et al. (2010) found that racial bullying and racial victimization were strongly related to individual factors such as race and gender. Being African-Canadians and being boys were associated with increased racial bullying of others. They found that students who engaged in racial bullying behaviors tended to engage in general bullying behaviors.

In summary, although a number of studies have examined similarities and differences in rates of bullying among children of different races, much still has to be learned, such as: (1) To what extent do rates of bullying vary depending on whether children are in the racial majority/minority? And if so, how? (2) Is bullying related to the status hierarchy (e.g., the economic and social mobility) of children of different racial and ethnic groups? (3) How do cultural views of and experiences with aggression (e.g., parenting, neighborhood and community characteristics) influence rates of bullying among peers?

Bullying in Urban, Suburban, and Rural Communities

Although bullying has often been seen as a problem primarily for urban schools, there appears to be no support for this view. In fact, bullying has been documented in diverse communities across the US (and around the world). In one of the few studies to examine urban, suburban, and rural differences in rates of bullying, Tonya Nansel and her colleagues (2001) found that students in grades 6 through 10 were just as likely to be bullied in urban, suburban, town, and rural areas. They found only very small differences in students' reports of bullying others, with suburban youth being slightly less likely than others to say that they bullied their peers "sometimes" or more often and rural youth being slightly more likely than others to have ever bullied their peers.

Children Involved in Bullying

Researchers and practitioners have focused much attention on understanding the characteristics and experiences of children involved in bullying – including those who are bullied, those who bully, those who bully and are bullied (bully/victims), and the majority who are witnesses or bystanders to the bullying.

Children who are bullied

Children who are bullied typically fall into one of two general categories – those who are passive or submissive, and a smaller number who are considered "provocative victims" or "bully/victims." The characteristics and experiences of passive victims will be discussed in this section; those of bully/victims will be discussed later. It is important to note that, although children are frequently referred to in the research and intervention literature as "passive," "submissive," or "provocative," these terms are not intended to be pejorative labels. Nor should they be used in any way to blame children for the bullying that they experience.

Characteristics of bullied children

Although there is no single profile of passive victims of bullying, research suggests that they are likely to share some common traits and experiences (Cook, et al., 2010). Olweus (1993a) noted that children who are bullied are likely to have one or more of the following characteristics:

- They are typically quiet, cautious, sensitive children who may be easily moved to tears.
- They may be insecure, have little confidence, and suffer from low self-esteem.
- They often have few friends and are socially isolated.
- They may be afraid of being hurt.
- They may be anxious or depressed.
- They tend to be physically weaker than their peers (especially in the case of boys).
- They may find it easier to spend time with adults (parents, teachers, coaches) than same-age peers.

As will be discussed later, low self-esteem, anxiety, and depression may be common consequences of bullying, but they also may be precursors to bullying, in some children. Research indicates that children with these characteristics are actually more likely to *become* victims of bullying (Cluver, Bowes, & Gardner, 2010; Fekkes, Pijpers, Fredriks, Vogels, & Verloove-Van Horick, 2006; Swearer, Grills, Haye, & Cary, 2004). It is likely that anxiety, depression, and poor self-esteem "signal" to peers that children may be easy targets for bullying.

In their meta-analysis of studies on bullying, Cook and colleagues (2010) concluded that a typical victim of bullying is one who has internalizing problems (e.g., is withdrawn, depressed, anxious), shows some externalizing behavior (e.g., defiance, disruptive behaviour), lacks good social skills, has negative beliefs about himself or herself (e.g., self-respect, self-esteem, self-efficacy), and has difficulty solving social problems.

Family variables may also contribute, to some degree, to a child becoming bullied (Cook et al., 2010). A child is more likely to be bullied if his or her family tends to be overprotective and sheltering because they think that child is anxious and insecure (Smokowski & Kopasz, 2005). A family's tendency to shelter a child may serve as both a cause and a consequence of bullying (Olweus, 1993a). Other family factors such as child maltreatment and domestic violence may also link a child with a high risk of being bullied by their peers (Ahmed, & Braithwaite, 2004; Baldry, 2003; Bowes, Arseneault, Maughan, Taylor, Caspi, & Moffitt, 2009; Cluver et al., 2010; Holt, Kantor, & Finkelhor, 2009).

Groups of children at high risk of being bullied
Although any child may be bullied by peers (and while it is not always evident *why* particular children are targeted), recent research has begun to focus attention on groups of children who may be at particularly high risk of being bullied. Relatively little research has been conducted on the relation between learning disabilities and bullying, but the existing findings suggest that children with learning disabilities are at greater risk of being teased and physically bullied (Martlew & Hodson, 1991; Mepham, 2010; Mishna, 2003; Nabuzoka & Smith, 1993; Thompson, Whitney, & Smith, 1994).

Children with Attention Deficit Hyperactivity Disorder (ADHD) also are more likely than other children to be bullied (and they also are somewhat more likely than others to bully their peers) (Kowalski & Fedina, 2011; Twyman, Saylor, Saia, Macias, Taylor, & Spratt, 2010; Unnever & Cornell, 2003a; Wiener & Mak, 2009). For example, in a study involving 1,315 middle school students in the US (Unnever & Cornell, 2003a), 14% of students reported that they had been taking medication for ADHD, of which approximately 34% had been bullied at least two or three times a month and 12% had bullied others at least two or three times a month. In contrast, only 22% of the students not taking medication for ADHD reported having been bullied and 8% had bullied others. Children with autism spectrum disorder (ASD) also appear to be at increased risk of being bullied and ostracized by peers (Kowalski & Fedina, 2011; Twyman et al., 2010). Twyman and colleagues found that children (aged 8–18) with ASD were three times more likely to report being bullied and ostracized than children with no special health care needs.

Children with special health care needs or chronic diseases may be frequent targets of bullying. For example, researchers have found higher rates of victimization among children with conditions that affect their appearance (e.g., cerebral palsy, muscular dystrophy, spina bifida, partial paralysis, acne, psoriasis and atopic eczema), and children with diabetes (Dawkins, 1996; Magin, Adams, Heading, Pond, & Smith, 2008; Storch, Lewin, Silverstein, Heidgerken, Strawser, Baumeister, & Geffken, 2004a, 2004b; Yude, Goodman, & McConachie, 1998), and epilepsy (Hamiwka, Yu, Hamiwka, Sherman, Anderson, & Wirrell, 2009).

Obesity may also place children at higher risk of being bullied (Falkner, Neumark-Sztainer, Story, Jeffery, Beuhring, & Resnick, 2001; Fox & Farrow, 2009; Gray, Kahhan, & Janicke, 2009; Griffiths, Wolke, Page, & Horwood, 2005; Janssen, et al., 2004; Pearce, Boergers, & Prinstein, 2002). In a study of more than 5,700 Canadian children aged 11–16, researchers found that overweight and obese girls (aged 11–16) and boys (aged 11–12) were more likely than normal-weight peers to be teased or made fun of and to experience relational bullying (e.g., to be socially excluded) (Janssen et al., 2004). Fox and Farrow (2009) found that, in a sample of 11–14-year-olds, overweight or obese children reported having experienced significantly more verbal and physical (but not social) bullying than their non-overweight peers. Some studies have examined gender differences in the relationship between bullying and obesity (Janssen et al., 2004; Pearce et al., 2002), but findings have been inconsistent. Underweight children may also become bullying targets. Wang, Iannotti, and Luk (2010) found that, among U.S. boys and girls in grades 6 through 10 in the Health Behaviour in School-aged Children 2005–2006 U.S. survey, underweight boys and girls were more likely to be victims of physical and relational bullying and underweight girls were more likely to experience relational bullying.

Finally, adolescents who identify themselves as lesbian, gay, bisexual or transgender (LGBT), those students who may be questioning their sexuality, and those who may be perceived as "too feminine" (boys) or "too masculine" (girls), can face unrelenting teasing and bullying by their peers (Eisenberg et al., 2005; Garofalo, Wolf, Kessel, Palfrey, & DuRant, 1998; Harris Interactive & GLSEN, 2005; Kosciw, Diaz, & Greytak, 2008; Williams, Connolly, Pepler, & Craig, 2003). Surveys of middle and high school students show that a great deal of verbal and physical bullying in schools is directed at students who are, or are perceived to be lesbian, gay or sexual minority youth. For example, the national School Climate Survey, conducted in 2007 by the Gay, Lesbian and Straight Education Network (GLSEN), concluded that nearly three-quarters of high school students surveyed heard derogatory and homophobic remarks "frequently" or "often" at school within the past year. Almost 90% of LGBT youth had been bullied verbally, and almost half had experienced physical attacks and threats. Bullying around issues of sexual orientation and gender expressions resulted in two-thirds of LGBT students feeling "unsafe" in school. Their rates of school avoidance were five times higher than a national sample of high school students (Kosciw et al., 2008).

Possible effects of bullying
Children who are bullied may experience problems associated with their health, well-being, and academic work. Research over the past decade confirms that many victims of bullying experience physical and mental health problems (Anthony, Wessler, & Sebian, 2010; Arseneault, Bowes, & Shakoor, 2010; Gini & Pozzoli, 2009). In their study of 2,766 Dutch school children aged 9–12, Fekkes, Pijpers, & Verloove-Van Horick (2004) compared health problems of bullied and nonbullied children and found that bullied children were approximately three times as likely to experience headaches, feel listless, and wet their beds. They were about twice as likely to have trouble sleeping, have stomach pain, feel tense, be tired, and have a poor appetite (Fekkes et al., 2004).

As these data would suggest, children who are bullied are more likely than nonbullied children to be anxious (Craig, 1998; Fekkes et al., 2004; Juvonen, Graham, & Schuster, 2003; Olweus, 1978) and to suffer from low self-esteem (Eagan & Perry, 1998; Hawker & Boulton, 2000; Hodges & Perry, 1996; Olweus, 1978; Rigby & Slee, 1993). Hawker and Boulton's (2000) analysis of peer victimization and psychosocial maladjustment suggested that victimization was very strongly related to depression (see also Craig, 1998; Fekkes et al., 2004, 2006; Hodges & Perry, 1996; Juvonen et al., 2003; Kumpulainen, Raasnen, & Puura, 2001; Olweus, 1978; Rigby & Slee, 1993). In a large sample of Norwegian adolescents aged 11–15 years, Undheim and Sund (2010) examined the relationships between being bullied, aggressive behaviors, and self-reported mental health problems. They found that the bullied youth reported more psychopathology and lower self worth than students not involved in bullying.

Bullied children also are more likely than other children to think about harming themselves or attempt to take their own lives. In a study of Australian children, Rigby (1996) found that those who were frequently bullied (i.e., at least once a week) were twice as likely as other children to wish they were dead or to admit to having recurring thoughts of suicide. In the United States, Klomek and colleagues (Klomek, Marrocco, Kleinman, Schonfeld, & Gould, 2008) found, in a self-report survey involving 2,342 high school students, that frequent exposure to five or six types of peer bullying (e.g., belittled about religion or race; belittled about looks or speech; physical victimization; subject of rumors or mean lies; subject of sexual jokes, comments, or gestures; cyber victimization) was related to a high risk of depression, suicidal ideation, and suicidal attempts among adolescents. They found that the more types of victimization to which students were exposed, the higher the risk for them to feel depressed, experience suicidal ideation, and make suicide attempts. Interestingly, the links between bully victimization and depression (and also between bully victimization and suicidal thoughts) are stronger for indirect as opposed to direct forms of bullying (Van der Wal, de Wit, & Hirasing, 2003). In other words, there may be more reason to worry about the psychological states of children who are ostracized by peers ("They pretend they don't see me") than children who are physically bullied ("They hit me"). Because children have such a strong need to belong and to be accepted by their peer group, many find it much more distressing to be excluded by peers than to be battered by them.

Bullying also may affect the academic work of bullied children. Research has documented that bullied children are more likely than nonbullied peers to want to avoid school (Kochenderfer & Ladd, 1996; Rigby, 1996; Smith, Talamelli, Cowie, Naylor, & Chauhan, 2004). They also have lower academic achievement than non-bullied peers, on average (Arseneault, Walsh, Trzesniewski, Newcombe, Caspi, & Moffitt, 2006; Eisenberg, Neumark-Sztainer, & Perry, 2003; Nakamoto & Schwartz, 2010). Although these findings indicate that there is a relationship between bullying and some academic problems, they do not necessarily imply that bullying *causes* these academic problems. Most studies linking bullying and poor academic adjustment are correlational; therefore, findings from these studies must be interpreted carefully, because correlational studies do not prove a causal relationship between bullying and academic functioning (see, e.g., Nakamoto & Schwartz, 2010). In a longitudinal study conducted on this issue, Buhs and colleagues followed nearly 400 children in the US from kindergarten through 5th grade (Buhs, Ladd, & Herald, 2006, Buhs, Ladd, & Herald-Brown, 2010). They observed that those children who were rejected by their peers in kindergarten (i.e., their kindergarten classmates said that they did not want to "hang out" with them) were more likely than others to be excluded and picked on by peers throughout elementary school. Children who were excluded by peers were, in turn, less likely to participate in class and ultimately performed more poorly on a test of student achievement. Students who were picked on were less likely to attend school. Although more research is needed to better understand the effects of bullying on children's attitudes toward school, their attendance, and their educational outcomes, there is reason for concern that the stress and distractions caused by bullying put children at academic risk. Similarly, in a longitudinal study of middle school students, Juvonen and colleagues (Juvonen, Wang, & Espinoza, 2011) found that middle school students' grade point averages and academic engagement (as rated by their teachers) were predicted by their perceptions that they had been bullied and also by their peers' perceptions that they had been bullied. The authors concluded that "the effect of peer victimization can account for up to an average of 1.5 letter grade decrease in one academic subject (e.g., math) across the 3 years of middle school" (p. 167).

The consequences of bullying can last long into the future. For some children, the devastating effects of bullying may be felt years after the bullying has ended. For example, in a study of young adults, Olweus found that boys who were bullied in junior high school were likely to suffer from low self-esteem and depression a decade after the bullying had ended (Olweus, 1993b). Other researchers have found that individuals who experienced frequent teasing in childhood were more likely to suffer from depression and anxiety in adulthood (Roth, Coles, & Heimberg, 2002). Roth et al. speculate that "children who are repeatedly teased may develop beliefs that the world is a dangerous place and that they have little control over outcomes in their lives" (p. 161). Fosse (2006) also provided some perspective on the possible magnitude of the problem. Fosse discovered that, among 160 young adults who had sought psychiatric treatment for the first time, 50% had been bullied during their school years, and the more severe bullying that they had experienced, the greater their psychiatric symptoms as adults.

Do children tell adults if they have been bullied?
Despite the high prevalence of bullying and the harm that it may cause, many children do not report their victimization to adults at school or at home. Research suggests that anywhere from 50% to 75% of students who are

bullied *do not* tell a teacher or another adult at school about their experiences (Boulton & Underwood, 1992; Fonzi, Genta, Menesini, Bacchini, Bonino, & Costabile, 1999; Harachi, Catalano, & Hawkins, 1999; Melton et al., 1998; Olweus & Limber, 2010c; Whitney & Smith, 1993). Older children and boys seem to be particularly reluctant to report being bullied (Melton et al., 1998; Olweus & Limber, 2010c; Rivers & Smith, 1994; Whitney & Smith, 1993). Children are somewhat more likely to talk with parents or other adults in their home about being bullied (Boulton & Underwood, 1992; Olweus, 1993a; Olweus & Limber, 2010c; see, however, Ortega & Mora-Merchan, 1999). They may be most comfortable reporting bullying experiences to their friends (Olweus & Limber, 2010c; Rigby, 2002; Rigby & Slee, 1999). Unfortunately, a worrisome number of children apparently do not tell anyone about their victimization (Harris, Petrie, & Willoughby, 2002; Naylor, Cowie, & del Rey, 2001; Olweus & Limber, 2010c). For example, Olweus and Limber (2010c) asked bullied children if they had told anyone about the bullying, and, if they had, whom they had told. Of particular concern were the percentages of students who had told no one that they had been bullied. More than one-fifth of girls and one-third of boys had not told anyone about the bullying.

Why are children reluctant to report bullying? For some (particularly older children), negative messages about "tattling" or "snitching" may cause them to think twice about reporting victimization. Boys may feel additional pressures to try to deal with bullying on their own and not to appear "weak" by seeking help from an adult. For other children, their reluctance to report bullying to school staff may reflect a lack of confidence in teachers' and other school authorities' handling of bullying incidents. For example, in a survey of high school students in the US, two-thirds of those who had been bullied felt that school personnel responded poorly to bullying incidents at school; only 6% believed that school staff handled these problems very well (Hoover, Oliver, & Hazler, 1992). As a boy remarked during a focus group convened by the developers of the National Bullying Prevention Campaign (Smith, January 3, 2003, personal communication), "Adults either way under-react to bullying or way over-react to it. They hardly ever get it right." With age, children are less and less likely to perceive that adults will be helpful in stopping bullying (Fonzi et al., 1999; Olweus & Limber, 2010c). For example, when students were asked how often teachers or other adults at school "try to put a stop to it when a student is being bullied at school", Olweus and Limber (2010c) found that, while about 50% of girls and boys in elementary grades believed that teachers tried to stop bullying "often" or "almost always", the percentage decreased with age. Approximately 45% of students in grades 6–8 and 40% those in grades 9–12 said that their teachers had tried to stop bullying "often" or "almost always."

In fairness to school staff, it can be extremely difficult for adults to identify bullying, particularly when the bullying is subtle, unreported, or denied by students. Students also may be unaware of efforts of staff to try to address bullying incidents sensitively and confidentially. Nevertheless, adults should take children's concerns to heart if we hope to increase the numbers who will report their victimization experiences.

Warning signs of bullying
Because children often do not report being bullied to adults, it is important for parents, educators, and other adults who work with children to be vigilant for possible signs of bullying. A child may have experienced bullying (or be a victim of ongoing bullying) if he or she:

- comes home with torn, damaged, or missing pieces of clothing, books, or other belongings;
- has unexplained cuts, bruises, and scratches;
- has few, if any, friends;
- seems afraid of going to school, walking to and from school, riding the school bus, or taking part in organized activities with peers (such as clubs);
- takes a long, "illogical" route when walking to or from school;
- has lost interest in school work or suddenly begins to do poorly in school;
- appears sad, moody, teary, or depressed when he or she comes home;
- complains frequently of headaches, stomach aches, or other physical ailments;
- has trouble sleeping or has frequent bad dreams;
- has little appetite;
- appears anxious, has low self-esteem (Olweus, Limber, & Mihalic, 1999).

If a child shows one or more of these characteristics, it is important to talk with the child (and his or her parents, teachers, other appropriate adults, and probably also his or her friends or peers) to determine whether the child may be bullied by peers and to help address whatever problems he or she may be experiencing (whether or not they are ultimately related to bullying).

Children who bully

Just as bullied children do not share all of the same traits or characteristics, there is no single "profile" of children who bully. Nevertheless, research suggests that children and youth who bully often have some common characteristics (Cook et al., 2010). Olweus noted that children who bully display one or more of the following characteristics (Olweus, 1993a):

- They have dominant personalities and like to assert themselves using force.
- They have a temper, are impulsive and are easily frustrated.
- They have more positive attitudes towards violence than other children.
- They have difficulty following rules.
- They appear to be tough and show little empathy or compassion for those who are bullied.
- They often relate to adults in aggressive ways.
- They are good at talking themselves out of difficult situations.
- They engage in both proactive aggression (i.e., deliberate aggression to achieve a goal) and reactive aggression (i.e., defensive reactions to being provoked; Camodeca & Goossens, 2005).
- They exhibit gradual decreases in interest in school.

Children who bully are sometimes stereotyped as "loners" who lack social skills, but this usually is not the case (Cairns, Cairns, Neckerman, Gest, & Gariépy, 1988; Faris & Felmlee, 2011; Nansel et al., 2001; Olweus, 1978; Juvonen et al., 2003). Some studies indicate that children who bully are less depressed, socially anxious, and lonely than their peers (Juvonen et al., 2003). Their classmates tend to rate them high in terms of social status, and their teachers confirm that children who bully often are the most popular students in the class (Juvonen et al., 2003; Langdon & Preble, 2008; Rodkin & Hodges, 2003). Faris and Felmlee (2011) found that children who picked on or were mean to other students enjoyed a relatively high status among their peers. Children at the very bottom of the status hierarchy among their peers were unlikely to be aggressive toward their peers because they lacked the capacity for it; those at the very top of the status hierarchy were unlikely to be aggressive toward peers because they had little cause to use it.

Although not all children who bully are popular, most have at least a small group of friends who support their bullying (Olweus, 1978, 1993a).

For example, Olweus and Limber (2010c) found that only 7% of "bullies" (compared to 15% of "victims" and 21% of "bullying/victims") said that they had no friends or only one friend in their class. Some studies suggest that children who bully are also good at reading the mental states and emotions of other children and in manipulating them (e.g., Sutton, Smith, & Swettenham, 1999a, 1999b).

Why do children bully?
There is no simple answer to this question, as children may bully for a variety of personal motivations, because of family dynamics, and even because of school, community, and societal factors. Researchers who have examined personal motivations for bullying have focused primarily on boys. There appear to be at least three primary motivations for boys' bullying (Olweus, 1993a; Olweus et al., 2007):

1. They have a need for dominance and power.
2. They find satisfaction in causing suffering or injury to others.
3. They are rewarded for their behavior. These rewards may be material (e.g., money, cigarettes, other possessions taken from their victims) or they may be psychological (e.g., prestige or perceived high social status).

Individual motivations for bullying behavior do not exist in isolation from other risk factors. Factors associated with the interpersonal relations of children and young people – with their family, friends and peers – can also strongly affect aggressive, violent, and bullying behavior and shape personality traits that, in turn, can contribute to bullying behavior. For example, a lack of parental warmth and involvement, inconsistent discipline/physical punishment by parents, and a lack of parental supervision contribute to children's bullying behavior (Cook et al., 2010; Duncan, 2004; Olweus, 1993a; Olweus et al., 1999; Rigby, 1993, 1994). Children who bully are more likely than their peers to be exposed to domestic violence (Baldry, 2003; Bowes et al., 2009; Holt, Kaufman Kantor, & Finkelhor, 2009) and be a victim of child maltreatment (Shields & Cicchetti, 2001). They also are more likely than other children to bully their own siblings (Bowes et al., 2009; Duncan, 1999; Holt et al., 2009).

If children are exposed to friends/peers with positive attitudes toward violence and to models of bullying, they will be more likely to engage in bullying behavior (Cook et al., 2010). Research seems to show that the influence of families is usually the greatest in this respect during childhood, while during adolescence friends and peers have an increasingly important effect (Krug, 2002). Bullying is also more likely in certain school settings than others, for example where there are opportunities and rewards for engaging in bullying behavior, where indifferent or accepting attitudes toward bullying on the part of students or teachers are common (Olweus, 1993a), where insufficient adult supervision exists (Olweus, 1993a; Pellegrini & Bartini, 2000), and where students experience a lack of community or connectedness with schools.

The communities in which children and young people live are an important influence on their families, the nature of their peer groups, and the way they may be exposed to situations that lead to bullying and violence. In a community with social disorganization, overcrowded neighborhoods with high crime rates, and high rates of drug and alcohol use, there is high risk for bullying and violence (Krug, 2002). The presence of risk factors does not, of course, indicate that a particular child will engage in bullying or violent behavior. However, it does increase the possibility that an individual will participate in bullying, and multiple risk factors further increase that possibility (Hermann & Finn, 2002). Adults should take these factors into account if we hope to better understand why children bully.

Concern for children who bully
There is good reason to be concerned about bullying behavior – not only because of the effect that bullying can have on victims, but also because it can be a sign of other troublesome behavior on the part of children who bully. Children who bully are more likely than their peers to be involved in a host of other antisocial, violent, or worrisome behavior, including fighting, stealing, vandalism, weapon-carrying, school drop-out, school adjustment, and poor school achievement (Byrne, 1994; Gini & Pozzoli, 2009; Haynie, Nansel, Eitel, Crump, Saylor, Yu, & Simons-Morton, 2001; Nansel et al., 2001; Olweus, 1993a). Very high rates of children who bully report that they do not like school (Cook et al., 2010). For example, Olweus and Limber (2010c) found that among 3rd to 12th graders, 31% of children categorized as "bullies" said that they "dislike or dislike very much" school (compared to 23% of "victims"). Children who bully also are more likely than nonbullying peers to drink alcohol, smoke (Gini & Pozzoli, 2009; Nansel et al., 2001; Olweus, 1993a), and own a gun for risky reasons (i.e., to

gain respect or frighten others; Cunningham, Henggeler, Limber, Melton, & Nation, 2000). Bullying also may be an early indicator that boys are at risk of later criminal behavior (Olweus, 1993a; Pellegrini, 2001). In a long-term study conducted by Olweus (1993a) in Norway, boys who were identified as bullies in middle school were four times as likely as their nonbullying peers to have three or more criminal convictions.

Children who are bully/victims

As mentioned earlier, some children are bullied with regularity but also bully other children. Olweus and Limber (2010c) found that only 3% of girls and 4% of boys were identified as "bully/victims," compared to the other categories ("bullies only" – 4% of girls and 8% of boys; "victims only" – 14% of girls and 12% of boys; and "not involved"). These children, who are frequently referred to as "bully/victims," "provocative victims," or "aggressive victims," are more likely than their peers to be hyperactive (Kumpulainen & Raasnen, 2000), restless, and have difficulty concentrating (Olweus, 1993b, 2001). As a group, they are more clumsy and immature than their peers, and they often have trouble reading the social cues of other children. Bully/victims tend to be quick-tempered and may try to fight back when they feel that they have been insulted or attacked (even when this isn't the case; Olweus, 1993b, 2001). Not only do peers find it difficult to associate with these children, but teachers and other school personnel frequently report that these children are among the most difficult to work with in a school setting, even though this group of children make up the smallest proportion of students involved in bullying behavior.

Research confirms that there is particular reason to be concerned about bully/victims, as they have many of the social and emotional difficulties of "passive" victims of bullying and the behavior problems associated with children who bully (Cook et al., 2010). Compared with other children (children who are "passive victims," those who bully, and those who are not involved in bullying), bully/victims fare more poorly in a variety of areas, including problem behaviors, self-control, social competence, deviant peer influences, school adjustment and bonding, and depression (Haynie et al., 2001), and social adjustment, isolation, and anxiety (Gini & Pozzoli, 2009). In a study of nearly 2,000 6th grade students, Juvonen and colleagues (2003) examined self-reports, peer reports, and teacher ratings of bully/victims compared with other students. The bully/victims were the group of children singled out by their peers as the most avoided students at school. Teachers rated them as being very unpopular, having many conduct problems and being disengaged from school. Olweus and Limber (2010c) found that 34% of "bully/victims" reported they "dislike or very much dislike" their school, compared to 31% of "bullies only," 23% of "victims only," and 15% of "not involved" students, respectively. Similarly, one in five "bully/victims" (21%) said that they had no friends or only one friend at school (compared with 7% of "bullies only", 15% of "victims only", and 6% of "not involved" students).

Disturbingly, bully/victims also are more likely than other children and youth to report suicidal or self-injurious behavior and suicidal thoughts (Kim, Koh, & Leventhal, 2005). Finally, the authors of two retrospective studies of violent acts at school (including, but not limited to, school shootings) have noted that many of the violent youth in their studies had also been bullied (Anderson et al., 2001; Fein et al., 2002). Anderson and his colleagues speculated that these children "may represent the 'provocative' or 'aggressive' victims ... who often retaliate in an aggressive manner in response to being bullied" (p. 2702).

Children who witness bullying

Adults often view bullying as a problem between two children – a child who bullies and his or her victim. But bullying is more accurately understood as a group phenomenon in which children may play a variety of roles. Olweus (1993a; Olweus et al., 1999; Olweus et al., 2007) described eight such roles as part of a continuum that he referred to as the Bullying Circle:

1. the student who initiates the bullying;
2. followers or henchmen, who actively take part in the bullying but do not initiate it;
3. supporters, who openly support the bullying (e.g., they laugh or otherwise call attention to the bullying) but do not take an active role;
4. passive supporters, who enjoy the bullying but do not openly support it;
5. disengaged onlookers, who neither get involved nor feel responsible for stepping in to stop the bullying;
6. possible defenders, who dislike the bullying and think they should do something to help, but do not;

7. defenders, who dislike the bullying and try to help those who are bullied;
8. the student who is bullied.

It is important to note that these roles (particularly roles 3–7) are not static but rather may change from one situation to the next. In one situation, a child may be a passive supporter of bullying that involves a new student whom she doesn't know; in another she may defend a friend who is being bullied. During physical education class, a child may be a victim of bullying. Later that day, the same child may pick on younger students on his school bus. Children's roles depend on the particular social setting, and the interaction of students within that setting. The term "bystander" is often used to describe those who witness bullying and other acts of violence (e.g., roles 2–7 in the Olweus Bullying Circle) but do not themselves initiate the bullying or experience being bullied in a particular situation (Twemlow, Sacco, & Williams, 1996).

What is the percentage of children who witness bullying behaviors and what are their attitudes toward the bullying that they observe? In a recent study involving 9,397 4th–11th grade students in Canada, 68% of children and youth reported witnessing bullying in school at least "once or a few times" (Trach, Hymel, Waterhouse, & Neale, 2010). Most children have fairly negative reactions to bullying and positive or sympathetic feelings towards children who are bullied (Baldry, 2004; Olweus & Limber, 2010c; Rigby & Slee, 1993; Unnever & Cornell, 2003b). Unfortunately, sympathy often does not translate into action. Olweus and Limber (2010c) found that 91% of 3rd–5th graders reported that they felt sorry for a bullied student (compared to 82% of 6th–8th graders and 77% of 9th–12th graders). However, when asked what they would do if they see or learn that a student is being bullied, a minority said they would try to help (approximately 45% of 3rd–5th graders, one-third of the 6th–8th graders, and one-quarter of the 9th–12th graders).

How does the behavior of bystanders affect bullying? Joining in the bullying or giving even subtle positive feedback by verbal or nonverbal cues (e.g. smiling, laughing) is probably rewarding for those who initiate the bullying (O'Connell, Pepler, & Craig, 1999), whereas challenging their behavior or taking sides with the victim provides negative feedback for them. In their observational study, Hawkins and colleagues (Hawkins, Pepler, & Craig, 2001) found that when bystanders reacted on behalf of the child being bullied, they were often effective in putting an end to a bullying incident.

Researchers from Finland (Kärnä, Voeten, Poskiparta, and Salmivalli, 2010) recently examined whether the 3rd–5th grade bystanders' behaviors in bullying situations influenced vulnerable students' risk for victimization. They found that the likelihood of anxious or rejected children being victimized depended to a large extent on the social context in classrooms. "If classmates reinforced bullying, this exacerbated the risk for the vulnerable students, whereas the protective effect of defending was weaker" (p. 275). Others have found that children's attitudes towards victims may be influenced by their observation of each others' reactions. Gini, Pozzoli, Borghi, and Franzoni (2008) manipulated the bystanders' reactions in hypothetical scenarios and found that, when middle-school children imagined witnessing a bullying incident where other bystanders intervened to help a bullied child, they reported liking the victim more than in the condition where bystanders assisted the bully.

The gender and age of children may significantly affect their bystander behavior. A study of Canadian students in grades 4–11 revealed that younger students and girls were more likely than older students and boys to report taking positive action to directly intervene to help the victim, tell the perpetrator to stop, or talk to an adult about the bullying (Trach et al., 2010). Boys and girls were equally likely to report that they ignored or avoided the person(s) who bullied. With increasing age, students were more likely to report that they did nothing to stop the bullying (see also Olweus & Limber, 2010c).

In a Finnish study, Salmivalli (1995) categorized bystander roles into five groups: defenders of the victim, "bystander", assistant to the bully, reinforcer of the bullying, and outsider. Salmivalli found that boys were more closely associated with the role of bully, reinforcer, and assistant, and girls with the role of defender and outsider. Olweus and Limber (2010c) also found gender differences concerning students' attitudes toward bullying. Ninety-one percent of girls reported that they felt sorry for a bullied student, compared to 76% of boys. Boys were more likely than girls to say that they could join in bullying a student whom they did not like (Olweus & Limber, 2010c).

If most children are disturbed by bullying, why don't they try to put a stop to it? Many may be uncertain about how best to respond to the bullying or are afraid that they may make the situation worse for the victim. Others may feel that their actions would be fruitless unless other students supported them, and they doubt that they would find many supporters. Many likely are afraid that they will become targets themselves if they take action to stop bullying. The literature suggests that children and adolescents facing bullying problems as bystanders are trapped in a social dilemma (e.g., Salmivalli, 2010). On one hand, they understand that bullying is wrong and they would like to do something to stop it, but, on the other hand, they strive to secure their own status and safety in the peer group. It is not entirely clear why older children and youth appear to be less inclined to help a student who is bullied. It may be that with age, there is increasing stigma associated with helping bullied students or reporting bullying to adults, and their desires for status and safety in their peer group are greater. Older youth also may be less likely to believe that such actions will be helpful in stopping bullying (particularly seeking help from adults). Perhaps previous experience with non-existent or ineffective responses to bullying has jaded them or taught them that trying to help is futile and may put them at risk.

The reasons for children's inaction illuminate some of the negative effects that bullying can have on bystanders. As witnesses to bullying, they may feel that they are in an unsafe environment. Effects may include feeling: fearful, powerless to act, guilty for not acting, and tempted to participate (Olweus, 1993a; Olweus & Limber, 2007). Over time, if they do not see adults or other children intervening to stop bullying, they may feel less empathy for children who are bullied. ("If they have been bullied all this time, maybe they deserve it!") If unchecked in school (or in other environments where children gather), bullying can seriously affect the silent majority of students who are bystanders to bullying. In so doing, it can erode the social climate of the school, family, and community.

Conditions Surrounding Bullying

In order to prevent bullying, it is important to better understand typical conditions that surround bullying incidents, including common locations for bullying, and the number and identity of perpetrators.

Where does bullying take place?

Bullying tends to thrive anywhere in a school or a community where adults are not present or are not vigilant. Although "hot spots" for traditional forms of bullying may vary somewhat from school to school and from community to community, some consistent areas of concern emerge. On self-report surveys, children report that traditional forms of bullying are more common at school (in the school building or on school grounds) than on the way to and from school, such as on the school bus, at the bus stop, or elsewhere in the community (Craig & Pepler, 1997; Harris et al., 2002; Nansel et al., 2001; Olweus, 1993a; Olweus & Limber, 2010c; Rivers & Smith, 1994). Olweus and Limber (2010c) examined the most common locations for bullying, according to children who had been bullied once or more often within the previous couple of months. "Hotspots" for bullying at school included hallways and stairwells (cited by 31% of bullied children), the lunchroom (30%), playgrounds or athletic fields (during recess or break times, 29%), in the classroom when the teacher was not in the room (28%), and in the classroom with the teacher present (26%). Twenty percent indicated they had been bullied on the school bus and 6% had been bullied at a bus stop.

Number and identity of perpetrators of bullying

Children who are bullied typically indicate that they are bullied by one other child or by a very small group of peers (Melton et al., 1998; Olweus, 1993a; Olweus & Limber, 2010c). It is much less common for children to be bullied by large groups, although children who are bully/victims may be the exception to this rule. Bully/victims may, in some cases, be bullied by many peers – occasionally an entire class (Olweus, 1993a). Most often, children are bullied by same-age peers or older children. When bullied students were asked who it was who had bullied them, Olweus and Limber (2010c) found that more than 70% of students had mainly been bullied by one student or by a group of two to three students. Boys were more likely to be bullied by boys; bullied girls, on the other hand, were very likely to be bullied by both boys and girls.

Effective Bullying Prevention

In the past two decades, an increasing number of bullying prevention and intervention strategies have been designed and implemented to address bullying, including: (a) efforts to increase knowledge of and raise awareness about bullying (e.g., during school assemblies, staff in-services, PTA meetings); (b) efforts to report and track bullying incidents at school; (c) therapeutic interventions for children who bully and children who are bullied; (d) peer mediation and conflict resolution to address bullying; (e) curricula focused on bullying; and (f) comprehensive bullying prevention programs.

What are common misdirections in bullying prevention and intervention?

Unfortunately, a number of misguided intervention and prevention strategies have been developed in recent years by well-intentioned adults (Health Resources and Services Administration, 2006; Olweus & Limber, 2010a).

Zero tolerance policies

Some schools and school districts have adopted zero tolerance or "three strikes and you're out" policies towards bullying, under which children who bully others are suspended or expelled. At first glance, and in light of tragic school shootings, these approaches may appear to make sense. However, these policies raise a number of concerns. First, they potentially affect a very large number of students. Approximately one in every 10 children has bullied other students with some regularity. Clearly, it would be bad policy to expel 10% of the students from our schools. Second, a goal of bullying prevention initiatives should be to encourage students to report known or suspected bullying among their peers. Threatening to severely punish students for bullying may have an unintended consequence of discouraging children and adults from reporting bullying. Finally, as noted earlier, children who bully their peers are at risk of engaging in other antisocial behaviors (such as truancy, fighting, theft, vandalism, and drug use). They need positive, prosocial role models, including peers and adults at their school. Suspension and expulsion of students may be necessary in a small number of cases to keep children and adults safe at school, but these practices are not recommended as a bullying prevention or intervention strategy (especially when effective bullying strategies are not in place in community).

The American Psychological Association Zero Tolerance Task Force (2008) reviewed the research on the effects of zero tolerance policies in school settings and concluded that 20 years of zero tolerance policies as implemented in schools "failed to achieve the goals (i.e., to preserve a safe climate, to encourage a positive and productive learning climate, to teach

students the personal and interpersonal skills they will need to be successful in school and society, and to reduce the likelihood of future disruption) of an effective system of school discipline" (p. 860). The
application of zero tolerance in suspension and expulsion has failed to
improve student behaviour, but has created unintended consequences for
students, families, and communities (e.g., accelerated negative mental
outcomes for youth, increased reliance on the juvenile justice system and
raised cost, disproportionate discipline of students of color and students
with disabilities).

Group treatment for children who bully

Other, less drastic measures call for children who bully to be grouped
together for therapeutic treatment, which might include anger management, empathy-building, or skill-building. Unfortunately, these groups
are often ineffective, even with well-intentioned and skilled adult facilitators, and they may actually make bullying worse, as group members may
reinforce each others' bullying behaviors. Rather, children who bully
need to be exposed to prosocial peers who can model positive behavior
and help send a message that bullying is not acceptable behaviour
(Limber, 2011b).

Conflict resolution/peer mediation

Because of the popularity of conflict resolution and peer mediation programs to address conflict among students, many schools use these techniques to address bullying problems as well. This practice generally is
not recommended. Why? First, as we discussed earlier, bullying is a form
of victimization or interpersonal abuse (the physical or psychological
maltreatment of a less powerful person by a more powerful person or
persons), not conflict. Second, mediation may further victimize a child
who has been bullied. It can be extremely painful for a child who has
been bullied to have to face his or her tormentor in mediation. Third,
mediating a bullying incident may send inappropriate messages to the
students who are involved. The message should not be, "You are both
partly right and partly wrong, and we need to work out this conflict
between you." Rather, the appropriate message for the child who is bullied should be, "No one deserves to be bullied, and we are going to see
that it ends." The message for children who bully should be, "Your behavior is wrong, it against our school's rules, and it must stop immediately"
(Limber, 2011b).

As discussed in detail in Chapter 6, restorative justice practices (also referred to as accountability circles) may be helpful in prescribed circumstances, where well-prepared victims of bullying, remorseful perpetrators, and parents of involved students are all willing to meet with well-trained facilitators. In this carefully controlled process, children who are bullied are able to share the impact of the bullying on their lives, and children who bully have an opportunity to apologize for their actions and propose ways to repair the harm that they caused. Effective restorative justice practices require time, training, and careful preparation, and they bear little resemblance to most schools' mediation programs, which often are led by students.

Simple, short-term solutions

With increasing pressures to address bullying at school, many educators are (understandably) searching for simple, short-term solutions. Bullying may be the topic of a school-wide assembly, addressed in a once-a-month curriculum, or the focus of a staff in-service. Although each of these efforts may represent important pieces of a comprehensive, long-term bullying prevention strategy, they probably will not significantly reduce bullying if implemented in a piecemeal way (Limber, 2011b).

What works in bullying prevention?

In its landmark National Bullying Prevention Campaign, the Health Resources and Services Administration (HRSA), identified 10 strategies that represent "best practices" in bullying prevention and intervention (2011).

1. Focus on the school environment

What is needed to reduce bullying in schools is nothing less than a change in the climate of the school and in the social norms. As the HRSA campaign notes, "It must become 'uncool' to bully, 'cool' to help out kids who are bullied and normative for staff and students to notice when a child is bullied or left out" (2011). Doing so requires the efforts of everyone in the school environment – teaching staff, administrators, non-teaching staff, parents, and, students (and presumably also community members).

2. Assess bullying at your school
Because adults often are not very good at estimating the nature and amount of bullying at their school, it is helpful to assess perceptions of bullying among the student body, staff, and parents. One effective way of doing this is by administering an anonymous survey. Findings from the assessment can help motivate adults to take action against bullying that they otherwise may have overlooked or downplayed. These data can also help staff to tailor a bullying prevention strategy to the particular needs of the school. Finally, these data are important in helping administrators measure progress in reducing bullying over time. Moreover, it is imperative to involve key stakeholders (e.g., school staff, students, parents) in the process of assessment, including assessment design, analysis, and report, because the assessment process may itself be a powerful practice to obtain knowledge of and raise awareness about bullying.

3. Garner staff and parent support for bullying prevention
Bullying prevention should not be the sole responsibility of any single administrator, counselor, teacher, or individual at a school. In order to be effective, bullying prevention efforts usually require support from the majority of the staff, from parents, and from the community.

4. Form a group to coordinate the school's bullying prevention activities
Bullying prevention efforts appear to work best if they are coordinated by a representative group from the school. This coordinating group (which might include an administrator, a teacher from each grade, a member of the nonteaching staff, a school counselor or other school-based mental health professional, a school nurse, a school resource officer, and a parent) should meet regularly to review data from the school's survey; plan bullying prevention policies, rules, and activities; motivate staff; get feedback from staff, students, and parents about what is working and what is not working; and ensure that the efforts continue over time. A student advisory group also can be formed whose purpose is to focus on bullying prevention and provide suggestions and feedback to educators.

5. Train school staff in bullying prevention
All administrators, faculty, and staff at a school should be trained in best practices in bullying prevention and intervention. Appropriate training can help staff to better understand the nature of bullying, its harmful effects,

how to respond to bullying, and how to work with others at the school to help prevent bullying. Administrators should make an effort to train all adults in the school who interact with students, including teachers, counselors, nurses, media specialists, lunch room and recess aides, bus drivers, custodians, and cafeteria workers.

6. *Establish and enforce school rules and policies related to bullying*
Most school behavior codes implicitly forbid bullying, but some do not use the term "bullying" or make it clear how students are expected to behave with regard to bullying (as witnesses as well as participants). Developing simple, clear rules about bullying can help to ensure that students are aware of adults' expectations that they refrain from bullying and help students who are bullied. School rules and policies should be familiar to staff, and posted and discussed with students and parents. Appropriate positive and negative consequences should be developed for following/not following the school's rules against bullying.

7. *Increase adult supervision in places where bullying occurs*
Because bullying thrives in places where adults are not present (or are not vigilant), school personnel should look for creative ways to increase adults' presence in "hot spots" that students identify for bullying.

8. *Focus some class time on bullying prevention*
Bullying prevention programs should include a classroom component. Classroom meetings, which focus on bullying and peer relations at school, can help teachers keep abreast of students' concerns, build a sense of community, allow time for honest discussions about bullying and the harms that it can cause, and provide tools for students to address bullying and other social problems. Antibullying themes and messages can also be incorporated effectively throughout the school curriculum.

9. *Intervene consistently and appropriately in bullying situations*
All staff should be able to intervene on the spot to stop bullying. Designated staff (e.g., school counselors or administrators) should also hold sensitive follow-up meetings with children who are bullied and (separately) with children who bully. Parents of affected students should be involved whenever possible and appropriate. It may also be helpful to hold meetings with bystanders, because this group of students should be encouraged to report the bullying behavior they may witness among their peers, to influence

their peers with positive and prosocial role models, and to understand adults' commitment to prevent bullying behavior.

10.   Continue these efforts over time
There should be no "end date" for bullying prevention efforts. Bullying prevention should be woven into the everyday fabric of the school and continue over time.

Comprehensive approaches to bullying prevention

Comprehensive bullying prevention programs that embrace principles of best practice hold the most promise for significantly reducing bullying behavior among school children (Limber, 2002, 2004; Mulvey & Cauffman, 2001). In recent years, a number of school-wide, comprehensive bullying prevention programs have been developed that include classroom-level interventions but also include interventions targeted at the broader school environment.[1] Ttofi and Farrington (2009) conducted a systematic review and meta-analysis of 59 well-designed evaluations of 30 different school-based bullying prevention programs in schools. They found that school-based bullying prevention programs are effective in reducing bullying and victimization, which were reduced by 20–30% in experimental schools (compared with control schools). Ttofi and Farrington (2009) concluded that "[p]rograms inspired by the work of Dan Olweus worked best" (p. 22) and that the future efforts should be "grounded in the successful Olweus programme" (p. 23) (also see Ttofi, Farrington, & Baldry, 2008).

The Olweus Bullying Prevention Program (OBPP)
The OBPP was developed and initially researched and evaluated in the early 1980s in Norway. More recently, this comprehensive, school-wide program and programs inspired by the OBPP has been implemented and evaluated in the United States, Canada, Great Britain, Germany, and several other countries.

The goals and principles of the OBPP   The OBPP was designed to reduce existing bullying problems among students at school, prevent the development of new bullying problems, and improve peer relations at school

(Olweus, 1993a; Olweus et al., 2007; Olweus et al., 1999). To meet these goals, schools work to restructure their school environment to reduce opportunities and rewards for bullying and build a sense of community among students and adults in the school community (Olweus, 1993a; Olweus et al., 2007; Olweus & Limber, 2010a, 2010b; Limber, 2011a, 2011b). The OBPP is based on four principles. Adults at school should: (a) show warmth and interest in their students; (b) set firm limits to unacceptable behavior; (c) use consistent, nonphysical, nonhostile, negative consequences for violation of rules; and (d) act as authorities and positive role models (Olweus, 1993a; Olweus et al., 2007; Olweus & Limber, 2010a, 2010b; Limber, 2011a, 2011b).

The components of the OBPP   These principles, which have been derived from research on aggressive behavior (Baumrind, 1967; Loeber & Stouthamer-Loeber, 1986; Olweus 1973, 1978, 1979, 1980), have been translated into specific program components at several levels: the school, classroom, individual, and (in some contexts) the community level (Olweus et al., 2007; Olweus & Limber, 2010a, 2010b; Limber, 2011a, 2011b). Table 2.1 provides a summary of the components of the OBPP at each of these four levels, as typically implemented in the US. Several of the program components have proven particularly important in the implementation of the OBPP. These components include: Bullying Prevention Coordinating Committee (BPCC), training and consultation, administration of the Olweus Bullying Questionnaire, staff discussion groups, school rules, classroom meetings, on-the-spot and follow-up interventions, community involvement, and parent involvement (for a detailed description of these program components, see Limber, 2011a).

The implementation and evaluation of the OBPP has been found to result in significant reductions in students' reports of bullying and victimization (Bauer, Lozano, & Rivara, 2007; Black & Jackson, 2007; Olweus, 1993a, 2004a, 2004b, 2005; Limber, 2006a; Limber et al., 2004; Masiello et al., 2009; Melton et al., 1998; Pagliocca, Limber, & Hashima, 2007). It also has resulted in clear improvements in students' perceptions of the social climate of the classroom, and in reductions in students' reports of antisocial behavior (such as vandalism, fighting, truancy, and theft). For a detailed description of evaluations of the effectiveness of the OBPP in the diverse settings within the US, see Limber, 2011a, 2011b, Olweus and Kallestad, 2010, and Olweus and Limber, 2010a, 2010b.

Table 2.1   Components of the Olweus Bullying Prevention Program.

Levels	*Components*
School-Level	• Establish a Bullying Prevention Coordinating Committee • Conduct committee and staff training • Administrate the Olweus Bullying Questionnaire schoolwide • Hold staff discussion group meetings • Introduce the school rules against bullying • Review and refine the school's supervisory system • Hold a school kick-off event to launch the program • Involve parents
Classroom-Level	• Post and enforce schoolwide rules against bullying • Hold regular class meetings • Hold meetings with students' parents
Individual-Level	• Supervise students' activities • Ensure that all staff intervene on the spot when bullying occurs • Conduct serious talks with students involved in bullying • Conduct serious talks with parents of involved students • Develop individual intervention plans for involved students
Community-Level	• Involve community members on the Bullying Prevention Coordinating Committee • Develop partnerships with community members to support a school's program • Help to spread anti-bullying messages and principles of best practice in the community

Source: Olweus et al., 2007.

Summary

Although the experiences of children like Jack and Tara are not new, it has only been in the past decade that the research community (with several notable exceptions) and members of the popular press have focused attention on their plight. Numerous studies conducted since the early 1990s have confirmed that bullying affects millions of school children each year – either directly or indirectly. Victims of bullying can suffer serious physical health, mental health, and academic consequences. Children who bully are at higher risk of being involved in a wide variety of antisocial, violent, or otherwise troubling behaviors. The effects of bullying also can "bleed" into the school environment as a whole, affecting bystanders and adults as well. As Limber (2006b) noted, "Although being bullied, harassed, and excluded are common experiences for many school children, we need not and should not accept that they are *inevitable* experiences" (p. 326). In fact, comprehensive school-based approaches have been shown to reduce bullying among students at school when they are implemented with fidelity. While more research is needed to better understand and address the many different risk and protective factors for bullying, including the broader societal or cultural influences on bullying, researchers have made important strides over the past decade in understanding this phenomenon.

We know less about the very new phenomenon of cyberbullying, however. Research into this new modality for bullying is clearly in its infancy. In Chapters 3 and 4, we will outline what currently is known about the nature and prevalence of cyberbullying, as well as ways in which it is similar to and different from more traditional forms of bullying.

Note

1. For a listing and description of comprehensive (as well as curricular) approaches to bullying prevention (and other aggressive behaviors), visit: http://www.findyouthinfo.gov/programsearch.aspx.

3

WHAT IS CYBERBULLYING?

Technology ... has all but erased the reflection time that once existed between planning a silly prank (or a serious act) and actually committing the deed.

(Franek, 2005/2006)

Ten years ago, this book wouldn't have been written because no one would have needed it. A decade ago, technology had not advanced to the point where cyberbullying was even an issue. Times have changed, however, and, for better or worse, children and youth are keeping pace with the changes much more readily than adults. As a testament to this, ask any child or adolescent what acronymns such as PAW, A/S/L, and POS mean. Most will know immediately what they mean. Ask adults, and you likely will be met with blank stares. For those who don't know, they mean "parents are watching," "age, sex, location," and "parent over shoulder" (www.netlingo.com).

Although school-yard bullying such as that described in the previous chapter still occurs regularly, kids today are experiencing a new type of bullying that has been made possible through technological advances, such as cellular phones and the Internet. In addition, with the accessibility of free e-mail services, such as Hotmail, Gmail, and Yahoo ("Internet bullies," 2006), a single child who cyberbullies can communicate with a victim using multiple identities and multiple e-mail addresses. As mentioned in Chapter 1, this type of bullying is known as cyberbullying, online social cruelty, and electronic bullying. One Web site devoted to educating parents about cyberbullying appropriately defined it as "social terror by technology"

Cyberbullying: Bullying in the Digital Age, Second Edition. Robin M. Kowalski,
Susan P. Limber, and Patricia W. Agatston.
© 2012 Robin M. Kowalski, Susan P. Limber, and Patricia W. Agatston.
Published 2012 by Blackwell Publishing Ltd.

("Cyber bullying," 2006). On an ABC *Primetime* news segment (Ross, 2006), Diane Sawyer referred to cyberbullying as "emotional wilding" and "going for the emotional jugular." Whatever the specific phrase used to capture its essence, cyberbullying, broadly defined, refers to bullying that involves the use of e-mail, instant messaging, Web pages, Web logs (blogs), chat rooms or discussion groups, digital images or messages sent to a cellular phone, online gaming, and other information communication technologies (Health Resources and Services Administration, 2006; Patchin & Hinduja, 2006; Shariff & Gouin, 2005; Willard, 2006). In keeping with Olweus' (1993) definition of bullying, Peter Smith and his colleagues (2008, p. 376) defined cyberbullying as "An aggressive, intentional act carried out by a group or individual, using electronic forms of contact, repeatedly and over time against a victim who cannot easily defend him or herself."

Much of the attention in the popular press and professional literature has focused on sexual predators that seek out their victims through online venues such as Facebook and MySpace. This focus on sexual predators is not all that surprising given the seriousness of the issue, and the legal resources available to handle such cases when they do arise. In addition, most parents and teens understand the significance and discuss the dangers of sexual predators. The same cannot be said of cyberbullying. Significantly less attention – popular, academic, and/or legal – has been devoted to the topic of cyberbullying. The reality, however, is that the majority of children are more likely to be targeted by a person who cyberbullies than by a stranger they have met on the Internet who is trying to arrange an offline meeting. Figures 3.1 and 3.2 show the amount of popular and empirical attention that has been devoted to cyberbullying.

Defining Cyberbullying

Whenever researchers begin working in a relatively new area, there are, not surprisingly, conceptual issues that need to be worked out. Cyberbullying has certainly been no exception. Defining the parameters of cyberbullying (e.g., which communication technologies are involved, how they are misused, what is said to whom and with what effect) has proven somewhat difficult, in part because the methods used to cyberbully are varied. Complicating matters further, cyberbullying can sometimes be ambiguous in much the same way that interpersonal teasing is ambiguous. Is a heated exchange between two people IMing each other cyberbullying or simply an

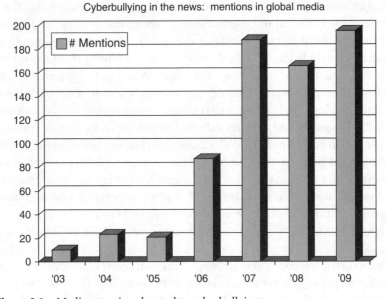

Figure 3.1   Media attention devoted to cyberbullying.
Note. Statistics from 2010 are not shown in the graph because there were over 3500 mentions due in large part to several suicides resulting in part from cyber bullying.

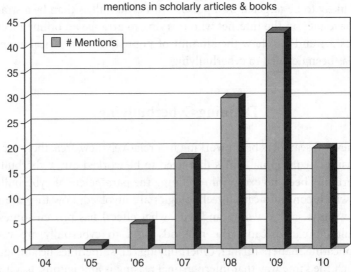

Figure 3.2   Research attention devoted to cyberbullying.

argument in print? As with interpersonal teasing, whether something is considered cyberbullying likely depends on who you ask. Targets of vicious e-mails or "verbal lynchings" as Diane Sawyer referred to them (Ross, 2006) are far more likely than perpetrators to identify the behavior as cyberbullying (see also Kowalski, 2000).

There is also confusion surrounding the ages at which cyberbullying may take place. According to Parry Aftab, a lawyer who specializes in Internet safety and who is the executive director of wiredsafety.net, cyberbullying must occur between minors. When an adult becomes involved, the behavior is labeled *cyber harassment* or *cyberstalking*. According to Aftab (2011), "adult cyber-harassment or cyberstalking is NEVER called cyber bullying." We would like to suggest that this behavior, while certainly deserving of the labels of cyber harassment and cyberstalking (and the legal remedies that follow), is also a type of cyberbullying. Indeed, the British National Association of Schoolmasters/Union of Women Teachers (NAS/UWT) highlighted the fact that teachers are often cyberbullied by their students. In one particular instance, the NAS/UWT lobbied for the rights of a teacher to be able to refuse to teach a student who had photographed her cleavage and distributed the image to classmates. Similar cases in which head shots of teachers have been superimposed on nude bodies had also been reported ("Pupils not the only victims of cyber bullies," 2006). More recently, a survey conducted by the Teacher Support Network and the Association of Teachers and Lecturers showed that 17% of teachers had been cyberbullied (Smith, 2007). One of the authors had a conversation with a newspaper reporter who talked about the dozens of e-mails she frequently gets haranguing her over a story she has written. Having been a reporter for many years, she said the viciousness of people's e-mails far surpasses anything they would write in snail mail letters or say to reporters over the telephone. As she related several examples of these e-mails, they were clearly examples of cyberbullying. A study with college students found that the majority of their experiences with cyberbullying occurred in college as opposed to in middle and high school (Kowalski, Giumetti, Schroeder, & Reese, 2012). Additional research has coined the term online incivility or cyber-incivility to refer to rude and discourteous behaviors online, a type of behavior that would certainly include cyberbullying (Giumetti, Schroeder, Hatfield, McKibben, & Kowalski, 2011).

Conceptual confusion about cyberbullying also stems from the fact that cyberbullying, like more traditional forms of bullying, can be both direct and indirect. Aftab (2011) draws an interesting distinction between *direct cyberbullying* and *cyberbullying by proxy*, or indirect cyberbullying. She defines direct attacks as sending messages direct to other children or youth. Cyberbullying by proxy involves "using others to help cyber bully the victim, either with or without the accomplice's knowledge;" in other words, getting someone else to do the dirty work (Aftab, 2011). Aftab argues that the latter is more dangerous because adults can get involved in the harassment. Most of the time, they are unwitting accomplices and don't know they are being used by the instigator of the cyberbullying. What Aftab refers to as "Warning" or "Notify Wars" are an example. Youth click on the warning buttons on their instant message (IM) screen, e-mail, social network or chat screens and alert the Internet Service Provider (ISP) that there is objectionable content in something the target has written. Targets who receive enough warnings eventually lose their accounts with a particular site. Children who cyberbully often set up their victims by making them angry so that they respond with an irate or hateful remark. Once the target responds this way, the perpetrator "warns" or "notifies" them. An unsuspecting adult then terminates the account, becoming an accomplice in the cyberbullying incident.

Cyberbullying by proxy also may occur when someone hacks into the victim's account and sends out harassing, inappropriate, and hateful messages to friends and family on the buddy or "friend" list. (A buddy list, most often associated with America Online (AOL), Facebook, and related Internet sites is a window that comes up that includes the screen names of friends, family, co-workers, and acquaintances whom you have chosen to include in the list and wish to be able to communicate with instantly once they sign onto the ISP; webopedia.com). Alternatively, the child who cyberbullies may be a friend with whom the target has shared his or her username and password, so access to the account is even easier. Recipients of the harassing messages assume that they are coming from the original user of the account (i.e., the target), who subsequently may lose friends, feel humiliated, and have his or her trust destroyed (Aftab, 2011).

In other instances of cyberbullying by proxy, perpetrators of cyberbullying may reset passwords on the target's account so that even the target is blocked from accessing his or her own account. Importantly, and highlighting the difficulty in always clearly identifying when cyberbullying has occurred, some individuals may reset a friend's password just in fun. What distinguishes "playful teasing" from cyberbullying is the aggressive intent behind cyberbullying. But, again, intent is in the eye of the beholder. Just as someone who realizes that his or her teasing has gone too far can say "I was only teasing," so, too, a person who cyberbullies can deny that there was any malicious intent behind the behavior; in other words, the target was being too sensitive.

In even more threatening situations, children who cyberbully will sometimes post information about their victim online that places their victim at considerable risk of harm. For example, they may post "information in child molester chat rooms and discussion boards, advertising their victim for sex. They then sit back and wait for the members of that hate group or child molester group to attack or contact the victim online and, sometimes, offline" (Aftab, 2011). Just such a situation occurred in Montana. A family of four, including 14-year-old twin girls, their mother and stepfather, had moved from California to Montana because they felt the town they lived in wasn't "white enough." The twin girls, Lynx and Lamb Gaede, created a band called Prussian Blue so they could use music to disseminate their views on the supremacy of the white race. Neighbors in the Montana town, concerned with the views of the new residents, posted fliers throughout the town that said "No Hate Here." However, according to news reports, Web sites, including hate groups, linked to the Prussian Blue site, then posted names, addresses, and phone numbers of individuals who had handed out the fliers (Redeker, 2006).

It should be clear now, why coming up with a single sentence or two that defines cyberbullying is difficult. Cyberbullying casts a wide net that captures a number of different types of behaviors. Still, at its core cyberbullying involves bullying through the use of technology such as the Internet and cellular phones. As with traditional bullying, cyberbullying also exists on a continuum of severity. On the less extreme end of this continuum, cyberbullying may, at times, be difficult to identify. At the other extreme, cyberbullying likely has contributed to murder and suicide (see, for example, www.ryanpatrickhalligan.org). As will be seen in the sections that follow, the methods that people use to perpetrate cyberbullying are as varied as the different types of behaviors that constitute it.

Types and Methods of Cyberbullying

A distinction needs to be made between the methods by which cyberbullying is carried out (e.g., e-mail, chat rooms, etc.), and the kind of behavior or exchange being transmitted via that method that leads to a label of cyberbullying. First, we will discuss behaviors that are likely to be classified as cyberbullying regardless of the specific means by which they are executed. Then, we will turn our attention to some of the most common mechanisms used to cyberbully others.

In one of the first books to address the topic of cyberbullying, *Cyberbullying and Cyberthreats*, Nancy Willard (2006), an attorney who is the Director of the Center for Safe and Responsible Internet Use, outlined a number of behaviors that she argues constitute cyberbullying. Included among these are flaming, harassment, denigration, impersonation, outing and trickery, exclusion, and cyberstalking. To this list, we will add happy slapping and sexting. Each of these will be discussed.

Flaming

Flaming refers to a brief, heated exchange between two or more individuals that occurs via any communication technology. Typically, though, flaming occurs in "public" settings, such as chat rooms or discussion groups, rather than private e-mail exchanges. If a series of insulting exchanges ensues, then a flame war has started (Willard, 2006).

At first blush, flaming would seem to occur between two individuals who are on an equal playing field with one another. However, an unsuspected aggressive act by one individual may create an imbalance in the playing field that is made all the greater by the fact that the target, at least in the short term, is unsure who else the perpetrator might bring into the flame war. So, what may appear to observers to be a level playing field may not be perceived that way by the individuals directly involved in the insulting exchange.

Harassment

Some writers and researchers have used the terms harassment and cyberbullying interchangeably. We mentioned earlier in this chapter Aftab's (2011) use of the term cyber harassment to refer to electronic bullying among adults. *Black's Law Dictionary* (2009, p. 784) defines harassment as "words, conduct, or action (usually repeated or persistent) that, being directed at a specific person, annoys, alarms, or causes substantial emotional distress in that person and serves no legitimate purpose" and further notes that some but not all types of harassment are actionable (i.e., persons may file suit). In the cyberbullying literature, cyber harassment generally is viewed as a unique form of cyberbullying that involves repetitive offensive messages sent to a target. Most often harassment occurs via personal communication channels, such as e-mail, but harassing messages may also be communicated in public forums, such as chat rooms and discussion groups. One form of harassment, referred to as text wars, involves one or more perpetrators and a single target. The perpetrator(s) sends hundreds or thousands of text messages to the target's cellular phone, leaving the target not only with a slew of harassing messages but possibly with a sizable phone bill as well.

Although conceptually similar, harassment typically differs from flaming in two ways. First, harassment is longer term than flaming. Second, harassment is more one-sided, with at least one offender and a single target. With flaming, on the other hand, there is a mutual exchange of insults between the individuals involved.

Harassment also occurs among a special group of online bullies known as griefers. Griefers are individuals who deliberately harass and bully other players in multiplayer online games. A griefer is less concerned about winning a particular game than he or she is about ruining the playing experience for other players (Coyne, Chesney, Logan, & Madden, 2009; Pham, 2002; Swartz, 2005). Typical griefer behaviors include extensive use of profanity, blocking certain areas of the game, and cheating (Merritt, 2009). Some griefers, although rare, resort to more extreme measures. Merritt (2009) reports a case where a griefer "rigged an epilepsy message-board with strobing graphics and animated objects that were specifically intended to trigger epileptic seizures." Several participants in our focus groups indicated that either they had been cyberbullied in this way or that they had friends who had been cyberbullied by griefers. In an investigation of the presence of griefers among second-life residents, 95% of the respondents indicated that they had come upon griefers (Coyne et al., 2009).

One particularly troubling form of harassment is perpetrated by "cyber trolls." These individuals post negative, harassing information on message boards, social network sites, Web pages, even on the memorial pages of recently deceased individuals (Famiglietti, 2011). In the latter case, some do it simply to be mean. Others do it to incite friends of the deceased and create a flame war (DesRochers, 2006).

Denigration

Denigration is information about another that is derogatory and untrue. The information may be posted on a Web page or it may be disseminated to others via e-mail or instant messaging. Included within this category of cyberbullying is posting or sending digitally altered photos of someone, particularly in a way that portrays them in a sexualized or harmful manner. In a cyberbullying case that was relayed to us, classmates recorded a song making fun of another classmate. They then placed the song on a Web site so that other classmates could listen to it. One of our focus group participants related a story about a classmate who was cyberbullied by other classmates who posted a picture of her online that was designed to make her look pregnant.

Online "slam books," which are created to make fun of students, represent a form of denigration. Students create a Web site where classmates' names are listed and students write mean and nasty comments about targeted students. Similar to this are negative lists that are posted online. For example, one individual created an online list of students that she identified as "ho's" of the school. Other lists may post information related to who is believed to be sleeping with whom.

Among college and university campuses, the online slam book was known as JuicyCampus.com. The site originated on August 1, 2007, and grew to include 500 college campuses and a million unique users monthly ("A juicy shutdown," 2009). The creator and CEO, Matt Ivester, tooted the site as "a platform that students have found interesting, entertaining, and fun" ("A juicy shutdown," 2009). Many students had a very different perspective of the Web site, however. Students would post commentary on the site, such as "Worst hookup" or "Top 10 sluts" to which others could post replies and commentary. Many individuals visited the site not to post information but simply to see if they were among those who were being defamed on the site (Lisson, 2008). "When asked about the possible dangers of the site, Ivester admitted that 'there are risks of cyber bullying,' but added, 'I don't think JuicyCampus causes those effects. We don't encourage lies to be posted on our website in any regard'" (Shah, 2008). Juicycampus.com was shutdown on February 5, 2009 due to "lack of revenue" according to Matt Ivester. Within a short period of time, however, a similar college gossip forum, www.collegeacb.com, replaced it and remains alive and well.

Impersonation

With impersonation, the perpetrator poses as the victim, most often by using the victim's password to gain access to his or her accounts, then communicates negative, cruel, or inappropriate information with others as if the target himself or herself were voicing those thoughts. In one case, a

15-year-old girl's online identity was stolen, and sexually explicit messages and profanity-laced messages were sent to her classmates and family from her social networking accounts by someone posing as this teenager. The student was humiliated and lost many friendships over the incident (Queally, 2011).

Additionally, the perpetrator may steal the target's password in order to be able to change the target's personal profile on buddy lists or on a social network site so that inappropriate or offensive information is included. Or they may steal the password so that they can send harassing e-mails to others as if they were coming from the target. As noted earlier, at the extreme, a cyberbully impersonator may post an offensive remark or comment on a hate group or some other type of group's message board pretending to be the victim, including the name, address, and phone number of the victim should members of the hate group decide to track him or her down. At this level, impersonation truly puts the victim's life in danger.

A recent method of gaining access to login information in order to impersonate someone is firesheep. Firesheep is an addon to the Firefox browser that shows when people on an open Wifi network are using an insecure site, such as Facebook or Twitter. The program, created by Eric Butler to "show the lack of security on many websites… and strongly encourage those companies to make their sites more secure" (Khalil, 2010), allows users to capture cookies sent over insecure connections and use that information to hijack another person's account (Khalil, 2010). Individuals with the addon can click "start capturing" and see the unsecured accounts of other individuals sharing the Wifi network. Depending on the encryption level of those accounts, they can then send messages from those accounts and alter information within the accounts (Machlis, 2010).

Outing and trickery

Outing refers to sharing personal, often embarrassing, information with others. This may take the form of receiving an e-mail or instant message from a target that contains private, potentially embarrassing information and/or photos and then forwarding that e-mail on to others. Trickery refers to tricking someone into revealing personal information about themselves and then sharing that information with others.

Exclusion/ostracism

Whether in the online or offline world, children often perceive that they are either "in" or "out". If they are not in the in-group, then they are in the out-group. Social psychologists have determined that people have a basic human need to be included by other people. Much of our social behavior is guided by our attempts to be included by others and to avoid being excluded, a situation referred to by some as "social death" (Sudnow, 1967; Williams, Cheung, & Choi, 2000). Not surprisingly exclusion in the online world, or cyber-ostracism, can have a serious emotional impact. Dr Larry Koenig (September 28, 2006, personal communication), a former family therapist and a leader in the development of programs for parents and children, summed it up well when he said "with cyber bullying you can absolutely destroy a child emo-tionally." Ask anyone who has been "defriended" on Facebook or related social network sites, and they can relay the sting attached to such ostracism.

Online exclusion can occur in any type of password-protected environ-ment or by a target being knocked off of buddy lists. In some instances, the ostracism may be perceived rather than real, as when someone doesn't respond as quickly to an IM or e-mail as you would like them to. According to Bill Belsey, the creator of www.bullying.org, a leading online source for information about bullying, and www.cyberbullying.ca, the first Web site devoted specifically to cyberbullying, not responding promptly in the online world is viewed as a "real social faux-pas."

Kip Williams and his colleagues (2000) conducted two studies looking at the effects of cyber-ostracism. In the first study, participants played a disk toss game in cyber space ostensibly with two other players. In fact, the play-ers were created by the computer. The researchers manipulated the degree to which the participant was included or excluded in the disk toss game. The more people were ostracized from the game, the worse they felt and the more their self-esteem dropped.

In a second study, the researchers used a simulated ball toss paradigm to determine the relationship between exclusion and the desire to re-establish social connections through conformity. As in the first study, researchers manipulated the degree to which participants were included or excluded in the ball toss game. The more excluded participants were, the more likely they were to conform to members of a completely different group than the group that had ostracized them.

Interestingly, this suggests that people who are cyberbullied, particularly through the method of cyber-ostracism, may join other groups online more readily than individuals who are not ostracized. These groups could be discussion groups or chat rooms, or they could be groups designed to seek revenge on the original source. Joining other groups and feeling connected again may help to alleviate some of the negative feelings associated with having been cyberbullied and ostracized. In addition, there is safety in numbers. Feeling connected to a group of other people may lead the victim to feel empowered to retaliate either individually or by enlisting the help of members of the new group.

Cyberstalking

Cyberstalking refers to the use of electronic communications to stalk another person through repetitive harassing and threatening communications. *Black's Law Dictionary* (2009, p. 444) defines "cyberstalking" as: "the act of threatening, harassing, or annoying someone through multiple e-mail messages, as through the Internet, esp. with the intent of placing the recipient in fear that an illegal act or an injury will be inflicted on the recipient or a member of the recipient's family or household." A counselor in the district where we conducted focus groups shared a story of a female band member who was stalked by a fan after posting her e-mail address on the band's Web site. A focus group participant, also a victim of cyberstalking, related the following story: "My ex-boyfriend got kind of crazy once. He started e-mailing me and saying that he was going to come to my house and kill me and stuff like he was watching my sister."

Video recording of assaults/happy slapping and hopping

In an effort to increase the humiliation experienced by the target of cyber-bullying, perpetrators often digitally record assaults on the target and upload those recordings to the Internet for hundreds of thousands to see and comment on. Importantly, it is often much easier to get the videos posted on the Web than it is to have them removed from the Web. One of the earliest examples of this was Gyslain Raza or the "Star Wars kid" described earlier.

A variant of this known as happy slapping began on subway trains and has taken hold in England. People, usually teenagers, walk up and slap someone, while another individual, also usually a teenager, captures the violence using a camera phone. The behavior often involves more than a "slap," however, and often constitutes assault with associated legal ramifications. In

2009, for example, two teenagers were charged with manslaughter following a happy slapping incident in which a 67-year-old man, Ekram Hague, whom they had perpetrated a happy slapping incident against as he left a house of worship, died from the injuries they had inflicted ("Attorney General," 2010). A variant of happy slapping, known as hopping, that typically involves direct assaults, is showing up with increasing frequency in the United States and elsewhere (Kohler, 2007). With both happy slapping and hopping, the video that is taken of the incident is then downloaded onto the Web for thousands to see. The victim could be someone known or unknown to the perpetrator. In one incident, an 11-year-old boy was mercilessly attacked in the hallways of his school while observers recorded the incident on their cell phones. Pictures of the boy were then e-mailed to friends of the perpetrator and other observers (Blair & Norfolk, 2004). In another incident, Triston Christmas died as a result of happy slapping. Triston was 18 years old when he was hit so hard that he was knocked backwards and hit his head on a concrete floor. The cell phone images show him bleeding as he tried to speak (Watt, 2006). He didn't die until a week later. While he lay on the ground after being attacked, his killer and the killer's friends went to a party and posted the image of Triston online.

In still other incidents, children have died by suicide after being the victim of happy slapping. In one instance in April, 2005, a 14-year-old named Shaun Noonan hanged himself after being physically bullied and happy slapped ("Bullycide memorial page," 2006). In a Web-based discussion forum on happy slapping, one respondent stated: "I live in London and can confirm this – I've seen this happen a couple times. It's sad but true. They generally 'attack' in groups and think it's really funny. But I've seen some people really messed up and scared by it" (Dybwad, 2005). As is true for other types of bullying behavior, depending upon the nature of the situation happy slapping incidents also may constitute crimes.

Sexting

Sexting refers to the sending or posting of nude or semi-nude pictures or videos via text messages or other electronic means. Prevalence rates of sexting vary depending on the survey used, the age of the participants surveyed, and the inclusiveness of the venue (texting, email, Web pages). A nationally representative survey conducted by the Pew Internet and American Life Project (Lenhart, 2010) of 800 children ages 12–17 found that 4% said that they had sent a sext via the cellular phone to another person; 15% reported receiving a sext. The older the child, the greater their likelihood of having been involved in sexting. In a survey conducted by the National Campaign to Prevent Teen and Unplanned Pregnancy, 19% of teens (13–19) said that they had sent via text messaging or posted online inappropriate pictures or videos of themselves. Thirty-nine percent of teens and 59% of young adults had sent or posted inappropriate messages. Thirty-one percent reported that they had received a sext from someone else. MTV and the Associated Press (2009) conducted a survey of sexting behavior and found that 10% of individuals aged 14–24 had sent a sext whereas 15% indicated that they had received a sext directly from someone else. Similar statistics were found by Hinduja and Patchin in their assessment of approximately 4400 respondents aged 11–18. Eight percent of the students indicated that they had sent a sext, and 13% said they had received a sext (Hinduja & Patchin, 2010b). In general, studies reporting higher levels of sexting include sexually suggestive comments in their definitions of sexting.

In terms of the recipients of sexts, among teens respondents in the National Campaign to Prevent Teen and Unplanned Pregnancy who had engaged in sexting, 71% of girls and 67% of boys had sent or posted the sext to a romantic partner; 21% of girls and 39% of boys had sent/posted the inappropriate picture or message to someone they wanted to be involved with; 15% of the girls and boys had sexted someone that they knew only from their online interactions (see also Lenhart, 2010). Although clearly some individuals engage in sexting for relational purposes and others do it because it seems to be the "in" thing to do, still others engage in sexting as a means of bullying and hurting others. For example, following the break-up of a relationship, one member of the former couple may forward nude images of the former partner to the student body at school as revenge for the break-up.

Sexting has personal, school-related, and legal consequences (Marshall & Stanfield, 2011). Those who are involved in sexting, as both victim and perpetrator, can face personal consequences such as embarrassment and anxiety. Individuals who send sexts and who are found with nude pictures or videos on their cellular phones can face suspension or expulsion from school. Additionally, youth involved with sexting may face substantial legal consequences, including felony charges of distribution of pornography and legal classification as a lifetime sex offender. In one case in Georgetown, Ohio in 2009, four teens ranging in age from 14 to 18 were arrested and charged with felonies because a picture of a nude girl was found on their cell phones. The 18-year-old in this case faced more serious charges than the three minors because he was legally an adult ("Teens face," 2009). Another 18-year-old found himself on the Florida sex offender registry after he sent a nude picture of his 16-year-old girlfriend to several friends and family following a fight (Feyerick & Steffen, 2009). Importantly, teens who receive sexts should report that information to an adult and then delete the picture. Deleting the image shows a clear lack of intent to distribute, reducing the likelihood that there could be any negative legal ramifications for them.

However, some researchers believe that youth who receive a nude picture from someone else, particularly a close friend, should delete the image without telling an adult. Although this perspective is controversial, the argument advanced by proponents of this perspective is that reporting the sexting to adults, even a parent, could cause legal problems for the recipient of the sext as well as the individual who sent it. For more information on this perspective, the reader is referred to the following Web site: http://cyberbullying.us/blog/you-received-a-sext-now-what-advice-for-teens.html.

Communication Modalities for Cyberbullying

Although it is clear from the descriptions of these behaviors that they can be carried out through any of a number of different communication modalities, some behaviors lend themselves more readily to certain venues than others. For example, flaming is more likely to be carried out over public communication venues whereas harassment is generally more likely to be limited to personal communication modalities such as e-mail. Because of the diversity of communication technologies that can be used to cyberbully others, we will briefly describe the most commonly used methods.

Instant messaging

As will be discussed in Chapter 4, instant messaging represents one of the most common ways in which teenagers cyberbully one another. Instant messaging, or "IMing", refers to real-time communication via the Internet with individuals on one's buddy or contact list. Cyberbullying through instant messaging can take a number of different forms (Aftab, 2011). Most obviously, perpetrators may send angry or threatening messages to someone else. Alternatively, they may create a screen name that closely resembles the target's screen name or they may use the target's actual screen name. They then send inappropriate communications to others as if they were the target. They may also send compromising photos or videos of another person via IM.

Electronic mail

Electronic mail, or e-mail, is one of the most frequently used means of digital communication. E-mails are a frequent method of cyberbullying others for two primary reasons. First, a single e-mail can be sent to hundreds and even thousands of people with a single keystroke. Someone wishing to harass or humiliate another individual can send an e-mail containing pictures or objectionable information about another individual to hundreds or thousands of people at one time. Second, although e-mails are generally easily traceable, there is no certainty that the person from whose e-mail account the e-mail originated was actually the individual who sent the e-mail. In some instances, individuals who cyberbully may sign up their targets on various pornographic sites and marketing lists so that they are barraged with offensive and harassing e-mails.

Text messaging

Text messaging is also known as Short Message Service (SMS). The speed with which youth today can send text messages to one another via cellular phones is astounding. Although not a method of real-time communication, text messaging is still an important mode of communication, particularly among teenagers, with some sending up to 3,000 texts a month! While certainly an invaluable tool for keeping in contact with others, cellular phones and text messaging also have a downside. Many a naïve college professor has realized only too late that pictures have been taken of a test via cellular phone and transmitted to others, or that students outside of class have text-messaged answers to test questions to their friends in the class.

Outside the academic setting, text messaging can also be used to cyberbully others. Stories abound of adolescent girls and boys receiving hundreds if not thousands of text messages because they upset someone. In addition to the harm caused by the messages themselves, there may be a financial cost associated with receiving the text messages.

Bash boards

Although often equated with chat rooms because they afford people the opportunity to have a virtual chat with one another, bash boards more closely resemble Internet polling sites. In fact, they are online bulletin boards where people can post any information that they want to about any person or any topic.

Social networking sites

Currently, there are hundreds of social network sites, millions of registered users, and hundreds of thousands of new users registering each day. The number of people communicating with one another via this modality is truly staggering. And, just in case users are away from their computers, they can download a social networking application on their smart phone so that they can readily access their favorite social networking site from wherever they are. Social network sites go by many different names. Among the most popular are Facebook, MySpace, LiveJournal, Friendster, Nexopia, Xuga, Xanga, LinkedIn, Twitter, Formspring, and Bebo. As defined by the Federal Bureau of Investigation ("Social networking sites," 2006), social networking sites are "websites that encourage people to post profiles of themselves – complete with pictures, interests, and even journals – so they can meet like-minded friends. Most also offer chat rooms. Most sites are free; some restrict membership by age." Social network sites would not be so popular if people did not enjoy the opportunity to use them to connect with old friends, maintain contact with current friends, or any of a number of other positive uses.

As noted by Swinford (2006), social network sites provide a "window on youth culture." Social network sites allow us to see who is doing what, where, and with whom. The news feed on Facebook allows almost real-time insight into what is happening in the lives of Facebook users (see Figure 3.3). Through these news feeds, we know who is friends with whom, who has ended a relationship with whom, who has posted new pictures, and who is having a bad day, to give just a few examples.

Changes to individual profiles on social network sites, particularly among young people, are frequent as they use their personal profiles to project particular images of themselves to others (Gonzales & Hancock, 2011; Livingstone & Brake, 2009; Mehdizadeh, 2010). Any changes made to an individual's profile are made readily available to "friends" who have access

News Feed

Lea Ann Dobson joined the group Brookstone Meadows Tennis. 8:15pm

Liz Johnson and Alison Richman are now friends. 6:39pm

Micah Lattanner and Gary Giumetti are now friends. 3:30pm

Jessica Dean invited you to the Clemson basketball game. 1:56pm

Sarah Louderback posted on your wall. 10:52am

Caroline King wrote on Whitney Chamber's wall, 8:15pm

Sarah Bagwell King joined the group CU Bound. 9:21am

Rebecca Fulmer and Stephanie Freeman are now friends. 2:15am

Kelly King is heading back to Clemson for an alumni weekend visit! 1:55am

Sarah Sheek and Zan Isgett are now friends. 1:02am

Jessica Doll posted on Lauren Carroll's wall. 12:42am

Noah Britt and Jordan Britt joined the group Twins are Awesome, 7:01pm

Erin Hunter and Lindsey Sporrer are now friends. 9:28pm

Frances Bagwell and Randolph Kowalski are now friends. 8:14pm

Jim Merck tagged Suzanne Tripp in the note It was a blast... And I thank you all. 7:54pm

Figure 3.3   Sample news feed.

to that person's profile. On the one hand, positive feedback from friends can be very affirming and can raise an individual's self-esteem. On the other hand, even the users of Facebook themselves say it's too much of a window on what Facebook users are doing in their day-to-day lives, leading even young people to become much more savvy in their use of privacy features (Patchin & Hinduja, 2010a, c).

Even with privacy features in place, the social network sites can often be a cruel window on what children and youth are doing. Swinford (2006) cites Chris Cloke, head of child protection at the National Society for the Prevention of Cruelty to Children (NSPCC), as noting that: "[i]t's a completely unregulated world out there. I'd compare it to a modern-day Lord of the Flies. Children say things that are much more extreme and vindictive than they would in their everyday lives."

Most recently, these social network sites can be used somewhat like bash boards with a different name "burn pages." "Burn pages" are often associated with certain schools and are used to post negative information or gossip about students at the school. In one recent case, a 14-year-old girl who attended Ranson Middle School in Charlotte, North Carolina, was slammed on the Ranson Burn Page. Pictures and sexually explicit comments were posted about her. Law enforcement was involved, and a request was made to Facebook to have the site shut down (Shayne, 2011). Miller, Thompson, and Franz (2009) include an example of a middle school burn book profile from MySpace in their article on how to safeguard adolescents in the digital age. Here is the content of that burn book:

This Is How You Do It

- Send us a picture of the person you hate!
- Tell us what you want it to say under the picture!
- We will put it up no matter what it says
- No one will ever know it's you!
- Send what you have to say in a message!
- Don't get mad at me for you being on the page! (Miller et al., 2009, p. 28)

A variant of social network sites are social Web sites where people can upload, share, and comment on videos. YouTube, Google Video, and similar sites have become very popular with teens. YouTube was founded in February 2005 by three PayPal employees. Today it is listed by the Web information company Alexa as the third most popular Web site after Google and Facebook, with over 2 billion views a day (YouTube, 2011). Relative to the general Internet population, youth in the 18–24 age range and individuals 65 and older are overrepresented visitors to youtube.com (Alexa.com). Approximately 35 hours of video are uploaded hourly, and YouTube's Web site lists its number of viewers as hundreds of millions (YouTube, 2011). Although some of the videos are intended to be funny, others are in very poor taste. Not surprisingly, a cursory search of YouTube quickly reveals instances of cyberbullying. Kazaa is a similar site that traditionally was used to share music. It was the Web site on which the video of the Star Wars Kid, described in Chapter 1, was originally posted (Dyrli, 2005).

Variants of social network sites have also been created in memory of deceased individuals who had profiles on social network sites. For example, MyDeathSpace.com contains tributes to former members of MySpace who are no longer living. Clicking on the individual's photo directs one to their MySpace page where people continue to post messages to the person. Although perhaps these sites provide cathartic value for some survivors, the sites also provide an opportunity for people to post comments and replies, many of them negative and inflammatory. It only takes a few minutes to find multiple instances of cyberbullying on this Web site, not all that surprising given that there is a section for hate mail. Posted within this part of the site's discussion forum are hate e-mails that have been sent to the Web site. In one instance, a mother, whose daughter had died and whose picture and MySpace page were posted on MyDeathSpace.com, had posted a comment about how offensive she found the site to be and how she would do everything in her power to have the site removed. A torrent of responses from proponents of MyDeathSpace.com followed, many of which fit the definition of cyberbullying.

Chat rooms

Chat rooms are places where people can go in virtual reality to talk with one another about any of a number of issues. Typically, a chat room is, at least on the surface, designed to focus on a particular topic or topics. Participants type in comments that then appear on the screens of other individuals signed into the chat room. Other chat rooms, however, are designed purely to provide visitors with a place where they can meet other individuals and communicate with them in real time. In some of these chat rooms, people pick an avatar or a symbol (e.g., an animal or a character) that they feel represents them. It is via this avatar that they communicate with others in the chat room (www.netlingo.com). As with any other virtual communication in real time, however, chat rooms provide a forum in which cyberbullying can occur. Members of the chat room can begin to denigrate a particular individual, they may ostracize a member of the chat group, or particular members may get into a flame war with one another.

Complicating matters further, people often assume identities in chat rooms that are very different from their real-world identity. They may fabricate their age, gender, occupation, or any other personally identifiable characteristic. Although this can be cathartic for the person trying to pretend to be someone other than whom they really are, in some instances cyber stalkers and sexual predators seek out their unsuspecting victims by fabricating their identities. Furthermore, in spite of the cathartic value to the communicator of taking on an assumed identity, fellow chatters often become angry if and when they find out they have been duped and have been chatting with someone other than whom they thought they were communicating with. For example, people in chat rooms and discussion groups often report communicating differently with another individual as a function of whether they believe that person to be male or female. One can imagine the chagrin and anger of an individual who has been sharing personal thoughts with a "woman" only to later find out it was a man (or vice versa). Such circumstances might set up a cyberbullying situation fueled by the anger of the individual who felt "duped."

Blogs

Blogs, or Web logs, refer to online journals. Blogs are extremely popular, although their use seems to be declining among teens recently (Lenhart, 2010). In fact, it is estimated that a new Web log is created every second (www.netlingo.com). One Web site devoted solely to tracking blogs, Technorati.com, searches Web sites according to blog topic. The purpose is to allow users to see what is being said about any of a number of topics and then weigh in with their own comments. In 2008, Technorati.com indexed over 112 million blogs (Solis, 2011). Although blogs can be used for any of a number of positive functions, they also can be used to cyberbully others. Youth may use these blogs to damage others' reputations or invade their privacy. For example, in some cases, jilted boyfriends or girlfriends may post a series of blogs containing degrading and embarrassing information about the ex-partner, even getting their friends to post negative information on the site as well.

Web sites

Web sites are places or locations on the World Wide Web that contain a home page, in addition to links to other possible pages. Many people have their own personal home pages used to promote their businesses, post personal information for the benefit of family and friends, or sell products. Web sites can also be set up, however, for the purposes of cyberbullying. In many instances, Web pages are created for the sole purpose of posting offensive information and/or pictures about another individual. For example, pictures may be taken of a classmate and then doctored in a way that portrays that individual in a sexually provocative manner. Personal contact information for that individual, including name, address, and phone number then may be provided on the Web site.

In other instances, Web pages are established to set up Internet polls. Internet polling may be used for the purpose of humiliating a target. Students, for example, might be encouraged to go to the Web site and vote for the ugliest girl in the class, or the fattest kid at school. Although sites that exist for the purpose of setting up such Web pages have abuse policies and reporting systems, they are often not closely regulated (Belsey, 2006).

Internet gaming

Many children and youth today play online interactive games on gaming devices such as X-Box Live and Sony Play Station 2 Network. (Many also play games on their home computers, in some instances paying a monthly subscription fee to participate.) Some of the games are single-player, text-based games, whereas others are complex, interactive, multiplayer games in a virtual world. Just as people expressed their frustration 20 years ago when playing Nintendo games, online players also vent their dissatisfaction with the playing of others. However, consistent with most other types of cyberbullying, the expression of dissatisfaction and frustration in the cyber world where people communicate anonymously using pseudo names tends to be more abusive, threatening, and demeaning. In addition, players can block other players from the game and they can gain unauthorized access to their game accounts (Aftab, 2011). One of the most popular massive multiplayer online games is World of Warcraft, with over 12 million subscribers at the end of 2010 ("World of Warcraft," 2010). Players join guilds in order to complete various tasks. Players can be promoted by the guild leader, but they can also be kicked out of the guild or demoted. This may cause quite a bit of emotional distress for some players. Importantly, many massively multiplayer online role playing games (MMORPGs) have worked hard to institute a sense of digital citizenship where players are more likely to report abuses and offenses. World of Warcraft has been a leader in this area. Being reported can lead to players being blocked from playing and many users take this digital citizenry very seriously. Online role playing games (which are more heavily monitored) can be training grounds for users to understand the importance of online civil behavior.

Who Cyberbullies?

Unfortunately, although there is much speculation about "cyberbullies" in the popular press, we actually know very little about the characteristics of these individuals or their various motivations. Below we will discuss what is known from the research literature about children who cyberbully, and we also will share speculations (our own and those of others), which will need to be further explored by research.

Characteristics of children who cyberbully

In Chapter 2 we explored the common characteristics of children who bully, which included (Olweus, 1993a):

- They have dominant personalities and like to assert themselves using force.
- They have a temper, are impulsive and are easily frustrated.
- They have more positive attitudes toward violence than other children.
- They have difficulty following rules.
- They appear to be tough and show little empathy or compassion for those who are bullied.
- They often relate to adults in aggressive ways.
- They are good at talking themselves out of difficult situations.
- They engage in both proactive aggression (i.e., deliberate aggression to achieve a goal) and reactive aggression (i.e., defensive reactions to being provoked) (Camodeca & Goossens, 2005).

Although it is reasonable to assume that children who cyberbully share some (or even many) of these characteristics, it is also likely that there are some important differences that will need to be explored through future research.

In Chapter 2, we also explored gender differences in traditional forms of bullying and noted that boys are more likely than girls to engage in bullying at school. When looking at similarities and differences in the types of bullying that boys and girls experience, research suggests that boys are more likely to be physically bullied by their peers (Finkelhor et al., 2005; Nansel et al., 2001; Olweus, 1993a; Rigby, 2002), whereas girls are more likely to be bullied through some indirect forms of bullying, such as rumor-spreading, as well as through sexual comments or gestures (Nansel et al., 2001). Interestingly, girls are more likely to report being occasional victims and perpetrators of cyberbullying. However, among those individuals who engage in cyberbullying, boys do so with greater frequency than girls (Kowalski & Limber, 2007). We will return to the issue of gender and cyberbullying again in Chapter 4.

Because of the suggestion that socially anxious individuals might be more likely to (a) use technology as a means of communicating with others and (b) engage in cyberbullying as revenge for bullying at school, we examined the relationship between a person's dispositional tendency to experience social anxiety and their experiences with cyberbullying (Kowalski & Limber, 2007).

As will be discussed in more detail in Chapter 4, our data showed that, among perpetrators, the highest levels of social anxiety were reported by 8th graders who cyberbullied others at least twice a month. The more frequent the cyberbullying, the higher the level of social anxiety, supporting our hypothesis that cyberbullying and social anxiety are linked. Importantly, however, in a comparison between individuals who cyberbully and those who are cyberbullied, social anxiety scores are higher among victims than perpetrators.

What motivates children to cyberbully?

Asking the question of "who cyberbullies?" also raises the question of "what motivates someone to engage in such a behavior?" Although there are a number of other personality traits that might be shared by many children who cyberbully, there probably is no single profile of such a child. Just as there is a variety of possible motives for engaging in traditional forms of bullying (see Chapter 2), there also is a long list of reasons why adolescents might engage in cyberbullying. Some engage in electronic violence somewhat inadvertently without realizing that what they are doing is actually cyberbullying, particularly when they are simply responding in kind to negative comments that have been sent to them in e-mails or instant messages. Other individuals, however, cyberbully with the express purpose of hurting and humiliating their victims. Still other children and youth cyberbully because they are bored and simply think that sending threatening or demeaning messages to another person would be fun. Their focus is on alleviating their own boredom, rather than thinking about the effects that their behavior could have on their victims. Some may cyberbully as a way of asserting power or channeling their aggressive energy. Others may gain satisfaction, prestige, or other rewards from cyberbullying. Still others may bully as a way to act out aggressive fantasies online. Parry Aftab (2011) recounted a meeting with a young boy who was what some might call the "perfect child" in real life – well behaved, polite, and a good student. However, online this boy became someone completely different – violent and aggressive. When asked why, his response was, "Because I can." In our focus group interviews with middle and high school students, a discrete number of motivations for cyberbullying continued to emerge. These motives included: boredom, power, meanness, as retaliation for being bullied, for attention, looking cool and tough, and jealousy. Other key reasons included that cyberbullying was safer than traditional bullying because it was anonymous and they were less likely to get caught and it was easier because it didn't involve face-to-face confrontations. Another motive is the pleasure of inflicting pain. As noted by Alex Pham (2002), a writer for the *Chicago Tribune*, in his analysis of griefers: "For a griefer, it's not the killing that is fun, because combat is inherent in many of these games. It's the misery it causes other players. 'Griefers feed on the negative reactions of the people they kill,' said Frerichs, who savors his evil online persona and saves every nasty e-mail he gets from the people he has antagonized. 'There's nothing sweeter than when you kill someone, and they spout insults at you for hours. That's when you know you got him. It sounds really cruel, but it's fun.'" Reeckman and Cannard (2009) in a series of interviews with students highlighted several motives for cyberbullying: to have fun, to feel empowered, to teach someone a lesson, to retaliate, to make the victim stronger, and because the perpetrator was fearful of targeting the victim face to face.

Parry Aftab (2011) has delineated four types of children who cyberbully: (a) the vengeful angel, (b) the power-hungry, (c) mean girls, and (d) the inadvertent cyberbully or "because I can." Although these four categories may provide a useful heuristic for considering different motives of children who cyberbully, empirical evidence is needed to determine if they have a basis in fact.

According to Aftab (2011), the "vengeful angel" views himself or herself as seeking justice to right wrongs that have been inflicted on them or others. Some of these cyberbullies are children and youth who have been victims of bullying at school and who are now retaliating. They may be the outcasts who have been victims of traditional bullying at school (Willard, 2006). Support for the fact that children often retaliate in one form or another after being bullied can be found in a study by the US Department of Education and the US Secret Service that showed that 75% of school shooters had been victims of traditional bullying (Fein et al. 2002; see also Leary, Kowalski, Smith, & Phillips, 2003). The Internet postings of Eric Harris and Dylan Klebold, who gunned down students and staff at Columbine High School, dramatically recounted their anger at being bullied. Similarly, Kimveer Gill, who killed one student at Dawson College in Montreal, Canada, in September, 2006, had numerous postings on vampirefreaks.com in which he wrote of his anger at being bullied: "Stop bullying. It's not only the bully's fault you know!! It's the teachers and principals fault for turning a blind eye, just cuz it's not their job ... Stop making fun of each other because of the clothes you wear or the way people talk or act, or any other reasons you make fun of each other. It's all the jock's fault" (Lackner, 2006). In some instances, the desire for retaliation may stem from feeling slighted in a relationship. Hoff and

Mitchell (2009) found that cyberbullying was often preceded by anger stemming from romantic break-ups. They noted that in some instances the rejector was the target and in others the rejector's new love interest. In other instances, the cyberbullying stemmed from envy and jealousy.

The "power-hungry cyber bully," according to Aftab (2011), most closely resembles the prototypical school-yard bully in his or her desire to exert control, power, and authority over others. Whereas the individual who engages in traditional bullying often uses, in addition to indirect strategies, direct verbal attacks or physical aggression to induce fear in others, the person who cyberbullies uses threats or humiliating postings to create fear. Unlike the vengeful angel, who most often acts alone, the power-hungry cyberbully thrives with an audience to watch or reinforce his or her actions. Aftab hypothesizes that there is a subset of power-hungry cyberbullies that seeks power over others but as a way of compensating for their own perceived inadequacies. These individuals may be victims of traditional bullying and may be smaller and weaker than many of their peers. Cyberbullying may be a means to retaliate and appear bigger than they really are, using technology at which they may be particularly skilled.

Included within the category of power-hungry cyberbullies are children and youth who have not been subjected to bullying at school but who bully online just to vent anger or hostility (Levine, 2006). These children may feel that their life is out of control for reasons that have nothing to do with peers at school or with school-yard bullying (e.g., divorce, separation, illness of a parent). Cyberbullying may provide a way for these children and youth to release the anger they have in response to their current life situation and to feel in control of something (or someone).

Aftab's (2011) category "mean girls" is used to refer to children who cyberbully out of boredom. As noted earlier, cyberbullying that is motivated by boredom occurs more for the pleasure and entertainment of the cyberbully than for any particular desire to hurt the victim, although clearly part of the entertainment value of cyberbullying would lie in knowing that their bullying had embarrassed or humiliated another person. Taking delight in the pain of others because it makes perpetrators feel "funny, popular, and powerful" was also observed by Mishna et al. (2010, p. 362).

This description, however, highlights the fact that the name "mean girls" is something of a misnomer. First of all, although cyberbullying is more common among girls than boys (see Chapter 4), boys engage in cyberbullying out of boredom as well. Second, the title implies that there is an inherent meanness in children and youth who are motivated to cyberbully because they are bored. Long before technology became what it is today, children and youth got into all kinds of trouble because they were bored. Boredom, however, does not equate with meanness. While it is certainly true that many people who cyberbully engage in the behavior to harm others, it would be inappropriate (and not very useful) to label children who cyberbully as "mean."

The "inadvertent" cyberbully consists of those individuals who become cyberbullies as they respond in kind to negative communications that they receive, or who are inadvertently brought into cyberbullying through cyberbullying by proxy.

To this list, we would add those perpetrators who cyberbully others who are perceived to be different in some way (Hoff & Mitchell, 2009). The literature on traditional bullying is clear that children with disabilities, for example, are more likely to be bullied than their peers. Although little research has been conducted on the cyberbullying experiences of children with disabilities, there is every reason to believe that they will be disproportionately targeted in the virtual world as they are in the real world (see Didden et al., 2009; Kowalski & Fedina, 2011).

How Cyberbullying Differs from Other Types of Bullying

A logical question for those interested in cyberbullying is the extent to which it is similar to and different from traditional bullying. We believe cyberbullying shares with traditional bullying the three primary characteristics of bullying that were discussed in Chapter 2: (a) the behavior is aggressive; (b) there is a power imbalance between the victim and the perpetrator; and (c) the behavior is repeated. Importantly, a power imbalance may be somewhat different in cyberspace than it is in a face-to-face interaction. Because of the nature of cyberspace (and particularly the anonymity it may present, something we will return to below), a child who might wield little power over a victim face-to-face may wield a great deal of power (and fear) in cyberspace. More specifically, there is power in being anonymous, in assuming a false identity, in having the ability to spread rumors and lies to a wide audience, and in being able to harass a victim anywhere and anytime (Dooley et al., 2009; Vandebosch & van Cleemput, 2008).

Furthermore, although typically bullying is defined as not occurring once or twice, but as being a repeated behavior, the picture becomes a bit murky in cyberspace. A single act (e.g., a nasty e-mail or an inflammatory text message) may be forwarded to hundreds or thousands of children over a period of time. Think how easy it is to copy, paste, and share an inflammatory message. Note how quickly videos go viral. From a victim's perspective, he or she may feel repeatedly bullied, to say nothing of the fact that the victim may reread the e-mail or text message himself or herself multiple times, again leading to the feeling of being bullied repeatedly. Even though there may have been only one initial act, it may have been perpetrated through many people and over time.

Some research has also shown that there is significant overlap in involvement in traditional bullying and cyberbullying. Hinduja and Patchin (2008) found that those who had perpetrated traditional bullying within the previous six months were 2.5 times as likely to also perpetrate cyberbullying (see also, Kowalski & Limber, 2011; Privitera & Campbell, 2009; Smith et al., 2008; Sourander et al., 2010). Other researchers, however, have found a relationship between victimization and perpetration of cyberbullying, but no relationship between involvement in cyberbullying and involvement in traditional bullying (Varjas et al., 2007). In either case, it is important to recognize that cyberbullying and traditional forms of bullying share some features in common but also differ in some important ways. We will discuss four of these differences.

The enemy you know ...

As bad as the thug in the school yard may be, at least he or she is a known entity. He or she usually can be readily identified, and potentially avoided. The child who cyberbullies, on the other hand, is often anonymous. Thus, the victim is left wondering if the perpetrator is a single person or a group of people. Is it a girl or a boy? Is it a friend or an enemy? A stranger or an acquaintance? Someone older or younger? Someone from school or elsewhere? Later in this chapter, we will return to this issue of anonymity and the implications it may have for both the victim and the perpetrator.

Accessibility

Most children who use traditional ways of bullying terrorize their victims at school, on the school bus, or walking to and from school. Although bullying also may happen elsewhere in the community, there usually is a circumscribed period of time during which traditional bullies have access to their victims. (And at the very least, most children who are bullied by peers can find respite at home, unless they also are bullied by siblings.) Children who cyberbully, on the other hand, can wreak havoc 24/7. A child in a study conducted by Glenn Stutzky, an instructor at Michigan State University, summed it up well when he said: "It's like being tethered to your tormentor" (Meadows et al., 2005, p. 152). In fact, most cyberbullying happens not at school but off school grounds (www.fightcrime.org/cyberbullying/cyberbullyingteen.pdf). Although certainly children and youth who are cyber bullied can turn their computers and their cellular phones off, as soon as they turn them back on the messages reappear, the comments continue to be posted on Web sites, and e-mails have accumulated.

Cyberbullying messages are too often accessible not just to the target but to others as well. Hurtful comments and images can be copied, pasted, and shared in a matter of seconds. Videos can quickly "go viral" as did the video of the "Star Wars Kid" Gyslain Raza (Boyd, 2009).

The fact that cyberbullying happens most often away from school as opposed to at school also limits the role that schools can play in intervening in cyberbullying situations. If the cyberbullying occurs using school computers, then school administrators can enact disciplinary measures. If the electronic violence occurs off of school grounds, even though it may affect school performance and relationships, school personnel may feel less obligation to intervene. We will talk more about this in Chapters 6 and 7.

Punitive fears

One way in which traditional bullies can wield their power is by threatening their victims if they tell anyone or if they fail to bring money or perform certain tasks. Thus, victims of traditional bullying may be most fearful of the bullying escalating if they tell someone about their victimization. Although fears of retribution also accompany cyberbullying, the fear of having computer and phone privileges revoked is even greater for many victims of cyberbullying. For many parents who hear that their child is a victim of electronic violence, this is, at first blush, the most logical initial step. However, given that the computer and cellular phone are key elements of the child's social life, to revoke technology privileges is to punish the victim (again!)

Bystanders

Most traditional bullying episodes occur in the presence of other people who assume the role of bystanders or witnesses (Atlas & Pepler, 1998). Although some of these bystanders may egg on the child who bullies or defend the victim, most stand by and simply witness the event. Their presence, however silent, still speaks volumes to both the victim and the perpetrator. To the perpetrator, the silence of a passive bystander comes across as support; to the victim, the mere presence of the bystander may amplify an already painful and humiliating situation.

With cyberbullying, bystanders may play a slightly different role and may be willing or unwilling bystanders. The role that a bystander plays also depends on the medium through which the cyberbullying occurs. In chat rooms, for example, a bystander could simply witness an exchange between a victim and a perpetrator or he or she could join in on the electronic bullying. In other instances, a cyberbully may use the screen name of an unassuming "bystander" to bully someone else, creating a cyberbullying by proxy scenario described earlier in the chapter. Although empirical data are needed to support or refute this statement, we would venture to guess that bystanders to cyberbullying are more likely to eventually take part in the cyberbullying themselves than are bystanders of traditional bullying. Why? First of all, cyberbullying requires neither the physical capabilities nor the social prowess that may be needed with traditional bullying. For example, size doesn't matter in cyberbullying; the smallest child could easily join in cyberbullying others. Second, as mentioned at other points throughout the book, the anonymity associated with the Internet, and the tendency to forget the human side of the target of cyberbullying, make it easier to join in on cyberbullying than traditional bullying.

In one of the few studies to examine the role of bystanders in a cyberbullying situation, participants were exposed to cyberbullying in an AOL chatroom between two other "participants", actually confederates of the researcher (Kowalski, 2011). The researcher was interested in the degree to which participants would intervene to stop the cyberbullying that occurred. Unfortunately, few participants actually did so, with some expressing a fear of getting involved.

The Phenomenon of Disinhibition

The anonymity afforded by the Internet can lead people to pursue behaviors further than they might otherwise be willing to do (Mason, 2008; Suler, 2004) When they cannot be identified, people often say and do things that they would not do if their identities were known, a phenomenon known as disinhibition. In a classic study within social psychology, Williams, Harkins, and Latané (1981) found that participants reduced the amount of effort they put into a group activity as long as they thought no one could single them out as withholding effort or engaging in social loafing. Once their identity became known, however, the participants exerted maximum effort. Ironically, it is their very anonymity that allows some individuals to bully at all. Children and youth who are smaller and physically weaker than many of their peers tend to bully others at school less frequently for the simple reason that they are outsized. Yet with electronic communications, they can hide behind an assumed identity and wreak havoc.

Because of the ability of people to hide behind pseudo names on the Internet as they bully others, some have referred to cyberbullying as the "cowardly form of bullying" (Belsey, 2006). Others have suggested that the anonymity associated with cyber technologies provides perpetrators with a "cloak of invisibility" (Carrington, 2006). Without the threat of punishment or social disapproval, people may carry their actions much further than they normally would (Sourander et al., 2010). Interestingly, however, this anonymity is more illusion than reality. As noted by Nancy Willard (2006, p. 47), "people are not totally invisible or anonymous when they use information and communication technologies. In most cases, they leave 'cyberfootprints' wherever they go." Still, even if they are identified, perpetrators can claim that someone else was using their screen name, so that they can distance themselves from any personal responsibility.

The anonymity afforded by electronic communications is a much bigger factor than one might think at first blush, and may be responsible for cyberbullying having such a strong intimidation factor associated with it. In a survey that we conducted examining the incidence of cyberbullying among over 3,700 middle school children, close to 50% of the individuals did not know the identity of the perpetrator (Kowalski & Limber, 2007). Among college students, this statistic jumped to 60% (Kowalski et al., 2012). Mishna and her colleagues (2009) found that many youth do not find out who cyberbullied them until much later, only to then determine that it was someone known to them, such as a classmate.

A respondent in one of our focus groups said: "I personally think cyber bullying is not something you think about and say oh I feel like cyber bullying someone. It might even be accidental but you might say something to someone that really hurts them and you might just keep at it. You might think you are having fun but you can't hear their tone of voice over AIM or e-mail so you don't even know if you are doing it." As conveyed in this statement, because cyberbullying occurs via technology as opposed to via face-to-face interactions, perpetrators cannot see the emotional reactions of their victims. In many face-to-face interactions, people modulate their behavior when they see the effect that their behavior is having on others (e.g., nervousness, increased anxiety, etc.). In other words, our behaviors in real life are often modulated by the emotional reactions of others. When we good-naturedly tease someone else, but realize based on their facial reactions that our tease has been misinterpreted or taken too far, we usually apologize and stop engaging in that behavior. When we cannot see that person's emotional reactions, as is the case with cyber technologies, there is no emotional meter that serves to temper our behaviors. As stated by a high school student being interviewed about cyberbullying: "It's hard to remember that the other person is really seeing it." It is almost as if some perpetrators fail to remember that they are actually communicating with another human being, albeit unseen.

The inability to read the emotional reaction of the other also extends from victim to perpetrator. There are no contextual cues for the victim to use to interpret the messages that they receive. In face-to-face interactions, victims can scan the faces of potential bullies or individuals they perceive to be hurting their feelings for signs that a tease is really just a tease. Teases that are accompanied by winks, smiles, or the like may convey information to the target regarding the prosocial nature of a tease (Campos, Keltner, Beck, Gonzaga, & John, 2007). When communicating electronically, however, targets cannot see the faces of the perpetrator. Thus, they have no means of "reading" the intentions of the perpetrator through nonverbal behaviors. With the exception of emoticons (e.g., smiley faces), e-mail, for example, is devoid of "off-record markers" (Kruger et al., 2005). As noted by Kruger and his colleagues (2005, p. 926), "this limitation is likely to be fertile ground for miscommunication and, in particular, a lack of awareness of that miscommunication."

In two studies investigating the discrepancy between how well people thought they communicated over e-mail and how well they actually communicated, Kruger et al. (2005) found that people believe they communicate better over e-mail than they actually do. In one of these studies, 12 participants were asked to write two statements about each of 10 topics (e.g., dating, Greek life). One statement was to be a serious statement and the other was to be a sarcastic statement. The sentences were then e-mailed to another participant who was asked to identify which statements were serious and which were sarcastic. Although participants estimated that 97% of their statements would be correctly identified by the receiver, in fact only 84% were correctly labeled as serious or sarcastic. The researchers concluded that e-mail senders overestimated their ability to communicate clearly because of egocentrism; in other words, because a message was clear to them, they assumed that it would also be clear to the receiver. When we communicate sarcasm, for example, over e-mail, we can "hear" the sarcasm in the sentences as we type them. However, the same sarcastic tone is not being played for the receiver. Thus, what may begin as "innocent" teasing over e-mail or instant messaging may be taken for something other than what was intended. The result could be a flaming war or some other type of cyberbullying.

Summary

One of the difficulties in discussing cyberbullying and in attempting to design intervention and prevention programs related to it, is that there is no simple definition of cyberbullying nor is there a single profile of a child who cyber bullies. Rather, cyberbullying is a behavior that can occur through multiple modalities (e.g. instant messaging, e-mail, chat rooms), appear in a number of guises (e.g., harassment, flaming, impersonation), and be perpetrated anonymously by individuals you would least suspect of bullying someone else. With time, however, and continued research, we should be able to better identify the circumstances under which cyberbullying is most likely to occur. Additional research related to cyberbullying will be discussed in the next chapter.

4

CURRENT RESEARCH ON CYBERBULLYING

Online aggression isn't just traditional bullying with new tools. It's widespread, devastating, and knows no downtime.

(Hinduja & Patchin, 2011, p. 48)

At the time that the first edition of this book was published, only a handful of studies had focused specifically on cyberbullying among children and youth, particularly relative to traditional bullying. Since the publication of the first edition, considerably more research attention has been devoted to the topic (see Figure 3.2, Chapter 3), yet so many questions still remain. These studies have used a variety of methods to obtain information about the frequency of cyberbullying, how children and youth are cyberbullying one another, and the effects of cyberbullying on both the victim and the perpetrator. The end result is that there are some slight inconsistencies in the actual numbers (e.g., frequencies) that are reported across studies. Although we will discuss many of these studies and report their findings, the variability in the precise frequency with which cyberbullying occurs, for example, is far less important than the consistent conclusions from the studies that cyberbullying is a problem and that more research needs to be conducted and policies developed to deal with the problem.

Important considerations to keep in mind when comparing studies are cultural similarities and differences in both the prevalence of research on the topic of cyberbullying and the prevalence of cyberbullying itself within a particular culture. Although clearly the frequency of cyberbullying is

Cyberbullying: Bullying in the Digital Age, Second Edition. Robin M. Kowalski, Susan P. Limber, and Patricia W. Agatston.
© 2012 Robin M. Kowalski, Susan P. Limber, and Patricia W. Agatston.
Published 2012 by Blackwell Publishing Ltd.

directly correlated with the availability of technology in a particular culture, among developed cultures cyberbullying is nonculture specific. In other words, cyberbullying has increasingly become an issue in most, if not all, developed countries. Reports on the prevalence of cyberbullying have emerged from all corners of the world, including the United Kingdom, Australia, Japan, Canada, Korea, and the United States, to name a few. Kraft (2006) summarized worldwide trends in cyberbullying and examined cross-cultural variations in the effects of cyberbullying. She found that victimization reports varied between 10% and 42%, and that, whereas the most popular medium for cyberbullying in Australia and the UK was the cellular phone, in the United States and Canada it was the Internet (see also Shariff, 2009).

Methods of Studying Cyberbullying

Most existing research on cyberbullying, whether in the US or abroad, has relied on surveys. Some of these have been anonymous paper and pencil surveys (e.g., Kowalski & Fedina, 2011; Kowalski & Limber, 2007), others have been completed online (e.g., Hinduja & Patchin, 2008; Kowalski & Witte, 2006), and still others have been conducted via the telephone (e.g., Ybarra, Mitchell, Wolak, & Finkelhor, 2006). One of the primary reasons for the extensive reliance on surveys is that they are easy to administer and can be completed by a large number of people in a relatively short period of time. However, surveys are not without their problems, as discussed in Box 4.1.

Another reason for the popularity of surveys is the difficulty associated with trying to recreate cyberbullying within a laboratory setting. With minors, in particular, there can be ethical concerns and challenges associated with laboratory investigations of cyberbullying. Using an adult sample, however, Kowalski (2011) created a simulated cyberbullying situation within a laboratory to examine the extent to which bystanders would intervene to put an end to cyberbullying occurring in an online chat room. Participants entered an AOL chatroom with three other "participants" (actually confederates). Two of the confederates began to cyberbully the third. To manipulate status, one of the perpetrators indicated that he or she was a graduate student. The confederates begin discussing the presence of parents and older individuals on Facebook. As shown in Box 4.1, as the conversation progresses, the individuals who cyberbully (identified as "Facilitator" and "Participant01) make increasingly disparaging remarks toward the target

Box 4.1 Cyberbullying script

Facilitator has entered the room. 10:11 am
Participant01 (confederate) has entered the room. 10:11 am
Participant02 (confederate) has entered the room. 10:11 am
Participant03 (participant) has entered the room. 10:15 am

Facilitator 10:16 am

Hi. I'm supposed to start this chat room discussion, probably because I'm a graduate student. The topic is: "How do you feel about adults (over 35) being on facebook?" What do you guys think about this?

Participant02 10:17 am

I don't really understand y older people would want to be on facebook

Participant03 10:17 am

I think that the point of facebook is to be able to connect with friends and old people need to do that too

Facilitator 10:17 am

It's a social networking site and a good way to share pictures I'm older and about to start my career and would like to keep up with my college and grad school friends

Participant03 10:18 am

I do not like it though when they dont know how to use it that annoys me

Participant01 10:18 am

Yeah, I agree with the grad student. I'm about to graduate and trying to find a job. And i still want to keep up with my friends that already graduated. But its creepy for really old people to be on facebook

Participant02 10:18 am

yea, but adults can communicate with email or something else

Participant03 10:18 am

but facebook makes it soooo much easier

Facilitator 10:19 am
well i just think its easier. what do you think participant 3?

Participant03 10:19 am
think about what?

Participant02 10:19 am
i still think its a little creepy

Participant01 10:19 am
Why is it creepy to have older people looking at your profile? Do you have something to hide participant2?

Participant02 10:20 am
no its just different

Participant03 10:20 am
yeah i agree when my 50 year old elder from church trys to friend me but i just ignore it and set up privacy

Facilitator 10:20 am
p2 you probably have dirty pictures of you or something. you should delete those.

Participant02 10:20 am
ummmm ... i limit my profile

Participant01 10:20 am
what are you trying to hide p2?

Facilitator 10:21 am
p2 you must be a stupid freshmen. employers have ways of getting around that...you idiot

Participant03 10:21 am
I dont think p2 is trying to hide anything this is an opinion a lot of people have and rightfully so

Participant02 10:21 am
i'm not looking for a job and i dont want old perverts creeping on me

Facilitator 10:21 am
If you're trying to hide something people can still see all your wall posts from all of your sexcapades

Participant01 10:22 am
I'm sure a lot of people on campus know how you get around anyway.

Participant02 10:22 am
that's not true. you don't even know me!!!

Participant03 10:22 am
haha this is a little rediculous

Participant02 10:22 am
didnt yall enjoy your college years?

Facilitator 10:22 am
sure i enjoyed undergrad bu I wasn't sketch and didn't end up with an std like you ; clearly you're enjoying your college years too much

Participant02 10:23 am
i don't even know what to say to that

Facilitator 10:23 am
yeah why fight a losing battle ... a slut is a slut

Participant03 10:23 am
we should get back onto the topic we started with
sound good?

Participant02 10:23 am
look, i just think facebook is more for college students because that was the way it was originally intended

Participant03 10:24 am
p2 has a good point

Facilitator 10:24 am
You just don't want your parents seeing all that filth you have posted. Then they will realize what a slut you are.

Participant01 10:24 am
I bet your mom is a slut too

Participant03 10:24 am
University study.... not so good of a point

Facilitator 10:24 am
haha and your dad and your brother and your sister

Participant02 10:24 am
  why would you bring my family into this?

Facilitator 10:24 am
  cause the apple doesn't fall too far from the tree

Participant03 10:25 am
  Whats everyones favorite kind of cheese!

Participant01 10:25 am
  what a bunch of whores!!!

Facilitator 10:25 am
  What p2? you don't have anything else to say?

Participant03 10:25 am
  p2 dont respond
  STOP RESPONDING

Facilitator 10:25 am
  exactly. That's because you know it's all true

Participant01 10:25 am
  Do you even know who your real dad is?

Participant03 10:25 am
  no its because they dont want to deal with imature people like you

Facilitator 10:26 am
  what a pussy

Participant03 10:26 am
  you said youre a grad student? act like it

Participant02 10:26 am
  I can't deal with this anymore. I'M LEAVING

Participant03 10:26 am
  good

Participant01 10:26 am
  that was dramatic…

Participant02 has left the room. 10:26 am

(identified as Participant02). The actual participant is identified in the script as Participant03. The goal was to examine the degree to which the actual participant (Participant03) would intervene to put an end to the cyberbullying that was occurring with the two confederates. Although very few participants actually did intervene, in the example provided in Box 4.1, the participant actually did stick up for the target of cyberbullying.

One additional method that has been used to study cyberbullying has been focus groups. In our own research using focus groups, a series of questions were created to allow investigators to probe not only the frequency of cyberbullying but also more specific information about actual incidents of cyberbullying that the adolescents had experienced or witnessed. A female and a male interviewer conducted 12 focus groups with small numbers of female and male students, respectively, from four suburban Georgia middle and high schools representing different socioeconomic backgrounds. Additional individual interviews were conducted with targets and perpetrators of cyberbullying as well as with the mothers of individuals who had been cyberbullied. (For a more detailed presentation of information from these focus groups, the reader is referred to Agatston, Kowalski, & Limber, 2011). As will be seen throughout the chapter, a key advantage of focus groups is that they provide much more information about specific incidents and feelings related to cyberbullying than can be conveyed on a survey. Ultimately, our knowledge about cyberbullying likely will best be enhanced by both quantitative (e.g., survey) studies and qualitative (e.g., focus group) approaches, as they provide different insights into the phenomenon.

How Common Is Cyberbullying?

As the methods used to study cyberbullying have been somewhat variable, not surprisingly exact statistics related to the prevalence of cyberbullying are difficult to obtain. Reported frequencies of cyberbullying depend on the country in which the data are collected, how cyberbullying is defined, the timeframe of participants' responses (e.g.,whether participants are asked if they have *ever* been cyberbullied or been cyberbullied *within the past couple of months*), and the ages of the respondents. To illustrate the role that these variables play in affecting prevalence rates reported, we can look at just a few studies. A 2009 study conducted by Cox Communications included interviews with 655 teens between the ages of 13 and 18. Fifteen

Box 4.2   Popularity and problems of surveys

In spite of the popularity of survey use in investigations of cyberbullying, and most other research topics for that matter, there is no research that is devoid of problems, including methodological issues and analytical issues. Research on cyberbullying is no exception to this. Two online surveys that have been done are good exemplars of this: Parry Aftab's online survey found at www.wiredsafety.org, and our survey (Kowalski & Witte, 2006). Both of these surveys have provided very useful data related to cyberbullying that will be discussed in the pages that follow. The online nature of these surveys meant that anyone could go to the Web site and complete the survey. At first blush, this would seem to be an ideal situation that would increase the representativeness of the sample and the number of people who could respond. However, the wiredsafety.org survey was housed on the Web site itself. Thus, people who accessed the site to fill out the survey represented those individuals who were probably already concerned about the issue of cyberbullying or who were interested in learning more about it. A link to our own survey (Kowalski & Witte, 2006) was posted on two social network sites: LiveJournal and Nexopia. Although this was a useful way to gain access to individuals willing to complete the survey, the fact that potential participants were visiting a social network site when they saw the link to the survey suggests that they might have been more regular Internet users than someone who did not regularly access a social network site.

We mention these difficulties so as to encourage readers to critically evaluate any research study, whether related to cyberbullying or not, whether written in a book, the popular press, or an academic journal article.

percent reported that they had *ever* been cyberbullied online, 10% reported being targeted via cell phone. Seven percent reported having *ever* cyberbullied another online, 5% via cell phone. Telephone surveys conducted with preteens between the ages of 6 and 11 living in the US showed that 17% had been cyberbullied *within the previous year* (www.fightcrime. org/cyberbullying/cyberbullyingpreteen.pdf). Of these cyberbully victims, 23% reported that the cyberbullying had occurred via e-mail, 12% via instant messaging, 19% through comments posted on a Web site, 18% in a chat room, 11% via embarrassing photos distributed without the victim's consent, and 7% through text messaging. A similar study conducted with *teens* between the ages of 12 and 17 (www.fightcrime.org/cyberbullying/ cyberbullyingteen.pdf) indicated that 36% of the teenagers had been cyberbullied *within the previous year*. The means through which the cyber-bullying had occurred included: 44% via instant messaging, 34% through e-mail, 30% through comments posted on a Web site, 19% via text messaging, 14% in chat rooms, and 13% through the distribution of embar-rassing photographs of the victim without his or her consent.

In our own research (Kowalski & Limber, 2007), 3767 students in grades 6 through 8 completed an anonymous pencil and paper questionnaire ask-ing them about their experiences with traditional bullying and with cyber-bullying. Eighteen percent of the students reported having been electronically bullied at least once *within the previous 2 months* and 6% had been electronically bullied *at least two to three times a month*. Eleven percent of the students reported having electronically bullied someone else at least once *in the previous 2 months* and 2% had electronically bullied *at least two to three times a month*. In this study, instant messaging was the most com-mon venue through which the middle school children reported being vic-tims and perpetrators of cyberbullying. Among the middle school targets, 67% had been bullied through instant messaging, 25% had been bullied in chat rooms, and 24% had been bullied through e-mail messages. Perpetrators, similarly, reported using instant messaging (56%) most fre-quently to cyberbully others, followed by chat rooms (23%), and e-mail messages (20%). A related study (Agatston & Carpenter, 2006) involving an anonymous survey administered to 257 middle school students showed that 18% of the students (27% of the females and 9% of the males) reported having been cyberbullied *at least once in the previous 2 months*. The most common means through which the cyberbullying had occurred were instant messaging (52%) and via Web sites (52%). The increased preva-lence of Web sites as a vehicle for cyberbullying among targets in the sample compared to the Kowalski and Limber (2007) study, whose data had been collected in 2005, likely reflects the increasing prevalence of social network sites as tools of interpersonal communication among adolescents. As these studies highlight, care must be taken when examining prevalence rates to also examine the parameters within which those statistics were obtained.

Data from the 2007 National Crime Victimization Survey (Robers, Zhang, & Truman, 2010) revealed that 4% of students in grades 6–12 had

been cyberbullied during the school year. Half of the targets had derogatory information posted about them on the Internet; the other half
reported being threatened via instant messaging. Of those who were cyberbullied, the majority (73%) reported that it had occurred once or twice
during the school year. However, 5% said that it happened a couple of
times a week.

In sum, studies typically find that between 10 and 40% of children and
youth report that they have been targets of cyberbullying, allowing for variability in time parameters, age, and the like (Tokunaga, 2010). However,
Juvonen and Gross (2008) reported a victimization prevalence rate of 72%
within the past year and Aftab (2011) states that 53% of 900 respondents
reported ever being victims of cyberbullying. She estimates that approximately 85% of 12- and 13-year-olds have *ever* had experience with cyberbullying. It is important to note, however, that Juvonen and Gross (2008)
asked participants the degree to which they had been targets of "mean
things" which they defined as "anything that someone does that upsets or
offends someone" (p. 499). And, Aftab's survey was located on the wired-
safety.org Web site, where people to go find out information about cyberbullying. Thus, respondents might be expected to have some prior
experience with cyberbullying.

In the next couple of pages, we will briefly discuss prevalence rates of
some additional key studies that have been conducted on cyberbullying
over the past few years, many of which highlight the specific venues (e.g.,
instant messaging, social network sites, texting) through which cyberbullying occurs. This is in no way intended to be an exhaustive list of
research studies on cyberbullying. These studies are summarized in
Table 4.1.

In the first study to systematically investigate cyberbullying, researchers
with the National Children's Home in Great Britain (NCH, 2002) surveyed children and youth between the ages of 11 and 19 and found that
16% had *ever* been bullied via mobile phone text messaging, 7% via
Internet chat rooms, and 4% through e-mail. Between March and April of
2005, NCH teamed up with Tesco Mobile to conduct a mobile bullying
survey ("Putting U in the picture – Mobile bullying survey 2005," 2005).
In response to a paper and pencil survey, 20% of the children and youth
aged 11–19 said that they had *ever* been cyberbullied. Fourteen percent
had been bullied via text messaging, 5% in chat rooms, and 4% through
e-mail. Eleven percent of the respondents admitted to ever cyberbullying
someone else.

Table 4.1 Key investigations of cyberbullying.

Study	Year	N	Ages	% Cyberbullied	% Who Bullied
National Children's Home	2002	856	11–19	16% via txt msg; 7% via chat rooms; 4% via email[1]	–
Mobile Bullying Survey	2005	770	11–19	20%[1]	11%[1]
Online Victimization Survey	2000	1501	10–17	6%[1]	–
YISS-1	2004	1501	10–17	4%[1]	12%[1]
YISS-2	2006	1500	10–17	9%[2]	–
Smith et al.	2006	92	11–16	22%[3]	–
Patchin & Hinduja	2006	384	< 18	29%[1]	11%[1]
Fight Crime Pre-Teen	2006	503	6–11	17%[2]	–
Fight Crime Teen	2006	512	12–17	26%[2]	–
Kowalski & Limber	2007	3767	Grades 6–8	18%[3]	11%[3]
Agatston & Carpenter	2006	257	Grades 6–8	18%[3]	5%[3]
Youth Internet Safety Survey	2006	> 700	> 11	11%[3]	3%[3]
National Crime Victimization Survey	2007	>10,000	Grades 6–12	4%[2]	–
Raskauskas & Stoltz	2007	84	13–18	50%[2]	–
Hinduja & Patchin	2008	1,378	<18	32% boys; 36% girls	18% boys; 16% girls
Juvonen & Gross	2008	1,454	12–17	72%[2]	–
Cox Communications	2009	655	13–18	15%[1]	7%[1]
Wired Safety	2011	> 900	> 7; 50% over 16	53%[1]	23%[1]

[1] Ever cyberbullied or cyberbullied others.
[2] Cyberbullied or cyberbullied others within the last year.
[3] Cyberbullied or cyberbullied others within the last 6 months.

In another British study (Smith, Mahdavi, Carvalho, & Tippett, 2006), 22% of the participating students, ranging in age from 11 to 16, reported that they had been cyberbullied at least once *in the 2 months preceding the survey*. The most common methods through which the cyberbullying had occurred were phone calls, text messaging, and e-mail.

A study sponsored by the National Center for Missing & Exploited Children found that one out of 17 American respondents (6%) between the ages of 10 and 17 reported having been threatened or harassed via the Internet (Finkelhor, Mitchell, & Wolak, 2000). The researchers defined harassment as "threats to assault or harm the youth, their friends, family, or property as well as efforts to embarrass or humiliate them." Almost three-quarters (70%) of the harassment episodes had occurred to children who were at least 14 years of age. The most common means by which the harassment had occurred were instant messaging (33%) and chat rooms (32%), followed by e-mails (19%; Finkelhor et al., 2000).

During the fall of 1999 and the spring of 2000, data were collected from 1501 regular Internet users in the US between the ages of 10 and 17, along with one parent or guardian of each participant, to compare characteristics of aggressors, targets, and aggressor/targets (individuals who were both victims and perpetrators of Internet harassment or online bullying; Ybarra & Mitchell, 2004). Nineteen percent of the respondents had *ever* been involved in online aggression (i.e., threats or harassing comments made via the Internet), 4% as online victims only, 12% as online aggressors only, and 3% as aggressor/targets only.

In a follow-up study, the second Youth Internet Safety Survey (YISS-2; Ybarra et al., 2006), 9% of the respondents, aged 10–17, indicated that they had been threatened or harassed over the Internet during the previous year. Ybarra et al. noted that this was a 50% increase over the frequency of Internet harassment found in the YISS-1 study. Almost a third (32%) of the victims reported that they had been harassed at least three times in the previous year.

Building on the research of Ybarra and Mitchell (2004), Patchin and Hinduja (2006) conducted an Internet-based survey of cyberbullying. A link to the survey was provided on the Web site of a popular female vocalist. Although anyone with access to the Web could respond to the survey, the majority of the respondents were from English-speaking countries, most notably the US (59%), Canada (12%), and the UK (9%). Among respondents younger than 18, 11% confessed to perpetrating cyberbullying, and 29% reported having been the target of cyberbullying. Almost half (47%) of the under-18 population indicated that they had observed cyberbullying while online. Among victims, the most common venues for cyberbullying were chat rooms (22%), followed by instant messaging (14%), and e-mail (13%). Perpetrators were most likely to cyberbully via chat rooms (8%) and instant messaging (5%).

Additional data were collected by one of the authors of this book through an online survey examining over 700 respondents' (predominantly college students) use of personal pages and their experiences with cyberbullying (Kowalski & Witte, 2006). The data revealed that 11% of the participants reported *ever* having been cyberbullied, with only 3% reporting that they had *ever* cyberbullied someone else. As with our survey of middle school children (Kowalski & Limber, 2007), instant messaging was the most common venue for victimization, with 42% of the respondents saying they had been cyberbullied through instant messaging, followed by chat rooms (23%), and e-mail (13%). Perpetrators of cyberbullying equally favored instant messaging (33%) and chat rooms (33%). Box 4.3 contains a sample of the content of some of the cyberbullying that occurred. We also asked participants whether their friends had ever cyberbullied or been cyberbullied and, if so, how. Participants with friends who had been victims of cyberbullying reported that those friends had been cyberbullied primarily through instant messaging (37%), followed by social network sites (33%), and e-mail (10%). Fifty percent of the friends who had perpetrated cyberbullying had done so through instant messaging.

As mentioned earlier, Juvonen and Gross (2008) found that 72% of their 1454 respondents aged 12 to 17 reported at least one incident as a victim of "mean things." The most frequent venue by which the "online incidents" occurred was instant messaging. Importantly, and as will be discussed in more detail later, 85% of the individuals experiencing mean things online also experienced bullying at school.

Hinduja and Patchin (2008) examined the cyberbullying experiences of 1378 youth under the age of 18. Over 32% of the boys and 36% of the girls had ever been victims of cyberbullying. Eighteen percent of the boys and 16% of the girls had ever perpetrated cyberbullying. The most common venues for cyberbullying were chat rooms and instant messaging.

Raskauskas and Stoltz (2007) surveyed 84 participants 13 to 18 years of age and found that approximately 50% of the sample reported being a victim of cyberbullying during the school year. A quarter of the sample reported perpetrating cyberbullying during the school year. Thirty-two percent of those who had been cyberbullied were targeted through text-messaging, 16% through Web sites and chatrooms, and 10% through picture-phones. Text messaging was also the most frequent method of perpetrating cyberbullying, followed by Internet bullying.

Box 4.3   Content of cyberbullying

Victims

- "A death threat."
- "Angry and malicious things said that wouldn't have been said in person."
- "I was mocked. Anything I said would be insulted. Anything about me was insulted, i.e., physical features, personality, the way I speak, etc."
- "Just threatening to beat me up and shoot me."
- "This guy was mad at me and threatened to make me out to be a whore and get his new girlfriend to beat me up and stuff like that."
- "Me trying to cheer someone up, and them saying I was full of crap for saying they weren't worthless … that I knew nothing … then came personal attacks against me."
- "Sexual stuff."
- "Someone knows my friend's screen name and is using it against her. This person is ruining her reputation and says things that my friend would never say."

Perpetrators

- "I made fun of them."
- "I used to find random people's screen names through chat rooms, and if they had the name of their girlfriend/boyfriend in their profile, I would IM them pretending to be that person and then I would pretend to dump them."
- "Calling them a noob."
- "My friend got on Facebook and changed some detailed information on the person's profile."
- "It was actually a website, like www.hatedevin.com (that wasn't it, but it was similar). Mostly how much a kid in their class annoyed them."

Age Differences and Cyberbullying

Research has revealed age-related variations in the prevalence rates of traditional bullying. As discussed in more detail in Chapter 2, rates of victimization from traditional bullying are higher in elementary school, with decreases in frequency in middle and high school (Olweus & Limber, 2010c). However, the frequency of *perpetrating* traditional bullying peaks in late middle and early junior high school. Support for this was found in the Kowalski and Limber (2007) study. Among individuals who had bullied others at school at least once (through "traditional" means), 8th graders bullied significantly more frequently than either 6th or 7th graders.

As with traditional bullying, there appear to be age-related variations in children's experiences with cyberbullying (Tokunaga, 2010). According to the published literature, middle school seems to be a critical time during which problems with cyberbullying emerge. The Fight Crime survey (www.fightcrime.org) with preteens described earlier supports this conclusion. Among preteens, children in the 6–8-year-old range were significantly less likely than children in the 9–11-year-old age range to have been cyberbullied within the previous year (13% and 21%, respectively). In the 2007 National Crime Victimization Survey (Robers et al., 2010), 10th and 11th graders experienced higher rates of cyberbullying than students in grades 6–9.

Even among middle schoolers, variations in rates of cyberbullying are observed. In our own research (Kowalski & Limber, 2007), we found significant differences by grade in the frequency with which youth had cyberbullied others, with 6th graders being significantly less likely to be involved with cyberbullying as either bullies or bully/victims than 7th or 8th graders, and somewhat less likely to be targets of cyberbullying (see also Hinduja & Patchin, 2008; Williams & Guerra, 2007; Wolak, Mitchell & Finkelhor, 2007). Grade differences were also observed among victims as a function of the method by which the cyberbullying occurred. Eighth graders reported being victimized through instant messaging at a significantly higher rate than 6th or 7th graders. Similarly, 8th graders also reported a higher rate of victimization via text messaging than 6th graders. Sixth graders used instant messaging to perpetrate cyberbullying less frequently than 7th or 8th graders. Sixth graders also used text messaging less often than 8th graders did. Similar findings were observed by Smith et al. (2008) who found that age differences depended on the method being used to cyberbully. Specifically, text messaging, picture bullying, and instant messaging were more common among older than younger students.

Importantly, though, cyberbullying is not limited to just adolescents. Although research on cyberbullying among older populations is limited, the few studies that have been done show that electronic bullying is alive and well among older populations, most notably college students (Hoff & Mitchell, 2009; Kowalski et al., 2012). In a study by Kowalski et al. (2012), 35% of a college student sample said that their first occurrence of cyberbullying was during college. Among those who had been cyberbullied, 44% reported that the majority of the bullying occurred during college, 30% during high school, and 26% during middle school. As technology use spreads to younger and younger ages, these statistics will likely shift to reflect greater percentages of cyberbullying occurring at younger and younger ages. Nevertheless, the point remains that cyberbullying is not localized to the adolescent population.

Gender Similarities and Differences

Over the past two to three decades, research on aggression has shown that males engage in more direct forms of aggression, such as hitting one another, and females engage in more indirect forms of aggression, such as gossiping or spreading rumors about one another (Bjorkqvist, Lagerspetz, & Osterman, 1992; Lagerspetz, Bjorkqvist, & Peltonen, 1988). Bjorkqvist et al. defined indirect aggression as "a kind of social manipulation; the aggressor manipulates others to attack the victim, or, by other means, makes use of the social structure in order to harm the target person, without being personally involved in attack" (p. 52).

A qualitative analysis of why girls are more likely than boys to engage in indirect aggression revealed some interesting insights. Owens, Shute, and Slee (2000) conducted focus groups with 54 teenage girls in Australia. The researchers concluded that girls engage in indirect aggression to eliminate boredom and because of friendship processes, including attention seeking, assuring that they are a member of the in-group as opposed to the out-group, belonging to the right group, self-protection, jealousy, and revenge.

In keeping with this, it is not all that surprising, then, that some studies have found cyberbullying to occur more frequently among girls than among boys (E. Mishkin, personal communication, January 20, 2006;

Hoff & Mitchell, 2009; Kowalski & Limber, 2007; Robers et al., 2010; Smith et al., 2006; Tokunaga, 2010). For example among 6th–12th graders who participated in the 2007 National Crime Victimization Survey, 2% of boys but 5% of girls said they had been cyberbullied during the school year. Among the middle school students who completed our survey about cyberbullying (Kowalski & Limber, 2007), 25% of the girls and 11% of the boys said that they had experienced cyberbullying *at least once* in the previous 2 months; 5% of girls and 2% of boys indicated that they had experienced cyberbullying "2 or 3 times a month", and 3% of girls and 2% of boys said they had been cyberbullied about "once a week" in the previous 2 months. However, at the highest frequency level – those electronically bullied "several times a week" – boys (1.4%) slightly outnumbered girls (1.2%), although this difference was not statistically significant.

In this same study, 13% of the girls and 9% of the boys said that they had perpetrated cyberbullying *at least once* within the previous 2 months. An equal percentage of girls and boys (1%) said they had electronically bullied others "2–3 times a month." Fewer girls (.7%) than boys (1.2%) said they had engaged in electronic bullying "once a week" in the previous 2 months. Twice as many boys (.8%) as girls (.4%) reported that they had electronically bullied others "several times a week."

For comparison purposes, we assessed the frequency of traditional bullying among girls and boys in our study (Kowalski & Limber, 2007). We found that 40% of the girls and 38% of the boys reported having been bullied at school *at least once* during the previous 2 months. A breakdown of prevalence rates at higher frequency levels showed that an equal percentage of girls and boys (6%) reported having been bullied "2 or 3 times a month;" 3% of girls and 4% of boys said they had been bullied "about once a week;" 3% of girls and 5% of boys indicated that the bullying occurred "several times a week." Among perpetrators, 27% of the girls and 35% of the boys indicated that they had bullied someone else (in traditional ways) *at least once* within the previous 2 months. Observations at the higher frequency levels showed differences between girls and boys; however, these differences were not statistically significant. Three percent of girls and 5% of boys had bullied other students "2 or 3 times a month;" 1% of girls and 1% of boys had bullied others "about once a week;" twice as many boys (2%) as girls (1%) had bullied others "several times a week."

Importantly, some studies have found no significant differences in experiences with cyberbullying between males and females (e.g., Hinduja

& Patchin, 2006, 2008; Mishna et al., 2010; Slonje & Smith, 2008; Williams & Guerra, 2007; Ybarra & Mitchell, 2004). Other studies have observed no gender differences overall, but found differences between males and females in the frequency with which particular venues were used to cyberbully others. For example, Hinduja and Patchin (2008) found that males and females did not differ in their overall prevalence rates of being victims of cyberbullying. However, females were more likely to be targeted via e-mail than males. Similarly, Alonzo and Aiken (2004) noted that males had a greater tendency to engage in flaming than females. Smith et al. (2006) found that girls were significantly more likely than boys to be cyberbullied. More specifically, however, they found that incidence rates for girls surpassed those for boys for all methods except for Web pages and picture editing (see also Keith & Martin, 2005).

These gender differences as a function of type of cyberbullying are important in interpreting prevalence rates across studies, and suggest caution in making quick global generalizations about particular patterns of difference in cyberbully victimization or perpetration as a function of individual difference characteristics, such as gender.

Data from the Fight Crime surveys with preteens and teens (www.fightcrime.org) show mixed findings regarding gender differences. In the preteen survey, no significant differences in the frequency of experiencing cyberbullying were observed between boys and girls. Fifteen percent of the boys and 19% of the girls reported having been cyberbullied within the previous year. Among teens, however, a significant difference was obtained. Almost twice as many females (44%) as males (28%) reported having been cyberbullied within the previous year.

Participants in our focus groups acknowledged the link between gender and cyberbullying. When asked what could be done to prevent cyberbullying, respondents in one of our focus groups said the following: "It depends on if it's a guy or a girl or how mean they are. Some people are just going to do it anyway. Girls are harder to stand up to. Cause like guys can be like 'stop bothering me.' I'm not afraid that a guy is going to hit me, but girls are like catty. They get back at you in a more subtle way."

In keeping with this sentiment, a male focus group respondent, when asked what he would do if he were cyberbullied at home by a student, said he would "print out the pages and say – 'what's up, man?'" Another male student responded similarly: "Just go up to them and be like 'how come you didn't say it to my face?'" None of the female focus group respondents indicated a similar response.

Racial and Ethnic Issues

In Chapter 2, we discussed the fact that research on racial and ethnic differences in regards to traditional bullying has not received a great deal of attention. This issue has received even less attention among cyberbullying researchers. What little research has examined racial similarities and differences in participants' experiences with cyberbullying has not found significant differences as a function of race (Hinduja & Patchin, 2008). Ybarra and her colleagues (2007) examined the experiences of 1515 youth ages 10–15 with online harassment. They observed no differences in experiences among youth of different races. Similarly, Hinduja and Patchin (2008) in a study of 1378 youth under the age of 18 found no racial differences in cyber victimization or perpetration. Importantly, 80% of this sample was Caucasian. One possible explanation for these findings is that race and ethnicity are not distinguishing characteristics in the virtual world. Thus, people of different racial and ethnic groups are less likely to be identified as belonging to particular groups online and thus less likely to be victimized for their racial group membership. On the other side of the coin, status online may not be determined by personal variables such as racial group membership to the same degree that it is in the real world, so race may be less likely to play a role in perpetrating cyberbullying. Additional research is needed to explore these hypotheses.

Characteristics and Experiences of Children Involved in Cyberbullying

A cursory look at the references accompanying this book or the dates of the studies on cyberbullying highlights the infancy of this line of investigation. Although researchers are getting a good picture of the frequency with which cyberbullying occurs, they know less about the characteristics of targets and perpetrators of cyberbullying, a topic to which we now turn our attention. One feature that has received increasing attention is the overlap between children's experiences with both cyberbullying and traditional bullying (Raskauskas & Stoltz, 2007).

Overlap with traditional bullying

Ybarra and Mitchell (2004) found that many of their respondents who were perpetrators of cyberbullying or victims were also targets of conventional bullying. Fifty-six percent of aggressors/targets of online aggression also reported being the target of offline bullying (compared with 49% of the aggressor-only and 44% of the victim-only respondents). As the authors note, "for some youth who are bullied, the Internet may simply be an extension of the schoolyard, with victimization continuing after the bell and on into the night" (p. 1313). For others who have been victims of conventional bullying, the Internet may provide them with a means to bully others "as compensation for being bullied in person" (p. 1313). Importantly, consistent with research on traditional bully/victims, Ybarra and Mitchell (2004) found that cyberbully/victims experienced a higher frequency of problem behaviors (e.g., drinking, smoking) and poor psychosocial functioning (e.g., depression).

In our own research (Kowalski & Limber, 2011), to assess more directly the links between traditional bullying and cyberbullying, we examined participants' responses to the two questions asking them whether they had been bullied at school or had bullied someone else two or three times a month or more. Based on these responses, participants were divided into four categories: victims (8%), bullies (8%), bully/victims (4%), and neither (80%). Because we were interested in the relationship between traditional bullying and cyberbullying, we examined the percentage of individuals within each of these four categories who had been electronically bullied two or three times a month or more and the percentage of individuals within each of the categories who had electronically bullied others two or three times a month or more. Among victims of traditional bullying, 4% had cyberbullied and 18% had been cyberbullied. Among traditional bullies, 23% had cyberbullied and 4% had been cyberbullied. Bully/victims reported the highest percentages associated with being a victim of cyberbullying (43%) and with perpetrating cyberbullying (31%). Among individuals who had not experienced traditional bullying, only .8% had cyberbullied and 2% had been cyberbullied (see Table 4.2).

Table 4.2 Relationship between traditional bully status and cyberbullying experience.

Traditional bullying status	Cyberbully victim	Cyberbully perpetrator
Victim only	18%	4%
Bully only	4%	23%
Bully/victim	43%	31%
Not involved	2%	.8%

Similarly, based on whether they had been the victim of, or perpetrated, cyberbullying two or three times a month or more, we divided our participants into four cyberbullying groups: cyber victim, cyberbully, cyberbully/victim, or neither. We then examined the percentage of individuals within each of these four groups who had been the victim of, or perpetrated, bullying at school two or three times a month or more. Among the victims of cyberbullying, 56% had been a victim of school-yard bullying and 17% had perpetrated bullying at school (see Table 4.3). Among cyberbullies, 9% had been victims of traditional bullying, whereas 77% had perpetrated traditional bullying. Bully/victims again stood out as the most problematic group. Seventy seven percent of individuals who were both victims and perpetrators of cyberbullying were also victims of traditional bullying. Seventy five percent perpetrated traditional bullying. Nine percent of respondents who had not been involved with cyberbullying had been a victim of traditional bullying, and 9% had perpetrated traditional bullying. The overlap between bullying others traditionally and cyberbullying others suggests that cyberbullying may be an extension of traditional bullying. The overlap between victims of cyberbullying and victims of traditional bullying may suggest the same thing. The disinhibition effect described in Chapter 3 likely comes into play among the 9% of perpetrators of cyberbullying who had been targets of traditional bullying. Importantly, we also examined the relationship between being a cyberbully and being cyberbullied, as well as between being a traditional bully and being bullied at school. The correlation between cyberbullying and being cyberbullied ($r = .43$) was quite high. In other words, cyberbullying and being a target of cyberbullying tended to go along together. Conversely, the correlation between being a traditional bully and being traditionally bullied was much lower at only .22.

Table 4.3 Relationship between cyberbully status and traditional bullying experience.

Cyberbullying status	Traditional bully victim	Traditional bully perpetrator
Victim only	56%	17%
Bully only	9%	77%
Bully/victim	77%	75%
Not involved	9%	9%

Characteristics of victims and perpetrators

In addition to gender discussed earlier, research on cyberbullying and Internet harassment suggests that there are other characteristics that may be linked to being a victim or a perpetrator of cyberbullying. Significantly more research attention has examined characteristics associated with targets as opposed to perpetrators of cyberbullying (Wong-Lo & Bullock, 2011). Indeed, virtually no research has focused on perpetrators of cyberbullying. Li (2006) found that half of the victims of had above average grades, whereas fewer than a third of individuals who prepetrated had above average grades. Hinduja and Patchin (2008) found that targets of cyberbullying were more likely than those who had not experienced cyberbullying to have off-line problems including perpetrating assaultive behaviors, school problems, and substance use. Ybarra et al. (2006) noted that victims of Internet harassment were more likely than individuals who were not victims to harass others online, to have social problems, and to be victimized in other situations (see also Dilmac, 2009). They were also more likely to use instant messaging, blogs, and chat rooms, a finding not all that surprising given what we now know about the preferred venues for cyberbullying (see also Juvonen & Gross, 2008; Shariff, 2008). Parallel findings were obtained in Kowalski and Witte's (2006) online study. Relative to nonvictims, targets were more likely to spend time using e-mail, instant messaging, online shopping, blogging, Web surfing, personal pages, and gaming. No differences were found between the two groups in the amount of time they spent doing research online or talking in chat rooms. Researchers often couch this latter finding within the routine activities theory of victimization, suggesting that differences in victimization reflect individual differences in lifestyle choices of victims (Cohen & Felson, 1979; Mesch, 2009). As it applies to cyberbullying, individuals who are targets of cyberbullying spend a higher percentage of time online and disclose a greater amount of personal information when online than nonvictims.

Our own research (Kowalski & Limber, 2011) has found a relationship between social anxiety, self-esteem, and cyberbullying (see also Dempsey, Sulkowski, Nichols & Storch, 2009). In addition to completing measures assessing involvement in traditional bullying and cyberbullying, nearly 4000 middle school students completed Leary's (1983) Interaction Anxiousness Scale and Rosenberg's (1965) Self-Esteem Scale. The Interaction Anxiousness Scale is a 15-item measure of an individual's dispositional level of social anxiety: how nervous they typically feel in social situations. A representative item includes "I often feel nervous in casual get togethers." Scores are summed and can range from 15 to 75, with higher numbers indicating higher levels of social anxiety. Rosenberg's Self-Esteem Scale is a 10-item measure of how an individual feels about himself or herself. A representative item from this scale is "I feel that I have a number of good qualities." Participants' scores on the self-esteem scale can range from 10 to 50, with higher scores indicating higher self-esteem.

We compared the levels of social anxiety and of self-esteem among individuals who were cyberbullies, cyber victims, cyber bully/victims, and those not involved in cyberbullying. We conducted these analyses twice for social anxiety and twice for self-esteem to allow us to examine levels of these individual difference measures among individuals who reported experience with cyberbullying at least once within the previous 2 months and those who had experienced cyberbullying at least two to three times a month within the previous 2 months. The data from these analyses are shown in Table 4.4. Using the criterion of occurring at least once in the previous 2 months, victims

Table 4.4 Cyberbullying status, social anxiety, and self-esteem.

Status (involved at least once)	Social anxiety score
Cyberbully only	35.4
Cyber victim only	38.2
Cyber bully/victim	37.4
Not involved	36.3
Status (involved at least 2–3x/month)	Social anxiety score
Cyberbully only	36.7
Cyber victim only	40.5
Cyber bully/victim	41.6
Not involved	36.3
Status (involved at least once)	Self-esteem score
Cyber bully only	20.4
Cyber victim only	19.2
Cyber bully/victim	19.2
Not involved	22.7
Status (involved at least 2–3x/month)	Self-esteem score
Cyber bully only	20.8
Cyber victim only	18.1
Cyber bully/victim	15.1
Not involved	22.1

of cyberbullying had higher social anxiety scores than children not involved with cyberbullying (see also Juvonen & Gross, 2008). Children who were not involved with cyberbullying had higher self-esteem than children in all of the other three groups. Using the more stringent criterion of cyberbullying occurring two to three times a month or more, cyber victims and cyber bully/ victims had higher social anxiety scores than cyberbullies and those children not involved with cyberbullying. Cyber victims and cyber bully/victims had lower self-esteem compared with children not involved with cyberbullying and also with children who bullied. Similar findings were found by Patchin and Hinduja (2010) who observed that both cyber victims and perpetrators had lower self-esteem than individuals not involved with cyberbullying. They noted, however, that the relationship was stronger between self-esteem and victimization than between self-esteem and perpetration.

Children and youth who experience social anxiety may choose to avoid friends and withdraw from social situations as a means of avoiding the socially anxious feelings associated with those situations. Unfortunately, as discussed throughout this book, the fact that children who cyberbully can attack 24/7 and that much "social" interaction for adolescents now takes place online makes it difficult for youth to completely avoid "social" settings that produce adverse feelings. The results of this study suggest that social skills training and practice in safe settings may be in order for children who are cyberbullied. Because of the correlational nature of these findings, it is not possible to know whether anxiety and low self-esteem may lead to cyber victimization or whether they might result from being cyberbullied (a focus of the next section).

An additional variable that appears to be related to victimization is parental mediation. Mesch (2009, p. 387) defines parental mediation as "activities carried out by parents to protect their children from exposure to online dangers." He makes a distinction between restrictive mediation and evaluative mediation. Restrictive mediation involves activities such as limiting the amount of time that a child or adolescent spends on the Internet or using filtering software to limit which Internet sites a child is allowed to visit (Mason, 2008). Evaluative mediation involves discussions with the child or adolescent about Internet safety, the creation of rules with the child regarding online activities, and the placement of the family computer in a central location (Mesch, 2009). Mesch found that parental mediation did, in fact, play a critical role in distinguishing victims and non victims of cyberbullying. Relative to victims, nonvictims were more likely to have computers in public spaces in their home, to have established rules for Internet use with their parents, and to have parents who had installed filtering software on the computers. Victims were also more likely than nonvictims to have profiles on social network sites, to participate in chat rooms, and to disclose personal information online.

Possible Effects of Cyberbullying on the Victim and Perpetrator

Research examining the effects of cyberbullying on both victims and perpetrators is still in its infancy (Mason, 2008; Wong-Lo & Bullock, 2011). Drawing firm conclusions from this research is further complicated by the fact that the effects of cyberbullying on the victim are highly variable. There have been a number of accounts of youth committing suicide after having experienced cyberbullying, as in the case of Ryan Patrick Halligan, or murder, as in the case of a 6th grader in Japan who retaliated against a friend and classmate who had made derogatory comments about her on a Web site ("Archive of CRN home page topics," 2004). In other cases, the cyberbullying has little to no apparent effect on children. Importantly, behaviors such as suicide are always determined by multiple factors so it would be incorrect to say that cyberbullying was the sole cause of such behavior.

More commonly, however, the effects of cyberbullying tend to parallel those of traditional bullying. Victims of traditional school-yard bullying often report feelings of depression, low self-esteem, helplessness, social anxiety, reduced concentration, alienation, and suicidal ideation (see Chapter 2). Based on predominantly correlational research to date, victims of cyberbullying report similar effects of their victimization (Beran & Li, 2005; Hinduja & Patchin, 2005, 2007; Imamura et al., 2009; Juvonen & Gross, 2008; Kowalski & Limber, 2011; Mason, 2008; Mishna, Saini & Solomon, 2009; Patchin & Hinduja, 2010; Ybarra & Mitchell, 2004). These effects appear to be magnified the younger the victim (Reeckman & Cannard, 2009). A respondent in one of our focus groups, in talking about the effects of cyberbullying on one of her friends, said: "It made them be mean for a while. They just didn't want to do anything with anyone, they didn't want to deal with it. It affected their mood, their relationships. It affected them academically. They stopped coming to school for a few days." The long-term effects of being a victim of cyberbullying stem in part from the intentional nature of the behavior. "It's not just the fact of getting hurt ... people get hurt in accidents. It's the fact that someone made a choice to intentionally hurt you" (Akwagyiram, 2005).

Data from Kowalski and Witte's (2006) online study highlight the emotional toll that being a victim of cyberbullying can take. When asked, "How did you feel when you were cyberbullied?" participants reported feeling angry, sad, depressed, hurt, stressed, and confused. One participant wrote that she felt "meek and small ... very alone and helpless." Alternatively, another respondent, although clearly in the minority, stated that he felt "engaged, like in a fight or combative sports activity." This individual went on to say: "I look at what most consider 'bullying' as a challenge or invitation to 'play.'" Another respondent recounting the effects of cyberbullying on his friend said: "She actually has been thrown into a sort of a depression and contemplates suicide very often." Similar findings have been reported by Patchin and Hinduja (2006, 2010b; Hinduja & Patchin, 2010).

An interesting comparison is the responses of perpetrators to the question "How did you feel when you cyberbullied someone?" Among the responses in Kowalski and Witte's online study (2006) were the following: aggressive, vindictive, happy, pleased. Another individual said: "Right, as they deserved it, like I was giving them a taste of their own medicine." Although longitudinal data do not yet exist providing empirical support for this, many researchers and writers on cyberbullying (e.g., Ybarra & Mitchell, 2004; Willard, 2006) believe that the long-term effects of cyberbullying are as negative as those that accompany traditional bullying. Cross-sectional data obtained by Kowalski and Limber (2011) supported this hypothesis. As serious as the physical and psychological effects were following traditional bullying, these effects were magnified with cyberbullying. Nine hundred and thirty-one 6th through 9th graders were divided into four groups based on their responses to questions examining whether they had been the victim of or perpetrator of cyberbullying: victims only, bullies only, bully/victims or not involved. Children who were cyber "bully/victims" had the highest rates of anxiety, depression, and school absences. Children not involved in cyberbullying had the highest levels of self-esteem and grades and the fewest physical health problems. Additionally, Ybarra et al. (2007) found that children who were targeted by internet harassment were eight times more likely than other young people to report carrying a weapon to school in the previous 30 days.

One reason for possible amplified effects following cyberbullying may be that adolescents cannot escape cyberbullying. A child who is bullied at school is at least free from the actual bullying when he is away from school or not riding the school bus. A child who is electronically bullied is never really free unless he or she ceases to communicate electronically, a behavioral choice that has other implications, such as cutting off the child's social communication network. Therefore, even as the teen sleeps, he or she could be inundated with text messages or e-mails containing harassing or denigrating communications.

Also, in comparison to traditional bullying, the public nature of cyberbullying increases the potential negative impact of the cruelty relative to traditional bullying. As horrible and embarrassing as it is to be humiliated and belittled in front of one's peer group at school, such humiliation may be multiplied by hundreds of thousands in cases like the Star Wars Kid described in Chapter 1. Instead of knowing who the bully and the observers were, cyberbully victims may walk around often unsure of who the bully is and most definitely unsure of how many countless people are aware of, or have contributed to, their humiliation.

Depending on the modality that cyberbullying takes, in some instances the danger associated with cyberbullying can be very real indeed. Perpetrators who impersonate another individual and post hate messages (and personally identifying messages) in chat rooms may be placing that individual at risk of physical harm. Discussants in the chat room offended by the hate messages may decide to use the identifying information to track down the person ostensibly posting the message.

There has been some discussion, although as yet no empirical data, regarding the extent to which social networking sites may facilitate a "suicide contagion effect" (Zayas, 2006). Previous research on copycat suicides that was published long before the existence of social network sites showed an increase in suicides following the publicizing of a suicide on the front page of a newspaper. Referred to as the Werther effect (Becker & Schmidt, 2005), researchers found that individuals who had been contemplating suicide were more likely to actually make the attempt if they saw a newspaper story about an individual who resembled them in some way. The Internet suicide contagion effect may work in much the same way. One MySpace user changed his screen name to Goodbye immediately before committing suicide. Another left a message on his MySpace page for his friends and family not to be sad when he was gone (Zayas, 2006). Psychologically vulnerable people with characteristics similar to these individuals might view these sites and decide that they, too, could be successful at a suicide attempt or be somehow "better off."

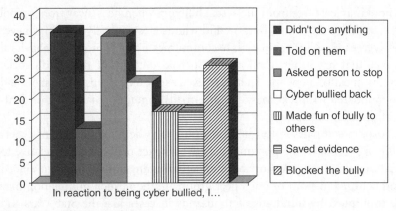

Figure 4.1 Reactions of victim.

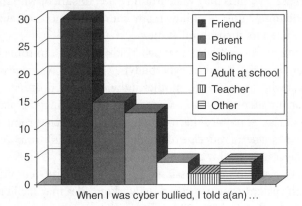

Figure 4.2 Who victims told.

An additional consequence of cyberbullying for at least some perpetrators is guilt and regret (Dempsey et al., 2009). Although, certainly, some people who bully, either electronically or in the traditional sense, feel no remorse for their actions, others do, particularly those who are more tuned in to the negative effects that bullying has on the victim. One of our focus group interviews that was conducted with a person who had cyberbullied a student at another school highlights this regret. When asked how he or she felt about the content of what they wrote, the perpetrator stated: "Well, now I realize … how bad it really did sound. I mean, I know this sounds totally lame, but I really did not realize how threatening it really was." In response to the question "Do you regret what you did?," the person who cyberbullied responded: "Yeah, one because it probably, I mean, not scarred her for life, but because it probably did something to her mentally or something, like made her more scared or something, and two because I lost some of my parents' trust and I have to regain that again and who knows how long it's going to take."

The effects that follow the cyberbullying may drive the responses to the cyberbullying. Victims who feel sad, anxious, and depressed may withdraw from both online and face-to-face encounters. Targets who feel hurt and angry, on the other hand, may retaliate, seeking revenge for the cyberbullying (Hoff & Mitchell, 2009). Unfortunately, most cyberbullying victims do nothing (see Figures 4.1 and 4.2). At least among adolescents, few tell anyone about the cyberbullying, and, among those who do tell, few tell an adult (Hoff & Mitchell, 2009; Li, 2006).

Conclusions

As research on the topic of cyberbullying continues to develop, presumably programs and policies will be put in place with the intent of decreasing the incidence of cyberbullying. As with traditional bullying, however, it is unlikely that cyberbullying will disappear completely. Thus, additional research using a variety of methodologies is needed to investigate the characteristics of targets and perpetrators of cyberbullying, as well as bystanders. We need to know more about who does what to whom with what effect, so that prevention and intervention efforts, such as those that will be discussed in the next two chapters, can take a more focused approach to increase their effectiveness.

5

WHAT PARENTS CAN DO

Brandy[1] is a 9th grader at a large suburban high school outside of Atlanta, Georgia. She is pretty, popular, and a cheerleader. She also has a profile on a social networking site called Xanga that includes pictures of herself and diary type entries of her personal interests and activities. One day over the summer break, she receives a post to her site that says, "Go to my Xanga, bitch!" When she clicks on the link, she is connected to another blog site that is dedicated to her. This blog, also on Xanga, contains profanity and demeaning language describing her as an ugly, fat whore. The tone of this blog is very dark, and sinister music begins playing as the screen comes up. The headline of the Xanga site reads, "Tomorrow You Will Die." The screen name of the person who owns this blog is listed as F*** you, F*** me. The unidentified blogger has listed his or her personal interests as "stalking and murder."

Though Brandy is upset about the content, she decides to keep it to herself and not respond to the postings on the blog because she thinks the person just wants to get a reaction out of her. She avoids telling her parents about the incident as well.

Six weeks later, another posting is added to the Xanga site dedicated to Brandy that reads, "Hey you f****** bitch. I know where you were the other night. You will f****** well die if I can help it ... How does it feel to be so hated ... You tell me when I see you tomorrow ... I'll see you tomorrow because I'll be beating the s*** out of you!!! Enjoy living, whore, enjoy living while you can. You won't be living for long. I'll make sure you die s-l-o-w-l-y. F****** die ass***e!!!"

Cyberbullying: Bullying in the Digital Age, Second Edition. Robin M. Kowalski, Susan P. Limber, and Patricia W. Agatston.
© 2012 Robin M. Kowalski, Susan P. Limber, and Patricia W. Agatston.
Published 2012 by Blackwell Publishing Ltd.

Brandy McClain did what many young people do when they receive cyberbullying messages on a Web site, or in an instant message, text message or e-mail. She told a friend, but avoided telling her parents. Fortunately for Brandy, her friend thought it was serious enough to tell her own mother, who in turn told Brandy's mother about the site.

Imagine for a moment that you are Brandy's mother, Mrs McClain. After the call from another parent, you access the social networking site called Xanga and are confronted with words on a dark screen that threaten to kill your daughter the next day. Imagine the fear and pain such a site would cause you. As Mrs McClain said later, "I didn't know whether to let her go to school the next day. She was supposed to be in a pep rally. Would someone try to kill her?" Mrs McClain also described the flood of emotions and panicky thoughts going through her mind. "You start to become paranoid. You begin wondering about all of your child's friends and look at them differently. Everyone is a suspect when you don't know who wrote such a thing. I started wondering if I should home school my child!"

What did Mrs McClain do? She started where many parents start when they are concerned about a threatening message targeting their child. She called the school counselor at Brandy's high school. Unfortunately, many school counselors are not sure what to do when confronted with this form of bullying. Many believe that, if cyberbullying happens outside of school, there is little that the school can do to assist the families. Although school personnel may have limited options to discipline the offender (see also Chapter 7), there are always steps they can take to assist the family of the victim. Chapter 6 will discuss the steps that school personnel can take to help students affected by cyberbullying. This chapter will focus on steps that families can take to prevent and address cyberbullying problems.

Admittedly, Brandy's school counselor faced a difficult challenge. She didn't know who posted the threatening site targeting Brandy and whether or not the offender was a fellow student. Fortunately, the school counselor referred Mrs McClain to the school district's student assistance program, knowing that it led many of the bullying prevention efforts for the school district and was beginning to focus attention on cyberbullying as well. The counselor also did a very wise thing: she suggested that Mrs McClain contact the police because the posting involved a physical threat.

Parental Involvement in Prevention and Intervention

As was the case for Brandy, the students in our focus groups indicated that most cyberbullying occurs outside of school hours, when children are at home under their parents' supervision. This is consistent with the Fight Crime: Invest In Kids (2006) survey data that reported that *teens* received 70% of harmful messages at home, and 30% of harmful messages at school. However, their data on preteens suggest a more equal distribution, with preteens reporting they were as likely to receive harmful messages at school (45%) as at home (44%). While the current generation of parents has been termed "helicopter parents" or "Velcro parents" for their tendency to "hover" unnecessarily over their children's school and extracurricular activities or to "stick" too close to their children, this rarely applies to parents' supervision of children's use of technology. Many families would benefit from parents spending more time discussing online behavior and monitoring their children's online activities.

*Parents often are not present in the online
environment of children*

As discussed in Chapter 3, social networking sites such as MySpace and Facebook have grown immensely popular among teens and young adults. The Pew Internet and American Life Project reports that 73% of teens have a social networking site (Lenhart, 2010). When these sites gained popularity among youth several years ago, older adults were less familiar with and less likely to have a profile on a social networking site, thus leading to a situation where young people were frequently unsupervised as they developed their online profiles. More recently, there has been an influx of older adults using social networking sites and increasingly asking their teens to "friend" them as a condition of using such sites. This can be one piece of a useful strategy of monitoring teens' involvement on such sites; however, it is still critical to set up agreements and have regular discussions about positive use of social media with our children. Parents' conversations with their children need to move beyond personal safety and avoiding harmful online content to the importance of uploading and sharing content in a considerate and constructive manner and taking care to protect one's privacy. The parent and child should discuss the importance of treating others well online and the responsibilities of digital citizenship. Having a conversation about what it means to be a positive digital citizen in terms of what we view, share, upload and download is a critical conversation for parents and new users of social media to have. Parents who routinely discuss bike helmet safety and "home alone safety tips" are often silent when introducing a new piece of technology such as a cellular phone or laptop into the home environment. These discussions are even more critical today as concerns about privacy increase. A recent Zogby International Poll (Common Sense Media, 2010) found that three out of four parents think social networking sites are not adequately protecting children's privacy.

Why don't children report cyberbullying?

In our case example, Brandy avoided telling her parents about the cyber threats she was receiving. It is very likely that children will avoid telling their parents about a cyberbullying incident unless families have discussed cyberbullying ahead of time. The Fight Crime: Invest In Kids survey found that, although 51% of *preteens* who had been cyberbullied told their parents, only 35% of cyberbullied *teens* had done so (2006). Research studies conducted in the United Kingdom (Smith et al., 2008) and Australia and Austria also show lower rates of reporting among students who were cyberbullied versus being bullied by more conventional means (Dooley et al., 2009). Communication with a daughter or son is the key. Parents need to listen closely to what children say about their online experiences and familiarize themselves with the sites and modalities children use for online interaction.

The students in our focus groups gave interesting responses as to why they and their friends do not always tell their parents about such incidents. Here are some of the student responses when asked why their friends did not tell:

"She was afraid if she told her parents she would get restricted, so [she] didn't want to let them know." "Yeah – or [their parents] would make them quit using [a social networking site]." – *middle school female*

"They might be scared to tell their parents, because they might say, 'I told you so, I told you not to have that blog.'" – *high school female*

"If you tell your parents a lot of times they'll want to get involved." – *middle school boy*

"They overreact." – *middle school boy*

The students' fears were supported by one middle school focus group participant who said that she was not allowed to instant message anymore because she had received intimidating instant messages from a former classmate.

It is tempting to view these new technologies in black or white terms, as good or evil, and to react accordingly. But children rarely benefit or learn when parents are reactive and respond immediately by restricting or punishing them. They benefit most when parents are proactive and educate. While parents may be inclined to blame technology and the Internet for putting their children at risk of harm, being anti-technology is unproductive. The reality is that the Internet is here to stay and is a valuable tool. While a child who abuses others over the Internet may need some consequences, such as restriction from certain sites or functions, the victim who did nothing wrong should not be punished by losing such privileges. Otherwise, the child may not tell a parent about the next incident. It is also important to find out the motivations of a child who engages in cyberbullying. Occasionally cyberbullying occurs as retaliation for on campus bullying. This also indicates how important it is for parents to have a calm conversation with a son or daughter in order to fully understand the dynamics of the bullying and whether it is necessary to notify school personnel of the situation.

Knee-jerk responses by parents that blame the victim are, of course, not limited to instances of cyberbullying. Consider, for example, the reactions of some parents to a child's disclosure of sexual abuse or assault. If a child tells her parent that someone touched her inappropriately, a parent may instinctively become upset and respond with a statement such as, "What do you mean? Why didn't you tell them to stop?" This or similar responses may further victimize a child by blaming him or her for someone else's actions. It also increases the likelihood that the child will try to avoid sharing any information in the future that could prompt such a response, such as having been at a party where drinking or drug use occurred.

Parents may benefit from beginning every response to disclosures, no matter how upsetting, with, "Thank you for telling me that. You did the right thing by letting me know." As challenging as it may be, parents who remain calm during disclosures will ensure that the lines of communication remain open with their child, and they will be in a position to provide guidance in the future when their child is faced with various challenges. Children tend to share more when they have learned that their parents can be trusted to respond in a stable and reassuring manner. We will also discuss the importance of educators responding appropriately to reports of cyberbullying in Chapter 6.

Warning signs that a child may be a victim
of cyberbullying

Because many young people are reluctant to tell an adult about cyberbullying, there are some warning signs that may indicate a child is being victimized, although these may also be signs of other problems.

- Child appears upset after being online.
- Child appears upset after viewing a text message.
- Child withdraws from social interaction with peers.
- Possible drop in academic performance.
- Child has been targeted by on-campus bullying.

The most obvious sign of a cyberbullying incident is when a child becomes
visibly upset or withdrawn after being on the computer or after viewing a
text message. A drop in grades or performance at school also could be a
warning sign of involvement in cyberbullying (Hinduja & Patchin, 2008;
Ybarra et al., 2007). However, as it also may be a sign of so many other
troubles, it may not be a very useful indicator of cyberbullying. Some students
in our focus groups seemed to minimize the impact that cyberbullying had
on the academic performance of friends who had been cyberbullied, claim-
ing their friends could separate cyberbullying from their schoolwork, as seen
in the following comments.

> *Interviewer:* Do you think the cyberbullying impacted their school work?
> "No – I don't think so." – *high school female*
> "No change." – *high school male*
> "Maybe, it depends on what was said." – *middle school girl*

However, one student discussed how her friend *had* been affected
academically:

> "It affected [her] academically. [She] stopped coming to school for a few days."

These students readily admitted, however, that the cyberbullying affected
their friends' social relationships and that they felt distrustful and fearful of
others in their social circle (especially if the cyberbullying was anonymous).

Here are some of the comments from a high school girls' focus group about their friends' social and emotional responses to being cyberbullied.

> "She thought the girls who did it were her friends, so she lost those friendships."
> "[She was] upset. She just wasn't friends with those people anymore."
> "She was scared, looking around all of the time."
> "He said, 'I don't even know who this person is.' I think he was kind of scared."

A middle school boy said the following:

> "[It] makes them think less about themselves. Because whenever someone is mad, they say things they shouldn't and then they [the targets] think less of themselves."

This comment came from a high school boy:

> "The kid I'm talking about takes everything too seriously. He got all … he started crying and stuff. It upset him."

It seems difficult to imagine being able to give the strongest academic performance when a student is fearful, anxious, and distrustful of peers at school. Kowalski and Limber's (2011) research on the effects of cyberbullying discussed in Chapter 4 has found that those who are involved in cyberbullying are more likely to report school absences than those who are not involved. In addition studies have found that students who are targeted by cyberbullying have also frequently experienced traditional bullying as well (Hinduja & Patchin, 2009; Kowalski & Limber, 2007, 2011).

Thus, paying attention to a child's social relationships and any changes in these relationships can help alert parents to instances of traditional bullying and cyberbullying. Some parents choose to read all of their child's e-mail and instant messages, but this can be construed as a huge invasion of privacy by young people, and rightly so. It is more helpful for parents to spend time talking with their children about appropriate ways to interact online and about their family guidelines for computer use. It is important for parents and children to reach consensus about the circumstances under which the children should notify the parents if they receive negative messages or view harmful material online. It also makes sense that if a son or daughter posts information to a social networking site, such as MySpace or Facebook, for the general public to see, the parent will view it occasionally. It is helpful if parents let their children know ahead of time that they will occasionally monitor their social networking site, but that they do not plan to read all of their children's communications on a daily basis. However, if the parents are alerted to instances of cyberbullying, they will need to monitor their children's communications more closely. Various Web-based and mobile phone monitoring software tools have recently been developed that allow parents to monitor social networking sites and texting on cell phones. Many of these new technologies only alert parents if there are specific terms or phrases used that might be of concern. Thus, youth still have some measure of privacy and parents are not bombarded with an overload of reports to review. Of course, a determined teen can certainly figure out "work arounds." Thus, nothing takes the place of regular discussions about treating others with respect, both online and offline.

Suggestions for Addressing Cyberbullying that Children Have Experienced

What can parents do if their child is cyberbullied? Because cyberbullying instances can vary dramatically from one another in method, intensity, and duration, there is no set course of action that parents can follow. However, we will provide some basic steps, as well as response options, that parents should consider when responding to cyberbullying directed toward a child.

Saving the evidence

Parents should teach their children to save any evidence of cyberbullying. While ignoring or blocking a sender's messages may be the best response for minor incidents of cyberbullying, it may still be useful to have copies of instant message conversations, e-mails, or other communications should matters escalate. Unless parents have added a specific program that routinely records all communications, most computers will not automatically save instant or chat messages that are sent to a child.

Children should be taught to print out any threatening or harassing e-mails or instant messages that they receive and to avoid deleting the e-mails. Instant message programs usually have a "save" feature, but children may need help in knowing how to use it. Parents should ask children to show them any messages that include threatening or harassing statements. If the parent and child do not know who sent the messages, the parent should save the messages to the computer's hard drive and then forward these communications to the Internet service provider or in extreme cases notify the police in order to try to trace the perpetrator.

Children also need to know that if they ever receive offensive pictures or are directed to a Web site that is offensive or frightening, they should turn off the monitor (not the computer) and notify a parent. Often children respond by shutting down the computer, which may erase the evidence. By turning off the monitor but leaving the computer on, they can stop viewing the upsetting material, but it will still be present for a parent to review (and if necessary save evidence). Older children can be instructed to save the Web pages and print out copies of offensive Web sites or social networking sites. It is important that they are told not to respond to the offensive comments unless they have conferred with an adult.

When to ignore, block, react, or report

An instant message from a friend that reads, "You idiot!" may seem upsetting to a child but may just lack a few critical words (e.g., "just kidding" or "jk") that would have conveyed quite a different sentiment. In such a situation, an appropriate response might be to ask for clarification or ignore the message. An individual who regularly communicates through the use of profanity or obscenities should be warned, and, if necessary, blocked from sending instant messages to a child. Instant message screen names and cellular phone numbers (used to send text messages to cellular phones) can be blocked. Of course, some users will set up new screen names to harass others. At that point, the cyberbullying may need to be addressed more directly by contacting the parent of the child who engaged in cyberbullying, possibly the school counselor if the students attend the same school, and maybe the police. Contacting the parent of the child who engaged in cyberbullying will be discussed later in this chapter.

Usually, the best response to a mean or nasty comment is no response. Students in our focus groups shared that responding often just aggravates the situation. Here are some of their responses to the question, "What would you do if you were cyber bullied by someone you knew?"

"Delete it." – *high school female*
"Ignore it." – *middle school male*
"I wouldn't pay attention unless it happened frequently." – *high school female*
"Ignore them. Block them." – *high school male*
"Block them so they couldn't e-mail me." – *middle school female*

A person who sends one mean e-mail, text message, or instant message can be ignored. Often this will end the cyberbullying, whether the identity of the individual is known or not. If the messages continue, the sender's messages can be blocked by using the blocking feature on an instant message account. WiredSafety.org explains how one can avoid receiving text messages temporarily by turning off the incoming messages function for a couple of days. This may stop the person from sending the text messages as he may think the phone number has been changed. E-mails accounts can also be set up to block incoming messages from certain senders. Social networking sites also allow the user to block, remove or "unfriend" someone who is sending or posting inappropriate or unfriendly messages and comments, and the comments can be deleted from the user's profile. This will be discussed further in the section on removing content on social networking sites.

Of course, ignoring or blocking offensive messages may not always stop them from coming. Occasionally, cyberbullying continues through the creation of new accounts and new screen names. Because the identity of the sender cannot be confirmed, the parents of the child who engaged in cyberbullying cannot be contacted. If, despite ignoring mean comments and blocking the sender's messages, the cyberbullying continues, parents may find it helpful to send one message indicating that the authorities will be contacted if the messages persist. Responding assertively has been helpful in some instances of cyberbullying. We give an example later in this chapter of a situation where this was used effectively by a parent. Youth may also find it useful to send a single message requesting that the behavior stop. However, it is important not to respond aggressively. Research on youth risky behavior online (Ybarra, et. al, 2007) as well as anecdotal evidence from discussions with youth suggest that aggressive responses usually escalate the cyberbullying.

Tracing e-mails and text messages

It is possible to identify the senders of e-mails and text messages in some situations. Students in our focus groups were asked, "What would you do if the cyber bully was someone you *didn't* know?" Some of their responses:

"Block them." – *high school male*
"Trace them." – *high school female*
"I worry about stalking. I might tell my parents just so they would know it was happening." – *high school female*

"I would wonder how they got my number if it were a text message." – *middle school female*

It is encouraging that some students are aware of such options as tracing and blocking inappropriate messages. Parents and children should also attempt to identify the individual doing the cyberbullying.

If threatening messages are coming through a cellular phone via text messaging, the phone number may be traced through a reverse look up directory or even through searching for the phone number on Google. Once identified, it can be reported to the mobile phone provider. Again, while one or two mean text messages would best be ignored, if continued harassment is occurring the abuse should be reported and if necessary the phone number can be changed. The Center for Safe and Responsible Internet Use recommends that abuse that occurs through e-mail be reported to the Internet service provider of the perpetrator (Willard, 2007). A copy of the abusive e-mail can be forwarded to their provider. There may be a specific e-mail address or an abuse reporting link on the support page of the Internet service provider that provides instructions for reporting abuse. Keep in mind the importance of reporting inappropriate messages as soon as possible. Internet service providers may only be able to trace information for a certain period of time. In addition, it is not uncommon for youth to learn who is engaging in the cyberbullying just from talking to supportive peers at school. Research from Mishna et al. (2009) found that while youth were sometimes unsure who the cyberbully was initially, they often discovered their identities later through conversations with their peer group. Thus, even when youth may be unable to trace the identity of the perpetrator at the time of the incident they will typically learn who posted or sent messages via word of mouth. Finding out who the sent the message may alleviate anxiety but steps should still be taken to ensure successful resolution of the incident.

Tracing and responding to postings to social networking sites and Web sites

Mrs McClain was asked by the student assistance counselor (and co-author of this book) if she had contacted the police and she replied that she had spoken with a detective at the high-tech crimes unit. He was pursuing a subpoena as required by Xanga.com in order to release the name of the Internet service provider that was used to post the material on the Xanga Web site. It was suggested by the author that she also let the school resource officer at the high school know about the threats, so that he could monitor the situation at the school in case the threats were from a classmate. Mrs McClain assumed that the offender was another student at her daughter's school. She was surprised to learn a few days later from the high tech crimes detective that the individual who had cyberbullied her daughter was, in fact, a 9th grade female student attending a different high school. The two students had been in middle school together previously. "They knew each other," Mrs McClain stated in a puzzled voice, "but they weren't really even friends."

Mrs McClain was fortunate to be able to identify the perpetrator of the cyber threats toward her daughter by contacting a high-tech crimes unit at her local police department. Many cities are adding cybercrime units and training detectives in cybercriminal behavior (Franek, 2005/2006). However, not every threatening statement posted on the Internet will be specific enough or deemed severe enough for the courts to allow law enforcement to pursue the identity of the perpetrator. The Center for Safe and Responsible Internet Use recommends that, if a site entry about an individual includes threats of violence, stalking, extortion, harassment, or is obscene or pornographic, the police should be notified (Willard, 2007).

Another parent who was interviewed for this book discovered an entry on a social networking site dedicated to her daughter, titled "Lisa Smith must die." The entry included comments about hating Lisa; however, there were no specific threats posted. Mrs Smith was referred to the high tech crimes police unit, but the district attorney's office would not issue a subpoena in this case. While Mrs Smith was disappointed in this outcome, she was successful in having the site shut down by posting the following assertive message on the Web site: "This is Lisa Smith's mother. This will be handed over to the police tomorrow. I will also be turning this in to the school. Your parents would not be proud. If you were smart, you would find better things to do with your time."

The next day, the site had been shut down by the person who had created it. In addition, it was suggested by one of the authors that Mrs Smith meet with the 7th grade counselor at Lisa's school to show her a printed copy of the Web site, and ask for her help. Mrs Smith was pretty sure some classmates were behind the Web site, and the counselor was more than willing to talk with teachers to ask them to be on the lookout for any incidents of bullying and listen for classmates' statements that might target Lisa. Regardless of whether one can determine the identity of the perpetrator, there are always steps to take to address the behavior.

As with instant messaging, text messaging, and e-mails, it is generally not recommended that the child targeted by cyberbullying or the child's parent respond to any of the mean comments or offensive material posted on a Web site. However, when the identity cannot be confirmed and the comments are continuing, it can be helpful for a parent to post one assertive comment as Mrs Smith did. Unfortunately, if the targeted child responds to the mean comments, the response may add fuel to the fire and encourage the perpetrator to respond in more aggressive ways.

Request that the Web site or social networking site remove the offensive material

As mentioned previously, minor incidents of cyberbullying such as one or two mean instant messages, posts, or a nasty text message are often best ignored. Information posted on a Web site, however, can continue to victimize a student when it is left up for everyone to see. Although parents may want to find the perpetrators and make sure they are punished, the child often simply wants the bullying to stop. Lisa, for example, just wanted the page to come down. Fortunately, her mother's post was successful in having the perpetrators remove the offensive material. She also could have requested that the domain host remove the offensive material.

Most social networking sites (as well as instant messaging programs) now have profile settings that allow a user to block other users from contacting them or posting comments on the user's Web site. If a user has set up a threatening Web site targeting a child, the parent or child can request that the social networking site remove the offensive Web site. The parent should also contact law enforcement in such instances. Most Web sites have an abuse policy that allows individuals to complain about material posted on the site. Parents can usually find the abuse policy as a link, as part of a help center, or sometimes under the "FAQ" (frequently asked questions) section on a site. Anyone can complain about an offensive site and request that it be shut down. Most sites have a link to their customer service department that allows individuals to report an offensive Web site in order to have it removed from the site.

Two popular social networking sites among teens are MySpace and Facebook. MySpace has a safety page with tips for users and parents as well as safety videos. They include information on cyberbullying and how to report cyberbullying. Facebook also has links to report abusive comments and fake profiles and provides useful cyberbullying information in their help section. In addition, Facebook provides a reporting option next to messages and comments that a user can click to report abusive or offensive messages. More recently Facebook has introduced a system that allows a user to ask a perpetrator to stop posting offensive comments or to remove inappropriate photos (Constine, 2011). For example, if someone has posted an unflattering picture of a user, the user can click on a link that provides an option to ask the individual to remove the picture. Another option involves blocking the person who posted the photo as a friend so that the individual will no longer be able to tag the user in a picture. In addition the user has the option to send a message asking a trusted authority (via email) for advice on handling the situation. The authority will receive a link to the offensive photo. However it may still be necessary to use the Facebook report form if perpetrators are not responsive to requests to remove unwanted content. A quick link to the Facebook reporting form can be found on the cyberbullyhelp.com Web site homepage.

Though not a social networking site per se, YouTube.com has become a popular site among young people for uploading and sharing videos that users have made, and it has included video clips involving bullying of classmates. YouTube.com has a feature in place that allows users to report such offensive videos that do not meet the site guidelines for appropriate videos, and they also have a Safety Center that includes information on and links to report cyberbullying. Users also have the option to block others from their channel so that they are unable to post comments.

Should Parents Ban Children from Social Networking Sites?

Although some parents respond to cyberbullying by banning the use of social networking sites altogether, by doing so they are asking their children to avoid a hugely popular pastime among students that allows for identity development and self-exploration. Younger children probably do not have the judgment to safely use sites designed for teens and adults, but older teens enjoy expressing themselves and exploring their identity online. Parents may choose to allow access for children who meet minimum age requirements, but they need to set some guidelines and occasionally visit the site. The current age limit for MySpace and Facebook is 13; however, it is easy for children to lie about their age and set up a profile. A parent should give approval for the social networking site only if their child agrees to the Web site guidelines, and gives the parent their profile name and password or agrees to some other form of monitoring. In addition, parents and children should review and set the privacy settings together. Connect Safely has an excellent online guide for setting the privacy settings for new users of Facebook. The child and parent should also agree that the parent will view the profile on occasion, at least until the child is in his or her later teens. There are also sites being developed now for children and preteens that market a safer online experience, such as Togetherville. Parents may find it helpful to use sites such as Togetherville, Club Penguin, and other social networking sites designed for younger children as a training ground for a child to learn how to safely and appropriately interact on such sites.

Social networking sites continue to be hugely popular during the college years (when a son or daughter is no longer under their parents' roof or control), so providing teens with age-appropriate rules for using social networking sites may be the best response among parents. The opportunity to use social media with parental guidance will better prepare youth for communicating responsibly when they are no longer living at home. The key for parents is to help their children understand that they are building a digital reputation that will follow them into the future. This will be discussed further in the section on monitoring a child's online reputation.

Contacting the Parents of a Child Who Cyberbullies

Authors of bullying prevention programs generally argue that it is risky or ineffective for the parent of a victim to contact the parent of a perpetrator of traditional bullying (e.g., Olweus, 1993a). Often the parents of the child who bullied are unresponsive or are defensive about the bullying and label their child's behavior as "kids being kids." It is not uncommon for parents to make statements such as, "I prefer to let the kids work it out," which assumes a level playing field for the parties involved. Unfortunately, with bullying we know that there is no level playing ground. It is an abuse of power similar in some respects to child abuse and domestic abuse (Olweus, 1993a).

Cyberbullying may be unique in that students who would not typically bully feel empowered to engage in bullying behaviors over the Internet. Reactive cyberbullying occurs when children who feel victimized or discouraged in their day-to-day life lash out, often anonymously, over the Internet.

Because the dynamics of cyberbullying are somewhat different from traditional bullying, it is appropriate to encourage parents of the victim to share evidence of the cyberbullying with the parents of the bully *in some situations*. The language of cyberbullying is often very threatening, offensive, and filled with profanity. It is hard for the average parent to defend their child when faced with a copy of such offensive language.

> After discovering the identity of the perpetrator, Mrs McClain was confused about what her next step should be. The detective stated that while she could press charges against the 9th grade female perpetrator, the student was basically a "good kid" from a "good family" who attended an honors program at a local high school. "I don't want to press charges," Mrs McClain confided to the author, "but I want to do something. I don't want her to think this is acceptable. Do you think it would be alright if I contacted her parents? The detective gave me their name and phone number. He said the mother was very responsive." "I think it would be alright," the author told Mrs McClain. "I would also be willing to meet with all of you if you think it would be helpful – a sort of mediation or accountability circle, if everyone is willing. Brandy can choose whether or not to be present. We don't want her to feel revictimized in any way."

In Mrs McClain's situation, the mother of the perpetrator, Mrs Jones, was very concerned about her daughter's behavior and very responsive to meeting in order to address the situation. After Mrs Jones agreed to meet Mrs McClain, the assistance program counselor contacted both parties and arranged to meet with both sets of parents as well as the student who made the threatening. Brandy did not want to be present during the session, but her parents did.

Mrs Jones was concerned about the cyberbullying incident when notified of its occurrence, yet when she went to view the actual Web site, it had been removed. After she was shown a printed copy of the blog entries that Mrs McClain had saved, Mrs Jones was shocked and outraged by her daughter's behavior. It was one thing to hear that her child had threatened another student; it was another to see a profanity-laced entry filled with shocking brutality. Few parents could justify such entries as just "kids being kids." As a result of viewing the evidence, Mrs Jones was very motivated to take steps to address the cyberbullying and monitor her child's online behavior.

In traditional bullying situations where the offenses happen at school, the school counselor or administrator usually contacts the parents of both the targeted student and the perpetrator. Parents of a child who has been bullied at school need to know that their concerns are being addressed, that the administration is meeting with the parents of the perpetrator, and that, if applicable, there will be consequences for the bullying behavior. These parents also can work with the administration to develop a "safety plan" that includes increased adult supervision and possible schedule changes of either party to help minimize their child's exposure to bullying behavior. Parents of the child who bullied need to be made aware of the situation and be aware of any consequences for current or future bullying behavior instigated by their child.

Cyberbullying, because it frequently happens outside of school, may require a different response. It often takes place between classmates but can also occur between students attending different schools, as our case example demonstrates. Thus, it may be appropriate in some cases for the parents of the bullied child to contact the parents of the aggressor. There is no guarantee that the parents of the perpetrator will respond in a helpful manner, but often the parents will take the situation seriously when provided with visual evidence of the bullying. In some cases, it may be effective to send a letter to the parents with a copy of the cyberbullying and a written request that the offensive messages stop. Parents of a bullied child may wish to outline their next steps if the cyberbullying continues, such as contacting law enforcement or an attorney (where appropriate), but this needs to be done in a sensitive and calm manner. Parents are advised to *describe* the bullying behavior, rather than label another child a bully.

Requesting Intervention Assistance from the School

Students in our focus groups shared that they would be more likely to tell a parent than any other adult about a cyberbullying situation. Parents may be able to investigate and handle the cyberbullying situation on their own or with community assistance, but in some situations parents may need the school's assistance to determine if cyberbullying or traditional bullying is occurring on campus. The school may also be able to provide resources and intervention assistance.

Share evidence with the school

Schools *need* to be aware of bullying situations that involve students at their school in order to effectively monitor the safety of students. It is helpful if parents print out a copy of the evidence of cyberbullying and share it with a school counselor or administrator, whether they know the identity of the perpetrator or not. The designated counselor or administrator can investigate whether bullying is occurring at school as well as over the Internet. Although schools may not be able to administer consequences for cyberbullying occurring outside of the school day (see Chapter 7), it is possible that incidents (either cyberbullying or traditional bullying) are occurring on campus as well. In such situations, the school may have policies in place to address bullying and cyberbullying that occur on campus.

School personnel can help monitor the situation

Sharing the evidence with the school will enable the administration to monitor potential bullying situations more closely and, where necessary, set up a school safety plan for the student. If offenses are determined to be occurring using school technology, the school district has a responsibility to address the situation. These incidents should be documented by the parent to provide the counselor or administrator with as much information as possible about when and where the incidents are occurring. If one student uses a cellular phone to cyberbully another student while at school, the administration may be able to intervene as well.

Requesting assistance from the school in contacting parents

If parents of a bullied child have reason to doubt that the parents of the cyberbully will respond appropriately to their requests that the cyberbullying cease, or if the cyberbullying is accompanied by traditional bullying at school, parents may need to request that the school counselor or administrator at a child's school contact the parents of the perpetrator to notify them of the incident. Be aware, however, that while public schools may be able to assist by alerting the parents of those involved through a phone call or letter sent home, they may not be legally able to discipline students for online comments or postings that occur at home, for fear of violating students' rights to freedom of speech and expression under the First Amendment (see Chapter 7). Private schools have more options in this area, and may be in a position to levy consequences for cyberbullying that occurs off campus. If the offenses are criminal in nature, the school resource officer may be able to assist or refer parents to the appropriate law enforcement official. Schools may also be able to provide educational materials or resources for parents on cyberbullying and Internet safety.

A school district may have counselors who are willing to assist the parties involved by arranging an informal resolution meeting. Chapter 6 of this book includes tips for counselors who wish to arrange an informal resolution or "accountability circle" strategy based on restorative justice principles. Such a strategy was used successfully with the McClain case.

Legal Options

Mrs McClain did not want to press criminal charges against the 9th grader who targeted her daughter, but she could have. Sometimes threatening to call the police or contact an attorney is enough to ensure that the cyberbullying stops. Police should be contacted if cyberbullying includes such things as:

- threats of physical harm to an individual;
- stalking or harassment;
- pornographic images;
- extortion (Willard, 2007).

In rare cases, parents may choose to file a lawsuit against the cyberbully or the cyberbully's parents. Courts have ruled in some jurisdictions that the parents of minors can be held financially responsible if the minor engages in wrongdoing that is a result of parental lack of supervision (Willard, 2007). Parents may wish to consult with a qualified and competent attorney if their child has been harassed or threatened in such a manner as to cause severe emotional distress, or if the child's reputation has been severely damaged by posting false information online. The parent of a child engaged in cyberbullying who has not been responsive to complaints will likely be more responsive to the situation when confronted with a letter from a parent or an attorney outlining possible legal actions.

Parents will find it well worth their time to monitor and guide their children's activities on the Internet, when faced with the prospect of being sued in response to statements written by their child online or having criminal charges filed against their son or daughter. This is another reason for parents to be proactive in educating themselves about the Internet and communicating their guidelines and expectations for how their children conduct themselves online. It would be a shame for a child's actions to lead to a criminal record for the child or other legal actions for the parent, but, unless parents take reasonable responsibility for their child's actions and recognize that parenting must continue in the virtual world, this is a possibility. Box 5.1 provides a summary of tips for responding to cyberbullying. (See Chapter 7 for more in-depth information on legal issues and cyberbullying.)

Box 5.1   Intervention tips for responding to cyberbullying

- Save the evidence. Print copies of messages and Web sites. Use the save feature on instant messages.
- First offense (if minor in nature) – ignore, delete, or block the sender. Instant message programs, e-mail, and cell phones usually have blocking features.
- If a fake or offensive profile targeting your child is set up on a social networking site, report it to the site. The link for reporting cyberbullying and fake profiles can be found under the help sections of many Web sites. MySpace and Facebook have a help center on their sites that provide a link for reporting offensive profiles. Make sure to copy the link (the Web site address) to the site for reporting purposes.
- Investigate your child's online presence. Set up an alert on Google, or search your child's name occasionally through a variety of search engines or social media monitoring technologies.
- If the perpetrator is another student, share evidence with the school counselor. Check to see if any bullying may be occurring at school.
- If the perpetrator is known and cyberbullying is continuing or severe, contact the child's parents and share your evidence (if you are comfortable doing so). Ask that they ensure that the cyberbullying stop and any posted material be removed.
- If the parent of perpetrator is unresponsive or the behavior continues, the parent of the bullied child may wish to contact an attorney or send a certified letter outlining possible civil/legal options if the behavior does not stop or material is not removed.
- Report the cyberbullying to the police or high tech crimes unit in your area if the cyberbullying contains threats, intimidation, or sexual exploitation.
- If your child expresses emotional distress or thoughts of self-harm, seek help from a school counselor or other mental health professional immediately.

Suggestions for Addressing Cyberbullying that
Children Engage in or Witness

Research on bullying has demonstrated that most young people do not find themselves in the role of bully or victim (Olweus, 1993a). The majority of young people are witnesses to bullying. They may play a variety of roles as witnesses or bystanders, including disengaged onlookers or possible defenders (a child who sees the bullying behavior and dislikes it, but is not sure what to do about it). Adults need to help young people understand that they have important roles to play as bystanders. Parents can talk with their children about the various options available to them when they see bullying behavior in the real world and cyberbullying in the virtual world. Too often young people witness bullying, feel badly, and do nothing.

Here are some of the students' comments about their feelings when witnessing cyberbullying behavior:

"I was surprised and stuff because I was friends with them and I knew they didn't like her but I thought it was lame to do that, I thought it was mean, so I was surprised they would do it." – *high school female*

"I felt bad for her because they were saying things about how she looked and stuff, and she couldn't help it." – *high school female*

"I just felt really bad because everyone was being so mean." – *middle school female*

"I felt bad for [her], because it was multiple girls doing it to one girl … on MySpace." – *middle school boy*

"I was mad." – *middle school boy*

Despite being upset or disappointed in their friends' actions, the bystanders did not tell an adult about the cyberbullying in the vast majority of the cyberbullying situations discussed in our focus groups. Thus, it is critical for parents to talk to their children about what to do when they witness cyberbullying. Increasingly youth are recognizing that they can use technology to provide positive messages of support to a targeted peer. "It is easier to be a positive defender through technology than it is face to face" commented one high school female in a discussion group with peer leaders (Agatston, Kowalski, & Limber, 2011).

If your child witnesses cyberbullying

Parents can help their children to become "empowered" bystanders by discussing the following strategies with their children.

Speak out against the cyberbullying

Children can let children who cyberbully know that they think their actions are wrong and that they need to stop. Some young people will feel comfortable speaking out against those who bully. These young people are assertive enough or have enough social support to do so. Others may not feel safe responding on their own, but they may recognize that there is "strength in numbers." Having a group of friends address cyberbullying face-to-face or online can bring positive results. These responses should be assertive; they should never be aggressive or antagonistic.

Support the student being bullied

Talking to peers who are bullied face-to-face (or in cyberspace) and letting them know that their peers think that the cyberbullying is wrong can provide much needed emotional support for targeted students. In the face of silence, many children who are bullied feel that everyone else believes, likes, or takes the side of the child who is engaging in cyberbullying. It is easy for a victim to feel friendless in such a situation. In the case of Lisa Smith (whose "Lisa Must Die" Web site was discussed earlier), her friends posted positive comments to the site to counteract the negative messages. In a follow-up interview about the incident, Lisa's mother commented that it helped her daughter weather the storm when she saw her friends' positive comments and messages of support posted online.

Tell an adult

Unfortunately, many bystanders as well as children who are targeted avoid telling an adult about cyberbullying incidents. As mentioned earlier, some are afraid to tell because they think they will lose their online privileges. Parents may find it helpful to clarify with their children that they will not be punished for another person's bullying behavior or their own reluctance to speak out to stop the cyberbullying that they witness. A parent's goal should be to help improve the situation, not to find fault. Parents can also discuss with their children which adults they feel they can trust or talk to when they need help or advice. While parents often prefer that their children come to them with a problem, it is helpful for young people to have a wider circle of adults to whom they can turn for support. If a classmate is being cyberbullied, the most appropriate adult to seek out may be the school counselor or a helpful teacher. Parents should explain to their children that these adults need to know about the situation so they can help stop the bullying.

The toughest social dilemmas that many children face are in the roles of a witness or a bystander. It is one thing to avoid engaging in mean, dishonest, or unethical behavior. It requires even greater moral fiber to take action when young people observe others engaging in such behavior. Parents may find it helpful to admit to their children that sometimes adults also fail to speak up or act when they witness inappropriate behavior. Think about how reluctant Parent A is to call Parent B even though she knows Parent B's child is engaged in harmful behavior that could be damaging to the child or to others. Parents may need to look in the mirror to make sure that they are leading by example.

If your child engages in cyberbullying

Imagine that the school counselor calls you to let you know that your daughter participated with her classmates in designing a Web site to make fun of a fellow classmate. On the Web site, students posted negative comments about the girl's physical appearance and called her sexually derogative names. Because the pages were printed out and shared at school, administrators are taking the position that the students should be disciplined for engaging in bullying behavior, and they request that you come to school for a meeting. How will you respond?

- You deny that your daughter could ever be involved in such behavior and threaten to get to the bottom of this. You ask for any proof they have that your child was involved and threaten a lawsuit if they are wrong.
- You accuse the school of overreacting and explain how this is just "kids being kids." You point out that slam books have existed forever and, even if it's mean, it's not that big a deal. "Do we really have to meet about this?"
- You listen carefully to their findings and express concern about your daughter and her classmates' behavior. You agree to come to the meeting and assure the school that you support its position to take cyberbullying seriously. You plan to have a serious discussion with your daughter as well, in order to better understand her role in the incident.

Few parents want to admit that their children are capable of cruel or bullying behavior. It has been our experience that many educators are very hesitant to use the term bullying in describing children's behavior to parents, because parents react so strongly to the term. "My child is not a bully!" and "Are you calling my child a bully?" are common responses from parents. Rather than becoming defensive, parents of students who engage in bullying behavior should recognize that most individuals are capable of either supporting or directly engaging in bullying behavior at some point in their lives. A child who engages in bullying behavior is not likely a "bully" every day of his or her life. The advent of the Internet and electronic communication, combined with the opportunity to post information anonymously, has influenced some young people to make negative statements online that they would be much less likely to make if their name were attached to the comment. In addition, some youth do not recognize how hurtful comments can be when they are caught up in a group "pile on" or in an online conflict that rapidly escalates. A courageous parent who is notified that his or her child has participated in online cruelty will recognize that this is a teachable moment and focus on educating their child and remedying the situation.

That being said, some young people who cyberbully also engage in other forms of bullying. If an investigation into the cyberbullying suggests that a child has bullied another student at school as well as online, the parents face a serious situation that may best be corrected through a combination of consequences, counseling, and possibly community service. The consequences and counseling should focus on correcting mistaken beliefs of entitlement, and the community service (if used appropriately) may help teach empathy. It also is important in this situation to monitor a child's Internet use much more closely. Installing tracking software is one way to verify that a child is only corresponding in a positive manner online and only accessing agreed upon Web sites.

If the child appears truly remorseful for his or her actions, it would be appropriate for him or her to write and apologize to the child who was bullied and the other family members that have been hurt. Forcing an apology is never a good idea, however, and will do more harm than good. The child who has been cyberbullied will probably recognize that the effort is insincere and may feel further victimized by the incident. The parents of the child engaged in the cyberbullying may want to have a school counselor review the apology note to make sure it appears sincere and appropriate before giving it to the family of the targeted child. The child who has engaged in cyberbullying should be encouraged to take steps to make amends for any harm caused. This could include correcting any false or harmful information that was shared online by contacting others who have viewed the information.

Parents should remember that every challenge that children face is also an opportunity for learning. Consider the lessons that children may learn from such an event. When parents catch a child experimenting with alcohol or other drugs or engaging in some other high risk behavior, it is common to be reactive and look at only the negative aspects of the incident. It is much more useful, however, to recognize that an opportunity is available to correct a situation that needs attention. This is an opportunity to teach again, guide again, and communicate values again to children who need to hear these messages. Parents may reflect that it is time to focus closely on issues that are important to them as a family. The alternative is for parents to take the position that their child should not be held accountable for his or her actions and that school administrators or other parents are overreacting. In this case, a child may conclude that his or her misbehavior was okay, but that being caught was unacceptable. Such lessons will do little to curb bullying and other antisocial behavior.

By teaching empathy and modeling compassion for others, parents will be less likely to see their children engage in bullying behavior. There is no guarantee, however, that, when faced with the dynamics of a peer group, children will always choose not to engage in bullying and other negative actions. Thus, parents need to actively discuss bullying behavior and bystander strategies to prepare their children for the situations they may encounter, both online and offline.

If your child is bullied but also engages in retaliatory cyberbullying

"One time I cyber bullied this person because [he] spread rumors about me ... I put up a whole [Web site] about [him]. I started a rumor that he cheated on his girlfriend, and his girlfriend actually broke up with him." – *high school male*

There are some incidents of cyberbullying that occur when a student who has been the victim of bullying at school decides to retaliate online. A student who lacks the social support or assertiveness skills to confront bullying behavior at school may occasionally use the anonymity that the Internet provides to respond to or attack a perceived bully. If a parent finds that his or her child has engaged in cyberbullying behavior, it is important to make sure that the child wasn't the recipient of other bullying behavior at school. A child who engages in retaliatory cyberbullying may fit the category of the "bully/victim" or "provocative victim" discussed in Chapter 2. These children may have poor social skills that put them at greater risk for being bullied at school and may benefit from a school-based support group that emphasizes the development of social skills (such as "friendship skills"). These children may also benefit from individual counseling, particularly if group supports are not available.

While retaliating online is not to be condoned, addressing the bullying at school will reduce the likelihood of retaliation online. Parents need to emphasize that such retaliation is inappropriate, yet empathize with the frustration their son or daughter may be feeling. It will be critical to request the school's help to address the bullying situation on campus; however, the parent of the child engaged in cyberbullying needs to take whatever steps are necessary to ensure that the cyberbullying ends. Parents will also need to support the school's policies around cyberbullying if it has occurred on campus or through the use of school technology. Yet they should also make sure that the school is aware of the bullying that influenced the retaliation.

Parents can request a meeting with the school to identify an appropriate adult for their son or daughter to approach should they experience additional bullying behavior at school. As mentioned previously, the school counselor or administrator can assist the parents and child in developing a school safety plan that includes increased adult monitoring of situations where bullying behavior typically occurs. This may include schedule adjustments (for either party, but preferably for the student engaged in bullying behavior), if necessary.

In addition, parents can set up a written agreement at home with a child that defines appropriate use of technology and clarifies that using the Internet to harass or demean others is not acceptable. The agreement needs to provide clear consequences, such as a loss of online privileges, should such behavior occur again. Parents can have their child sign a copy of the agreement and keep it for reference in case any other online infractions occur.

Suggestions for Parents to Prevent Cyberbullying

Many parents assume that, if they just speak with their children about respectful treatment of others, they will have done enough to prevent cyberbullying. After years of research, prevention experts have learned that adults cannot give a message one time and expect that children have received it and incorporated it into their actions. Many prevention specialists use the immunization model as an example. A flu shot can be effective in preventing the flu, but it needs to be repeated every year. The same holds true with messages about healthy behavior. Telling a child on one occasion not to use alcohol or other drugs will not be sufficient for him to navigate the teen years when underage drinking and drug use become more prevalent. Telling a child the Golden Rule on one occasion will not be sufficient to expect that she will always treat others as she would like to be treated.

It is, therefore, recommended that parents talk with their children regarding the dos and don'ts of each new piece of technology that enters the home (Franek, 2005/2006). Such discussions should include maintenance, safety, and constructive and destructive uses. In addition, parents need to make sure they are complying with the age limit policies of various online sites. Because parents are seldom present in the online world of children and youth, setting up a home environment that lends itself to supervision is crucial. One of the most basic tips on Internet safety for families is to place the computer in a family room or kitchen where it can be easily viewed by adults in the home. This reasonable guideline becomes trickier as more families go wireless and laptop computers, Ipads and tablets can travel from room to room and still access the Internet. Setting up family rules ahead of time that keep computers and mobile devices out of bedrooms and making use of monitoring tools will help prevent unmonitored access. It is also important for parents to discuss with children the importance of taking breaks from technology. The "always on" generation needs permission to disconnect and reflect away from the constant barrage of their peers' messages.

Holding weekly family meetings encourages communication about any issue impacting the family. These weekly meetings are an ideal time to bring up the ground rules for use of new technology and to discuss potential inappropriate uses of such tools. Parents can define and explain cyberbullying at such family meetings and remind their children of the family rules as new technologies are introduced. Parents can also invite children to share the many positive ways they are using technology and brainstorm the various ways social media can support positive relationships.

Not only must parents repeat and reinforce important messages in their discussions with their children, they also must help children apply these messages to new situations. This principle was in evidence in our efforts to address the new phenomenon of cyberbullying as part of the Olweus Bullying Prevention Program in Cobb County, Georgia, schools. Despite

our efforts to encourage students to avoid engaging in or supporting bullying behavior, we discovered that some students didn't recognize their mean
and harassing online behavior as bullying. This is an important lesson for
parents. Parents need to help children make the transition in their learning
by giving consistent messages about appropriate behavior and apply them
to new situations and settings, including online environments. "Take time
for training," was a favorite expression of psychologist Rudolph Dreikurs to
parents in his audiences (Dreikurs & Soltz, 1991). Parents need to look for
opportunities every day to educate their children and communicate their
values through discussions rather than lectures. Parents may find it helpful
to ask their children to share new experiences with them so that they understand the challenges teens face as they move through the adolescent years.

Talk about sexting

It is also important for parents to specifically discuss the practice of sending
nude or semi-nude photos via cell phone or computer, often referred to as
"sexting" (see Chapter 3). Conversations with tweens and teens that address
sharing appropriate images or photos can be expanded to talk about the
specific practice of sexting. Parents need to help youth recognize that,
despite media attention, the majority of teens do not send such images and
regard it as a mistake to do so (MTV/Associated Press Poll, 2009). Parents
can discuss with their children a variety of reasons why it is a bad idea to
send such images, including:

- It may embarrass the sender or recipient.
- It may impact the sender's reputation or recipient's reputation.
- The sender loses control of the image and how it is used.
- It may increase the sender's risk for being cyberbullied or experienc-
  ing blackmailing activities.
- The sender may experience serious legal, academic, or career-
  impacting consequences.

Students share advice with parents

In each of our focus groups, students were asked what adults could do to
prevent cyberbullying. They had limited advice for educators, because the

students perceived that most cyberbullying occurs after school hours. Some of the high school girls did have quite a bit of advice for parents, however. Here are some of their tips:

- Set age-appropriate guidelines.

  "I think in my case parents need to not let 11-year-old kids get on MySpace and stuff. I mean, I know that I started using the Internet at 13, but there wasn't MySpace and stuff then. They need to be a parent and take charge of what their kids do."

  "Tell kids not to put revealing information on their blogs and stuff."

  "A lot of parents say you can't have a blog but as long as they don't put anything personal on it I don't see a problem with it and then they would be more open with their parents and share more."

- Communicate about appropriate ways to deal with conflict.

  "I think parents need to talk to their kids more. Like in my family, when my brother and I fight, my parents stop us, but they don't talk to us about it, and they could just help us."

- Monitor their children's use of the Internet.

  "See what their kids are doing on the Internet. Limit their use."
  "I showed my Dad how to use the history to see where they are going on the Internet."
  "Some parents don't even know how much time their kids spend on the computer. They should at least talk to them about it and stuff."
  "I think they could help monitor it."
  "They should at least ask you what you are doing on the computer."

- Supervision, not snoopervision.

  "[Parents should] not record everything, I hate it when they do that, because I have a friend whose parents do that. They like look at all her history and cookies and stuff."
  "My mom does monitor me. Like my mom watched Oprah and it was on MySpace so then she came up and was standing behind me and I'm like, 'What are you doing?' and she says, 'I just want to make sure you are safe.'"

- Watch for warning signs.

  "Usually you can tell if your kid is being weird, or keeping to themselves, or if their parent comes into the room and they like jump or are clicking to get rid of stuff."

- Don't blame the victim (or punish them for someone else's behavior).

  "They might be scared to tell their parents [if they are cyberbullied] because they might say, I told you so, I told you not to have that blog."
  "Parents shouldn't punish before you do something – that's just going to make the kid sneak around more. Talk with the kid more about what's right and what's wrong and what's normal."

- Educate themselves.

  "They should have something for parents like a parent seminar or something that parents can go to about cyberbullying."

Explain the challenges of communicating online

Parents may wish to begin by explaining to children that communicating online is prone to miscommunication because of the lack of nonverbal cues. Individuals readily use nonverbal cues in day-to-day conversation to determine if someone is being friendly, teasing playful, or angry. Emoticons (smiley and frowny faces used in e-mails and instant messaging – ex: ☺ ☹) were developed to help users determine the emotional meaning behind messages. Parents need to explain to their children that it is more difficult to communicate accurately without nonverbal cues, and that they need to be careful to avoid sarcasm or other such emotions that can lead to hurt feelings. It is helpful to teach children to make use of emoticons so that misunderstandings can be avoided. Children should also consider whether the person on the other end of a cyber message will know that they are joking before they hit the send button.

Parents need to communicate regularly to their children that it is not acceptable to harass, spread gossip, or make mean or disparaging comments toward others online. Parents can also discuss with their children the importance of taking time to "cool down" if they are upset or angry with a friend or classmate before sending or posting a message online. Once an angry message has been sent, it may be forwarded to classmates or viewed by others and escalate a conflict. It is best to talk face-to-face with a friend or peer if they are having a disagreement. It is possible to retrieve an e-mail message, but only if the recipient has not yet opened it. This option may be a life-saver for users who experience an immediate feeling of regret after sending a negative or nasty e-mail. However, once the recipient has opened the message, it cannot be retrieved. This option came in handy to one parent we interviewed. When she realized her 11-year-old daughter had forwarded a threatening chain e-mail to another classmate, the mother was able to use this option to retrieve the message before it was viewed.

We are not invisible online

The phenomenon of "disinhibition" was discussed in detail in Chapter 3. Disinhibition is a term used to describe how people in cyberspace say and do things they wouldn't normally do face-to-face because they feel anonymous. Using an anonymous screen name or setting up a Web site anonymously may allow the user to believe he or she will not be held responsible for posting mean or offensive comments online. Parents should communicate to their children that they are not, in fact, invisible online. Any communications posted online or sent electronically can usually be traced back to the individual who originally posted or sent the message. Granted, not all communications will be deemed worthy of the effort; however, threats of violence, harassment, stalking, defamation, extortion, and posting pornographic images should be traced and many police departments have a high-tech crimes unit that will assist in such instances. Because parents can be held liable for a child's actions in many states, parents should discuss with their children that their actions could harm the entire family, as well as the children they are targeting.

Protect passwords

Parents should discuss with their children the importance of protecting their passwords to their social networking sites, instant message programs, and even to their online gaming accounts. A student who sends instant messages can easily pose as another individual if he or she is aware of an individual's screen name and password. In addition, teens have been known to alter their peers' social networking sites when their passwords are known. Unfortunately, a peer who is friendly one day may turn on a classmate the next day, or may simply be indiscreet, so passwords should always be kept private. Parents need to advise children to change their passwords periodically and especially if they suspect someone else knows their password. Parents, however, need to know their children's passwords, screen names, and account information should an emergency arise or if abuse needs to be reported.

Blocking versus monitoring

Parents have always had the difficult challenge of supervising their children, yet gradually allowing them more freedom as they become older and show more responsibility. Unfortunately, with the advent of the Internet, many parents assume that, if their child is home on the computer, he or she is safe. Thus, they allow their child complete freedom on the Internet. Making use of blocking software that screens material is one way of preventing children, who are naturally curious, from stumbling into sites that could be risky or harmful to them. Setting parental controls on a "kid or teen setting" still allows children to visit most sites of interest, but provides protection from violent, pornographic, or otherwise inappropriate sites. Sometimes a favorite site will be mistakenly blocked because of the terms used in the description of the site. In such instances, parents can set the parental controls to allow access to individual sites that they feel are appropriate and that their children routinely use. Overblocking of sites becomes an issue as children get older. Parents of teens may find it more useful to adopt monitoring rather than blocking software, since blocking can frequently restrict access to legitimate sites and may in some situations encourage youth to try to find "work-arounds." Monitoring software records a history of the sites that are visited so that a parent can discuss any objectionable content that has been viewed by a child. Online Family Norton is an example of a free parental control product that can be adjusted as a child ages. Objectionable content can be blocked for a younger-aged child, but the product also has a feature that allows a child to override a blocked Web site and send a message to a parent or guardian on why he or she thinks it is appropriate to proceed. Parents may also allow all content to be viewed, however the history of the sites visited is reported to the parent or guardian. Users are informed that Online Family Norton is monitoring the computer. John Halligan, who wrote the foreword to our book, recommends that parents let their children know upfront that monitoring software has been installed to ensure that the family's safety rules are followed and that inappropriate material or activity is not "pushed" on to the family's computer (J. Halligan, personal communication, January 17, 2007).

In cases where parents have reason to believe that their children have abused their online privileges, are engaging in highly risky behavior, or have abused others, they can install tracking software that records every site a child visits and every message a child sends, including chat, instant messages and e-mails. Spectorsoft and IamBigBrother are examples of such keystroke logging software. Keep in mind, however, that these programs communicate a lack of trust between the parent and child. As Larry Magid and Anne Collier (2007), the directors of Connect Safely write in their book *MySpace Unraveled*, these tools should only be used as a last resort.

Parents also can use a simple method to check the history of the Web sites visited online if they have reason to believe that their children are accessing inappropriate Web sites. The toolbar has a view key that allows the user to view the recent history, or the user can press the control key and the "H" key simultaneously to display the history on most computers. Figure 5.1 shows a screen shot of a computer with the history displayed on the left side of the screen. However, by middle school most youth know how to delete the history of a Web browser and also are aware of online tools that allow one to surf "anonymously."

Nothing takes the place of ongoing communication and discussions that facilitate reaching a consensus in a family regarding what types of sites are off-limits and why. Thus, communicating with a teenager about why it is inappropriate to view pornography or send mean messages to his or her peers may be far more useful than relying on a filtering program. However, parental controls do have benefits. They help prevent young children from stumbling into sites innocently. They also allow parents to set the time of day that certain features are available (such as instant messaging and online gaming) so that parents don't have to nag their children to get off of the computer in the evening or worry about children sneaking downstairs at night to play a favorite online computer game.

As more children have access to wireless networks outside of the home through mobile devices such as portable game players and cell phones, their ability to surf the Internet away from parental controls also increases (Olsen, 2006a, 2006b). In addition, tech-savvy teens can choose to log on to a neighbor's unsecured wireless network to circumvent the parental controls at home or log on at free Internet cafes. Parents should pay attention to the capabilities of the devices that they purchase for their children and take time to establish ground rules about acceptable and unacceptable uses of the wireless Internet devices they bring into their home.

Finally, parents need to explain to their children that they want to know if someone sends them inappropriate material or messages. This way, the parent and child can address the situation together before it escalates. Reassuring children that they will not be disciplined for someone else's abusive comments or actions will allow them to feel safe contacting their parents if they view something inappropriate.

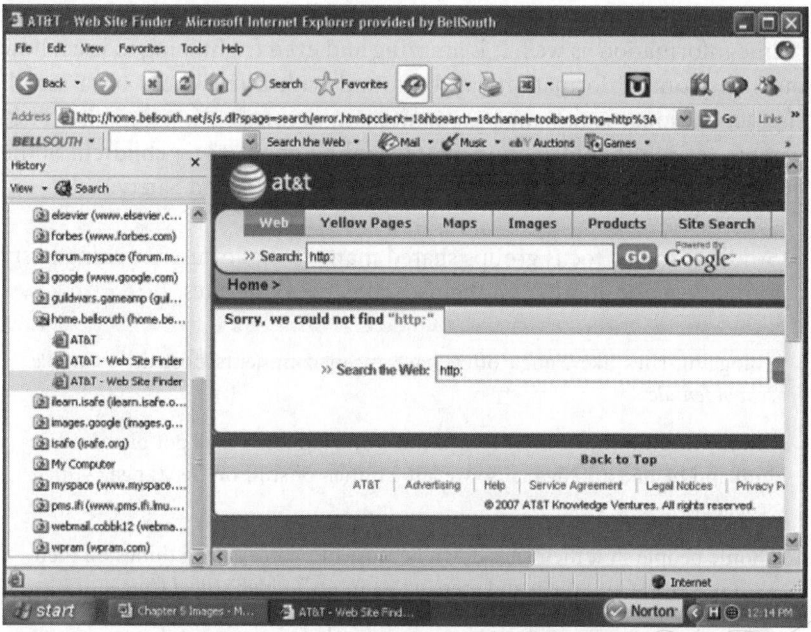

Figure 5.1 Computer screen with history displayed.

Monitor your child's reputation online

It is important for parents to explain to their children that, if they choose to use a social networking site, anyone can view their entries. Parents should give examples of how other parents, teachers, college admissions representatives and potential employers may seek information from social networking sites.

Parents and children need to discuss the potential repercussions of posting negative comments on other individuals' Web sites and how this could also affect their online reputation. Parents should "Google" their children's names occasionally (as well as their own) to see what is posted online about family members. Parents can simply go to the google.com search engine site, insert their child's first and last name in quotes, and search for what is posted online about them. Obviously, this works better if a child's name is not extremely common. Parents may also need to check for common misspellings of a child's name as well as their screen names. In addition, parents can use the google.com/alert function to set up regular searches of their children's names online. Google will notify a parent by e-mail every time a child's name appears online. Adults would be wise to monitor their own online information as well. It is amazing and even frightening to learn how much personal information can be found with a few clicks on a search engine. Various social media monitoring technologies now also alert parents to public information posted online about their children. Some popular tools include AOL's SafeSocial, Social Shield, and Safety Web.

Students in our focus groups shared many stories of users writing nasty comments to one another on their social networking sites.

"Blogging sites like Xanga often have mean comments posted." – *middle school female*

"In my neighborhood there was like this one kid and we all got pissed off at him and he had a Xanga ... so we left a bunch of stuff on his Xanga." – *high school boy*

"Some people shut their sites down because of people saying things on their sites or getting into them and messing them up." – *high school female*

"There is a teacher we didn't like ... so we kind of made fun of that teacher ... we have a Facebook blog of that teacher." – *high school male*

Blogging appears to be decreasing among teens in general (Lenhart, 2010), but it is still encouraged on some sites and users often write journal-like entries about their day. Students who share their secrets or emotional state on social networking sites or blogs may be ridiculed or targeted with nasty comments. Conflicts among peers that are aired on a social networking site can escalate into confrontations at school. Youth who allow peers to ask them anonymous yet very personal questions on sites such as Formspring.me may also be at greater risk of being embarrassed or humiliated online. Thus, youth need to be advised to avoid sharing very personal information that could be used against them or their classmates in cyberbullying situations. They also need to understand the risks involved in using sites that allow users to post messages anonymously.

Another repercussion that may significantly affect high school and college students is that an increasing number of college admissions representatives and employers search prospective candidates' names online to learn more about them (Hass, 2006). Do teens really want a college admissions counselor reading about their sexual escapades or drinking binges? Would a profanity-laced entry help their chances of being selected by a potential employer? An employer or college representative who views a personal profile that shows a lack of discretion may be quick to choose another applicant. Parents should help their sons and daughters recognize how entries posted today may affect their reputation and future in life-changing ways.

Resources for parents

Preparing a child to fully embrace digital citizenship is an important new role for parents. While it is challenging to parent in a world of rapidly evolving technology, it is a requirement to be an engaged and vigilant parent today. The good news is that the Internet can be a parent's friend in this area as well. Many Web sites exist that provide great learning tools for parents attempting to learn more about monitoring their child's Internet use and helping youth to use social media in pro-social ways. Connect Safely, the Net Family News, Onguard Online and WiredSafety provide excellent guidelines and tips for parents on how to supervise their children on the Internet and how to have important discussions about the role of technology in their lives. The Stop Bullying Now Campaign also has helpful tips for parents on bullying and cyberbullying prevention at the Web site www. stopbullying.gov. The following Web sites provide helpful information on Internet safety and/or cyberbullying, and the list includes our own Web site, www.cyberbullyhelp.com.

- connectsafely.org
- onguardonline.gov
- netfamilynews.org
- commonsensemedia.org
- stopbullying.gov
- cyberbullyhelp.com

Allow children to be the experts

Lastly, remember that children can be an important source of information in understanding the way that students at their school interact online. If parents allow their children to be the "experts" on occasion, they may find this helps to keep the lines of communication. Youth are often happy to show adults around the popular sites where their classmates spend time online. It may be humbling to admit that children may have more information about the latest technology than adults, but it is also a wonderful opportunity for parents to build a positive relationship with their children by letting them be the teacher for a change. Recognize that in discussing new media we need to be listening as much or more than we are talking!

Summary

Rather than forbidding Internet and social media use, parents need to educate children about both their rights and responsibilities as a digital citizen. Make sure that children understand that it is not acceptable to harass, spread gossip, or make mean or disparaging comments toward others online or through other digital devices, and that all of our actions create part of our "digital footprint." Parents should also set developmentally appropriate guidelines for introducing various technologies to their children.

In addition, parents need to help children understand the steps they can take if they are cyberbullied or witness a peer being cyberbullied. Empowering the bystanders to speak out against such actions will be one of the most effective strategies in reducing cyberbullying that parents and educators can pursue.

Note

1. The names of all individuals described in the real-life cyberbullying incidents have been changed to protect their identity.

6

WHAT EDUCATORS CAN DO

"I feel really bad for him because he already told my mom he didn't want to go to school because he didn't think he was going to make any friends, and now he feels left out of everything."

(sister of a 15-year-old boy
who was cyberbullied)

Several years ago one of the authors of this book was asked by an area superintendent to talk about cyberbullying at a principal's meeting that included her child's former principal. When asked by the principal why she was joining their group, she responded, "I am here to talk about cyberbullying." The principal's response? "What is cyberbullying?"

Since that time, the topic of cyberbullying has been featured frequently in the media, and educators have increasingly had to address issues pertaining to cyberbullying. In this chapter, we will examine how educators can intervene, provide resources to families, and help prevent cyberbullying. Our focus groups and individual interviews with students and parents suggest that currently few educators discuss cyberbullying in the classroom. While more school districts are adopting polices around cyberbullying, many schools are still reluctant to address the issue of cyberbullying in a comprehensive manner (i.e. by folding it into whole school approaches to prevent bullying). The authors hope that this chapter will encourage educators to take steps to prevent and intervene in cyberbullying behavior among their students.

Cyberbullying: Bullying in the Digital Age, Second Edition. Robin M. Kowalski, Susan P. Limber, and Patricia W. Agatston.
© 2012 Robin M. Kowalski, Susan P. Limber, and Patricia W. Agatston.
Published 2012 by Blackwell Publishing Ltd.

Is Cyberbullying a Problem for Schools?

As discussed in Chapter 4, findings from our anonymous survey of students suggested that cyberbullying is an issue for many students, with 18% reporting that they had been cyberbullied at least once in the previous 2 months (6% having been cyberbullied two to three times a month or more often), and 11% admitting that they had cyberbullied others at least once (2% admitting to doing so at least two to three times a month; Kowalski & Limber, 2007). Although most children are not cyberbullied on the school premises, half of those who had been cyberbullied noted that they had been targeted by another student.

Research from a Cox Communications survey of teens ages 13–18 years old found that 60% of males and 76% of females strongly agreed or some-what agreed that online bullying is a serious problem for today's youth (Cox Communications, 2009). In addition, 70% of males and 80% of females agreed that there should be stricter rules regarding online bullying.

These survey findings were supported by responses from middle and high school students in a series of focus groups that we conducted to better understand the extent of the problem and its effects (if any) on the school environment. While some students didn't feel that cyberbullying was a concern, others disagreed. Their responses varied greatly depending on whether they personally knew someone who had been cyberbullied. Some sample responses are included below.

Interviewer: Is cyber bullying a problem at your school?

"No." – *high school male*

"Not really." – *middle school girl*

"I think it is a problem but people keep it to themselves." – *high school female*

"Yeah – because it happens a lot." – *middle school male*

"Yes. It is a problem specifically at this school." – *high school female*

"I remember when I first started using the Internet I didn't know anyone who got cyber bullied, and now it's really bad, it's getting a lot worse as time progresses. I feel like it's getting worse among young people, like young teenagers, like middle school." – *high school female*

"Yeah, it's getting a lot worse – even among elementary school kids." – *high school female*

"I think it bleeds into the school." – *high school male*

One of the authors discussed cyberbullying more recently with a group of high school leaders. This was an informal discussion group, but some of the students' responses are useful in capturing current views among students.

- People can be meaner so much easier now.
- It is way more powerful than regular bullying.
- There are apps like Formspring that are easy to access (Facebook is blocked by the school district but Formspring is not) and people use it to anonymously say awful things about one another. People are figuring out how to keep things more private so it is harder to have evidence of the bullying too. People don't post things as publicly anymore (Agatston et al., 2011).

Examples of the cyberbullying

When students were also asked if they knew anyone who had been affected by cyberbullying, high school girls were particularly able to provide examples:

"My best friend in middle school, she had a Xanga (social networking site) and someone posted this horrible one about her, it was dedicated to her."

"I have heard of people knowing someone's password and going in and changing their MySpace."

"I only know it between people who know each other. Not like a stranger, so like if I didn't like her I might post something about her."

"I've heard of people going into chat rooms and picking on one person."

"I know someone who posted pictures of different people and they were just making fun of them."

"This one girl had the password to her MySpace or Facebook [stolen] and they put up all these bad pictures and stuff on it. Her parents found it and were very mad and they called the police about it."

"My brother has a MySpace and it has gotten really bad. The kids are really picking on him on MySpace. He just turned 11. I think it is ridiculous. They don't even know him."

"I know someone who got mean text messages."

"At my old school there was some kind of comment thing where all these kids ganged up on her. It wasn't really a blog site, just a comment Web site."

Does cyberbullying affect students?

While some students in our focus groups indicated that receiving mean online comments was no big deal and should just be ignored, many others were aware of students who were affected more negatively by cyberbullying. Below are some of the students' perceptions of the effects of cyberbullying on themselves and their classmates.

> "[It] makes them think less of themselves. Because whenever someone is mad they say things they shouldn't and then they [the targets] think less of themselves." – *middle school male*

> "[It] makes me really mad. It's personal – to me and her – and I got a really bad temper, so … it doesn't affect my schoolwork but when I see his name come up I really want to go get him." – *high school male* (responding to how he feels when he sees comments from a classmate who has targeted him and his girlfriend)

> "She would cry a lot. They said mean stuff and she couldn't get it shut down because she didn't have the password. She was really upset about it for awhile." – *high school female*

> "She thought the girls who did it were her friends, so she lost those friendships." – *high school female*

> "The stuff [the cyberbullies] said really affected [her]. I don't know how I could ever say something like that. It was just kind of ridiculous. It made [her] be mean to people for awhile. [She] just didn't want to do anything with anyone; [she] didn't want to deal with it. It affected [her] mood, [her] relationships. It affected [her] academically. [She] stopped coming to school for a few days." – *high school female*

> "She was afraid to walk around the school and was afraid everyone was going to gang up on her. The people that were [cyber] bullying her told other people so they all picked on her." – *middle school female*

As noted in Chapter 2, children who experience traditional forms of bullying have higher rates of anxiety, somatic complaints, depression, and suicidal ideation and poorer academic performance than non-bullied peers. Since our first edition of this book was published, research on the effects of cyberbullying on children (as victims or bystanders; see Chapter 4) has increased. Research by the authors suggests that students who report being targets of cyberbullying report effects similar to those experienced by targets of traditional bullying (Kowalski & Limber, 2007; see also Hinduja & Patchin, 2010b). In addition, participants in our focus groups believed that cyberbullying behavior could have serious effects on children. Those students who experience bullying at school *and* cyberbullying at home may be at particular risk. They may feel that they have no safe place left. Children cannot perform their best at school when they are fearful or believe that they don't belong.

How much cyberbullying takes place at school?

It is possible that some educators are not aware of the problem of cyberbullying because it often takes place outside of the school day, and students may be reluctant to tell teachers or administrators. While cyberbullying can occur on campus through the use of school technology, students in our focus groups noted that using the school system's technology to cyberbully was somewhat rare. Students seemed puzzled when asked about being cyberbullied at school. "How would someone cyberbully you at school?" was a common question that we received. Their responses indicated that most cyberbullying occurs after school through the use of instant messages, text messages, or posts on social networking sites. While students indicate it is sometimes possible to access instant messaging and social networking sites at school (despite their being blocked from the district server), or via mobile phones with Internet access, for the most part students in the focus groups avoided using these functions at school. However, students did mention that text messaging at school was one way that students might cyberbully each other at school. When asked if most students send text messages during the school day despite the school district's policy, many students laughed and said, "Yes, all day, every day." When we asked if they would tell an adult at school if they were being cyberbullied at school through text messaging, many students gave comments similar to this one:

> "No, because we are not supposed to have our cell phones on at school or be text messaging. So you can't tell an adult that you are being text messaged with mean messages because you might get in trouble for having your cell phone on."

However, some schools are moving toward allowing students to check messages and make calls between classes. This might allow some students to feel more comfortable in seeking assistance if they are experiencing harassment via cell phone at school. However, an additional concern is that many students felt there was no reason to tell adults at the school about cyberbullying, because there would be little they could do. The following are common responses when asked what adults at school could do to prevent cyberbullying:

> "It's not here so you wouldn't tell people." – *high school female*
>
> "I don't really think they can do much because it's at home, not at school, so I don't think they can do much." – *middle school male*

High school leaders in a recent discussion group shared their views on whether educators should intervene in cyberbullying behavior. Their comments suggest that we need to improve our responses as educators in order to help students.

> Do you think the school should intervene with off campus cyberbullying that disrupts school?
>
> "No."
>
> "It doesn't really help."
>
> "Our administrators did a mediation with some girls who were cyberbullying another student. It just got worse. They became more secretive."
>
> "There is not a lot they can do unless you have a copy/clear evidence."
>
> "Going to a counselor is better than going to an administrator."
> (Agatston et al., 2011).

Is cyberbullying discussed at school?

To gain a sense of how much the issue of cyberbullying was discussed in the home or school environment, students in our focus groups were asked if they had heard the term "cyberbullying" prior to the group. For the most part, students indicated that it was rare for a parent or teacher to talk with them about cyberbullying. However, students from one of the middle schools that is implementing a bullying prevention program indicated that cyberbullying was discussed in the classroom.

While some educators may insist that a child's online behavior is the responsibility of the parent, in reality educators frequently teach and encourage students' use of appropriate behavior and social skills through character education lessons, guidance lessons that teach conflict resolution, and health classes that teach refusal skills for drug prevention. Although parents need to take primary responsibility for their child's online behavior, as technology has become such an integral part of the classroom environment educators should make appropriate online behavior part of their technology instruction as well. Just as we recommend that bullying prevention (including cyberbully-ing) be infused throughout the curriculum, the topic of digital citizenship needs to be infused as well. Social media is increasingly being used as a teach-ing tool and proactive schools will be infusing digital citizenship lessons such as Common Sense Media's Digital Literacy and Citizenship Curriculum in order to "empower students to think critically and make informed choices about how they create, communicate, and treat others in our ever-evolving, 24/7 digital world" (www.commonsensemedia.org/educators).

What Can School Personnel Do to Prevent Cyberbullying?

In fact, there are many preventive steps that educators can take to help reduce the number of incidents of cyberbullying that occur in school and out of school. Two of the authors of this book have spent significant time training educators in schools to implement a research-based bullying pre-vention effort known as the Olweus Bullying Prevention Program. This sys-temic approach to bullying prevention has shown significant reductions in bullying behavior among students, but it takes a long-term commitment by the entire faculty to establish a climate that discourages bullying. Schools that already are implementing bullying prevention programs are at an advantage when combating cyberbullying. Educators, parents and students who are already working to address bullying behavior can include cyber-bullying as part of their prevention focus. The core components of an effec-tive bullying prevention program can easily be adapted to include segments on cyberbullying.

Assess cyberbullying

An important first step in implementing an effective bullying prevention program is to thoroughly assess the problem. As discussed in Chapter 2, one good way to do this is by having students complete an anonymous ques-tionnaire about bullying behavior at school. Including questions on cyber-bullying will help educators gain insight into the amount of cyberbullying that is occurring among their students. The most useful measures will define cyberbullying and include questions about cyberbullying through various mediums, including instant messaging, e-mails, text messaging, blogs, and social networking sites such as MySpace and Facebook. Such surveys not only will allow administrators to see how common cyberbullying is, but also they will help administrators to know if it is occurring during the school day or after school, and which mediums are most prone to abuse. It will be useful to be able to examine students' responses by grade and gender. For example, if cyberbullying peaks among 7th grade girls, prevention strategies targeting 6th graders may be particularly useful. Good assessment will help the school administration to craft policies and strategies to prevent cyberbullying from happening at school, effectively address cyberbullying that does takes place on school grounds, and work with parents to prevent and address cyberbullying that takes place away from school.

Provide staff training on cyberbullying

Many educators already discuss the importance of Internet safety with their students, but the topic needs to be broadened to include online civility and careful consideration of what we upload, post and share. Educators need to talk with students about what it means to be a "digital citizen" including holding discussions of rights and responsibilities, and proper "netiquette" (online etiquette) that defines and discusses cyberbullying and cyber threats. To do so effectively, educators will need some degree of training about bullying, cyberbullying, and children's use of social media.

Although it is not necessary for the entire faculty to be experts on cyberbullying, they should all be familiar with the issue, and certain staff members (i.e., counselors, administrators, and media and technology specialists) should be comfortable recognizing and responding to concerns about cyberbullying that affect their students and the school environment. Incorporating cyberbullying training into staff training on bullying prevention is one way that schools can educate their faculty on this important topic.

To fully understand the many ways that students use technology to bully and harass others, educators need training on the various popular forms of online communication that students use, such as instant messaging, social networking sites, internet voice calls with video, online gaming, and text messaging. MySpace and Facebook are becoming a cultural requirement among middle and high school students. Educators need to understand the appropriate uses of such technologies as well as the potential for abuse. Training should also include tips on preventing cyberbullying as well as how to intervene in a cyberbullying incident. It training should include a discussion of the school district's policies regarding bullying in general, and cyberbullying in particular. It also would be helpful if the training included resources for educators, such as sample lesson plans on cyberbullying and Web sites for additional information. Such training would allow educators to partner with parents in providing guidelines for children on appropriate uses of technology.

Define cyberbullying

One of the first things that schools must do when addressing bullying is to have a clear definition of bullying behavior that is understood by students, administrators, faculty, and nonteaching staff. The same is true of cyberbullying. If schools wish to prevent cyberbullying, they first need to define it and discuss it so that students and faculty members are clear about what cyberbullying is and what it is not. The definition should include the various methods that students employ to cyberbully one another, including e-mail, instant messages, text messaging, social networking sites, and blogs, as discussed in Chapter 3.

Educators and students should discuss why cyberbullying is hurtful to others (and sometimes unlawful) and what classmates can do to prevent the use of cyberbullying among their peers. Youth need to understand that treating others well online is a protective factor, since research indicates those who harass or embarrass others online increase their own risk of victimization (Ybarra et. al. 2007). Educators could include in such discussions the "when, why, and how" of reporting cyberbullying. Supporting documents could be sent home by the school so that parents can better understand cyberbullying and the school's policies on it, ways that they can help to prevent and address cyberbullying at home, and where to go for additional help, if needed.

Develop clear rules and policies about cyberbullying

As we will describe in more detail in Chapter 7, schools should develop policies that specifically address cyberbullying. Cyberbullying should be incorporated into existing anti-bullying policies and should also be incorporated under an existing "student use of technology" policy. The policy should include provisions that prohibit using district technology to access, send, create, or post material or communications that are damaging, abusive, obscene, threatening, or demeaning to others. The policy should use clear language and discuss expectations for students and staff, as well as consequences for violations. School districts should provide students and their parents with a copy of the policy that includes a definition of cyber-bullying, examples of cyberbullying, and consequences of such actions. Sharing this information with students and parents at the beginning of the year likely will decrease violations and/or avoid misunderstandings. Although public schools may need to limit most school-based consequences to students' abuse of technology while on campus (owing to legal protections that exist for free speech), they also should indicate what types of off-campus communications might be sanctioned by school personnel and include examples of cyberbullying that will be reported to the police. As discussed in detail in Chapter 7, government organizations (including schools) are very limited in their ability to censure speech that occurs off campus; however, private schools could conceivably have a policy that includes off-campus conduct if it disrupts the school day or interferes with the rights of students to feel secure. As always, schools should consult with their local attorney for guidance in drafting anti-bullying and acceptable use policies. By developing a comprehensive and easily understood policy, school personnel will clarify their expectations for student behavior. It can be helpful for parents and students to sign and return a copy of the district's acceptable use of technology policy to ensure that it has been reviewed.

Encourage the reporting of cyberbullying

Students need to know that there are supportive staff members available to whom they can turn if they experience bullying or cyberbullying behavior, and that these adults can help them problem-solve to deal with the issue. Establishing a school-wide reporting system has proven helpful for students who wish to report bullying behavior but are uncertain how to do so. Many schools make available, at various drop-off boxes around the school, forms that students can complete (anonymously or not) to report bullying. Including a section on cyberbullying in these forms will allow students a mechanism for reporting cyberbullying as well as other forms of bullying or troubling behavior. Increasingly, educators are using online report systems or report forms that can be downloaded from the school's Web site. Online methods may allow students to feel more protected and anonymous when making a report (Dooley et al., 2010). Students can be instructed to describe the cyberbullying incident and, where applicable, provide a Web site address if they are aware of a classmate being ridiculed or humiliated online. The sample form below may be used to report bullying behavior at school (Figure 6.1).

Middle School
Bullying/Cyber Bullying Report Form

(Please return to any staff member or to one of the drop
boxes located in the counselors' office)

Name: _____Team: _____

Date: _____Homeroom Teacher _____

What happened or is happening?

_____
_____
_____
_____
_____

How long has this been happening?
When and where is this happening? (Include Web site or
printed evidence if applicable)

_____

Did anyone see this happen? _____
Have you reported this situation? Yes/No
If so, to whom? _____

_____

How would you like to be contacted? (please check the
box(es) that apply and fill-in the proper contact information,
if necessary)

❑ Home phone: _____
❑ e-mail: _____
❑ I would like to speak with a school counselor
❑ I would like to speak with a school administrator
❑ I would prefer to not be contacted

Thank you for your report. Empowered Students like you
are making a difference at _____ Middle
School!

Figure 6.1   Sample reporting form.

Share resources with parents

Because most cyberbullying occurs outside of the school day, parents often
are the first to hear about cyberbullying from their children. Students in our
focus groups indicated they would be more likely to tell a parent than an
adult at school if they experienced cyberbullying. Because of this, parents

need to be aware of strategies for preventing and addressing cyberbullying. Schools can assist parents by sending parent newsletters home with information on cyberbullying and by providing seminars for them on the issue. Parents need to know about legal issues that might arise if their child harasses or threatens another online. They also could benefit from tips on how to educate themselves (and their children) about safe use of social media. As discussed in Chapter 5, there are many helpful Web sites that parents can use to teach their children to think critically about how their online actions affect themselves and others. Helpful Web sites include ConnectSafely, NetFamily News, Common Sense Media, and WiredSafety.org. Such Web sites also provide parents with suggestions for how to monitor their children's online behavior. The guidance office at a particular school may be the best resource for making such information available to parents. Parent letters or newsletters should include the following information for parents:

- appropriate online netiquette and the importance of treating others well online;
- guidelines for protecting one's privacy online as well as the privacy of others;
- definition of cyberbullying;
- examples of cyberbullying;
- how to report cyberbullying at school;
- tips on responding to cyberbullying (such as ignoring, blocking, or warning);
- safe use of social networking sites as well as other social media and how to report abusive behavior;
- when to notify the police;
- possible parental liability for youth online behavior;
- who to contact for more information or assistance.

Spend class time on the topic of cyberbullying

As mentioned previously, most students in our focus groups felt that educators could do little to address cyberbullying; however, one high school female had an important suggestion for educators:

> "Maybe introduce kids to cyberbullying at a younger age, talk to classes about it and signs of it so they'll know if it's going on and not be afraid to tell [their] parents and stuff."

This student already recognized the importance of spending class time to discuss bullying and cyberbullying and the importance of doing so in early grades. The importance of holding regular class meetings/discussions to address traditional bullying was noted in Chapter 2. It is important to incorporate cyberbullying and proper online communication into these classroom discussions to make sure that students understand that bullying is not acceptable in cyber space either.

Topics for classroom discussions on cyberbullying
What issues should be covered during classroom meetings on cyberbullying? Initially, teachers likely will want to ensure that children understand: (a) what cyberbullying is, (b) what the school's policies and rules are with regard to cyberbullying, (c) what mechanisms there are at the school to report cyberbullying, and (d) how best to respond to cyberbullying (such as when to ignore, block, or report it). Research suggests that it is not uncommon for youth to "cyberbully back" when targeted (Kowalski & Limber, 2007). Yet such responses often intensify and escalate cyberbullying. Thus, it is critical to facilitate discussions with youth on helpful versus harmful responses. If the use of social networking sites is popular among students, teachers should discuss the "appropriate use guidelines" from such sites. Many students believe they have a right to free speech that allows them to say anything online. The site guidelines and steps for reporting abuse would help dispel this myth. The role of the bystander to cyberbullying should be discussed as well, so that students understand that witnessing cyberbullying and doing nothing is a harmful choice. Helping students to develop empathy for class-mates who are targeted by cyberbullying is important, as students who taunt or abuse a classmate online do not witness the student's emotional response as they would with face-to-face bullying. Teachers can develop writing assignments where students take the perspective of someone who is experiencing bullying or cyberbullying behavior and discuss their reactions to the bullying behavior. Being able to take someone else's perspective is a corner-stone of empathy development and can assist students in their role as posi-tive bystanders working to develop a caring school climate.

Establish a climate that encourages bystanders to speak
out against bullying behavior
Feeling anonymous in cyber space appears to encourage some young peo-ple to develop unhealthy social norms for online behavior. The impulsivity of youth combined with a belief that "anything goes" online is a recipe for

disaster if there are no competing positive social norms. Counteracting these faulty social norms is a critical role for educators and parents to ensure a positive online environment.

One effective way to build more positive social norms is through activities that focus on positive roles that bystanders can play to stop bullying. As discussed in Chapter 2, young people may assume a variety of roles in instances of bullying. When a bullying incident occurs, the majority of students assume roles as bystanders (e.g., as disengaged onlookers or possible defenders). Although many students are disturbed by cyberbullying and other forms of bullying, they often are not sure how to respond when they witness it. With adequate role-playing and class discussions, these students can be encouraged to report cyberbullying behaviors when they observe them. Students can also learn about ways to support a classmate who is being cyberbullied (e.g., positive comments, letters, and instant or e-mail messages). Discussing the various steps that bystanders can take when cyberbullying occurs is a great class discussion topic. Possibilities include:

- Don't view the mean material.
- Don't gossip or spread rumors online or talk about it at school.
- Support the victim – post or send positive messages!
- If you know the person, invite him/her to spend time with you.
- Tell an adult at home and at school.
- Print the evidence to share with an adult.
- Discourage a student who is cyberbullying, if it is safe to do so, and make it clear that you think their behavior is wrong.

*Teach students to safely use the social Web through discussions
on online "netiquette," privacy, safe sharing, and monitoring
their online reputation*

Online netiquette skills are becoming vital as technology is increasingly incorporated into most career paths. Many schools encourage teachers to keep blogs or use wikis (a Web site that allows for collaborative work) where class and homework assignments are posted for students to review. Providing tips on appropriate posting and online etiquette as a way of incorporating more technology in the classroom is critical. As part of class discussions, teachers can help students set up class blogs, wikis, and private social networking sites where they can be taught appropriate online behavior. The students can choose whether the blogs will be public (for anyone's viewing) or private (solely for the viewing of and commenting by members of the class). As a class and with the teacher's facilitation, students can respond to comments made on the blog by their classmates and describe how those comments made them feel. There are Web sites available to help individuals and groups, such as a class, create social Web sites and blogs that might be used for this purpose. Include activities where students discuss how they decide what to share or post, how to assess if someone is a safe online friend, and the importance of avoiding in-person meetings with someone they have "met" online. Of course these lessons also apply to cell phones. Teens will also benefit from discussions about GPS and other location-sharing technologies that could publicize their whereabouts and lead to unintended consequences.

School counselors need to teach classroom guidance lessons on the importance of keeping a positive online reputation, as part of their lessons on careers and college. Such lessons should help students recognize how their personal profile on a social networking site can have a positive or negative impact on their future. Demonstrating how easy it is to search such sites and access personal information (without embarrassing anyone) will ensure that students learn that their postings are public information and, as such, may come back to haunt them in the future. School counselors should make sure that students are aware that individuals have lost jobs, faced criminal charges, and been removed from college athletic teams as a result of personal information and offensive statements they have posted on social networking sites.

Involve students in social norming campaigns

In order to change social norms around bullying and cyberbullying, it is very useful to involve youth in sharing information about the healthy choices that most youth are making. Using survey data can be an effective starting point to help youth see that the majority of their peers are making good choices online and avoiding bullying and cyberbullying behaviors. In addition, youth leaders are key in promoting bystander involvement so that there is social pressure to say or do something when youth witness abusive behavior, both online and offline. Trained peer leaders can also help educate their peers on how to respond to cyberbullying, when to involve an adult, and where to go for help.

Perkins, Craig, and Perkins (2011) have found that a social norms approach can be effective in reducing bullying behavior among youth. Their research demonstrated that schools that promoted positive peer behavior by designing posters that emphasized that the majority of youth did not support bullying resulted in less bullying behavior among students. This is a promising approach for cyberbullying as well. Youth can frame positive messages indicating that the majority of youth do not support spreading gossip and rumors online, and that the majority of youth believe it is important to treat others with respect online. Youth can develop positive posters, public service announcements, video broadcasts, and the like to help norm the positive behavior that many youth are engaging in but that is rarely recognized among peers and adults. Social norming campaigns may also be useful in the prevention of "sexting" (discussed in Chapters 3 and 5.) Instead of relying on threats of legal consequences to frighten youth into avoiding the behavior, a promising approach might be to remind youth that the majority of teens do not engage in sexting. Having students develop public service announcements (PSAs) and posters around the top reasons students think it is a "dumb idea" to engage in sexting and sharing statistics that 90–96% of teens have never sent a "sext" (Cox Communications, 2009; Lenhart, 2009) will help promote a positive message that most teens are making healthy choices around this issue as well.

Use students as experts

Many schools recognize the power of youth leadership in developing a climate that is inclusive and supportive of others. Young people regularly serve as peer helpers, peer mediators, and as school ambassadors where they develop skills that will serve them for a lifetime. Students also are able to serve as mentors to others by teaching skills and modeling healthy behavior. In many school districts, students have taught lessons on drug prevention, postponing sexual involvement, and media literacy, to name just a few. Making use of students' expertise in the area of Internet safety and cyberbullying can send a strong message to classmates and younger students. The peer group often has more legitimacy than the teacher in addressing social issues, so making use of student leaders to help teach lessons on social Web safety and cyberbullying is a great prevention strategy. The authors of this book have written a Cyber Bullying Prevention Curriculum for Grades 6–12 that makes use of peer leaders to facilitate lessons and discussions. Students from the class can serve as peer mentors or older students can teach the lessons to younger students. Students are also a great source of information on how best to address the "hot spots" for bullying or cyberbullying at an individual school. We have learned that the popularity of sites among students changes rapidly, and youth are often the first group to embrace a new technology. Thus, educators need regular input from young people about popular Internet sites and new technologies that have been embraced by their student population.

Community/school partnerships

While we have provided a variety of steps that educators can take to prevent cyberbullying, youth organizations also have an important role to play in the prevention of cyberbullying (and all forms of bullying). Many students engage in afterschool programs and activities that make use of computers and technology, and social skill development is often a goal of the many youth organizations in the community. These organizations can assist educators and parents by reinforcing the message of appropriate use of technology, netiquette, and personal safety by developing and implementing online safety/netiquette guidelines, lessons, group activities, and peer-to-peer mentoring.

A Guide to Social Networking Sites for Educators

Although we have referred to social networking sites throughout this book, it is critical that educators take time to familiarize themselves with one of the biggest social phenomena to affect youth and young adults in America. According to the Pew Internet & American Family Life Project, over 75% of American teens between the ages of 12 and 17 use online social networking sites (Lenhart, 2010). Individual entries on social networking sites are similar to a yearbook profile, but with so many communication features, they provide young people a way to "hang out together" in the digital world. Most sites include features similar to e-mail, bulletin boards to post messages to friends, and blogging features that allow users to post diary-like entries about their day. While adults still communicate online largely through e-mail, teens communicate primarily through instant messaging and through the tools on Facebook, MySpace or other similar sites. Adults who are unfamiliar with these sites would be wise to visit them in order to better understand their use by teens. Young people use these sites as a way to explore and define who they are. Many are quite comfortable (and in fact enjoy) sharing their most private thoughts and feelings online. Of course, as youth share personal information without discrimination, they can make themselves vulnerable to identity fraud, predators, or victimization by classmates.

Social networking sites are not without merit, however, and it important to accept the reality that such sites have become the teen hot spot in a "cyber neighborhood" similar to the teen hangouts many of us frequented as youth. As young people have less opportunity to hang out in the real world because of their heavily scheduled extracurricular activities or because of safety concerns, youth have carved out a way to interact, explore their identity, and share the subtleties of youth culture. Such interactions have always occurred; the difference is that adults were available to provide some supervision when the local teen hangout was a pizza place or bowling alley. Socializing primarily online, away from the eyes of a responsible adult, can lead to many of the problems that we currently face, i.e., Internet predators, cyberbullying, and cyber threats. The best solution lies in finding ways to make such sites safer through a combination of site-based strategies (tips on safe use and how to report abuse), and through increased supervision and sensible guidelines for use communicated by parents, educators, student mentors, and the community at large.

Obviously, bullying has always taken place, but the cyberbullying that occurs on social networking sites has the possibility to be more disruptive to the school day, since large numbers of students at a school may witness the incident and/or rapidly spread gossip and rumors to classmates regarding the attack. Having so many classmates aware of their humiliation, combined with the victimization occurring outside of the school day (typically a safer time of day for a bullied student), can lead to the bullied students feeling they have no safe place to go and nowhere to turn. Thus, educators must play a role in addressing students' use of social networking sites, whether these sites are banned from the school district server or not. The good news is that more adolescent users of social networking sites appear to be using privacy settings in recent years. Research from Patchin and Hinduja (2010c) found that 85% of adolescent users set their MySpace profile to private compared to just 39% in 2006. Regardless of their accessibility from school, the use of such sites at home may impact the learning environment when they are used to bully and harass classmates. In addition, many students access these sites at school through the use of cellular phones with Internet capabilities. Proactive educators should address these important lessons with students: the proper use of social networking sites, protection of privacy and students' "digital footprint," how to report problems on social network sites, and how to assist a victimized classmate are lessons that proactive educators address in the classroom.

What Can School Personnel Do to Intervene Effectively in Cyberbullying Incidents?

Although prevention efforts will often decrease the likelihood that students will be involved in cyberbullying incidents, school personnel will, undoubtedly, be faced with periodic instances of cyberbullying. In this section, we will discuss how educators can best respond when a cyberbullying incident comes to their attention.

Notify parents of all involved children (when known)

Based on the content and severity of the messages, the parent of a bullied student may wish to initiate contact with the parent of the student engaging in the cyberbullying behavior. Chapter 5 contains tips for parents about contacting other parents. If, however, the cyberbullying appears to be more serious in nature or disruptive to the school environment (e.g., if it has occurred repeatedly or has been viewed by many students), the parents of the targeted student may need the assistance of a counselor or an administrator at their child's school. In many cases, it will be important for the school administration to notify the parents of all parties involved. In determining whether or not it is appropriate to do so, and in order to notify parents effectively, educators should attempt to obtain evidence of the cyberbullying. This evidence can be obtained from the parents of targeted students or through the actual viewing of a Web site, e-mail, text message or other communication. Web pages can be saved by using the print screen button or screenshot command on a computer and saving it as a file. If a student or adult recognizes the phone number, the sender of a text message can be identified. (The phone company can trace a phone number if a student is not sure who is targeting him or her.) School personnel also should document the date and time at which texts were sent, to determine if the messages were sent during the school day.

Many issues come into play when a cyberbullying incident interrupts a school day. The cyberbullying may take place at school, which provides a much clearer response by the administration. Most school districts now have policies around the misuse of school technology that can be followed when cyberbullying occurs on campus. Far more common, however, is a cyberbullying incident that occurs outside of the school day. If the evidence confirms that those responsible are in attendance at the same school, and if the cyberbullying has created a disruption in the school environment or has the potential to do so, or if the bullying has interfered with the rights of students to feel secure, the administration needs to notify the parents of the parties involved. Even if the administration is uncertain whether formal discipline is appropriate, notification can still be effective in informally resolving the problem behavior. Educators may provide suggestions, support, and resources to the family of the targeted student as well as the family of the student engaged in cyberbullying behavior.

Provide suggestions about various response options

If the cyberbullying is a minor incident (calling someone a mean name) between two students that occurred on only one or two occasions, typically the best course of action is for the targeted student to ignore the behavior. A student who cyberbullies typically wants to see a reaction from the targeted student, and, if the comments are ignored, he or she may stop. Blocking or filtering future messages also may be helpful. Many technologies allow users to block or warn other specific users. Instant messages and cellular phones have blocking features, e-mails have filters, and social networking sites allow users to block individuals from commenting or posting on their site. These steps often will be sufficient to address minor incidents of cyberbullying. Educators may be able to assist students and parents by providing training on how to use the blocking, warning, and filtering functions of various technologies; however, it is likely that many teens are quite knowledgeable about how to use such tools. Additionally, research suggests that it is not uncommon for targeted youth to cyberbully back (Kowalski & Limber, 2007). This often escalates the problem behavior. Thus, educators can help families by reminding them how important it is to avoid aggressive responses to cyberbullying. It is also important to save the evidence in case the cyberbullying continues despite efforts to ignore or block the user. In the following sections, we will discuss steps to take if the cyberbullying is persistent or more severe.

Provide resources/tips on the removal of offensive material

Most social networking sites have user agreements that prohibit cyberbullying, cyber threats, impersonation, and other dangerous behaviors. Educators can assist students and parents by locating the various user policies on social networking sites such as MySpace and Facebook that explain how to report abuse or threats. MySpace has a frequently asked questions (FAQ) section that provides links to safety tips, as well as links to how to report identity theft, underage use, cyberbullying, and copyright violations. Students, parents, and educators can use the site procedures to report behavior that violates these user agreements. Facebook has a help center that provides advice to users and parents about how to report abuse. In addition, links are provided throughout Facebook that allow users to report inappropriate or abusive content. Facebook has added a new feature that allows the user to share the inappropriate comment or content with a trusted authority for advice. If a parent or student does not receive a timely response to a report of abuse, a school resource officer, counselor, or administrator can also file a report of abuse to Facebook. This can be particularly helpful in the case of a fake profile that targets a student. The cyberbullyhelp. com homepage has a quicklink to the Facebook report form, as it can be difficult to find.

School personnel can be valuable resources to parents by letting them know the various steps they can take to have offensive material removed. Sites such as Facebook and MySpace will routinely shut down a site if it is in violation of their "Terms of Use" policies (i.e., it includes exploitation, threats or harassment of others). Educators can also warn students that the site they have spent hours developing will no longer be accessible if they violate such guidelines.

Contact the police

Although laws vary based on jurisdiction, serious allegations such as threats of physical harm, sexual harassment, posting nude or compromising photographs, extortion or stalking behavior should be reported to the police immediately, and the police will conduct their own investigation (Willard, 2007). If a police report is made, school administrators should consult with law enforcement to determine if it is appropriate for the school to contact the parents of the parties involved. Law enforcement may not want the parents of the alleged perpetrator to be contacted in case evidence of the illegal behavior may be destroyed.

Share concerns with the school community

In many instances, simply providing referral resources and sending home a tip sheet on responding to cyberbullying will be an effective intervention for the family of the victim who has been targeted off campus. An example of such a tip sheet for parents exists on the cyberbullyhelp.com resource section. It is also worthwhile to send out a communication to all parents at a school or the parents of a particular grade level explaining that cyberbullying behavior has occurred among students at the school and inviting parents to partner with the school to monitor students' use of technology. These are teachable moments in the school community and should be used to encourage discussions around our rights and responsibilities as digital citizens.

Warn parents of children who have been threatened

School personnel should always warn the parents of a child who has been threatened online if they have been made aware of the threats. One of the individual interviews conducted in preparation for this book involved a parent who was not notified by the school when her child was cyberbullied online. Even though school administrators were contacted by a parent regarding negative postings on a Web site that were threatening in nature, the administration did not notify the parents of the other targeted students, and they remained unaware that their child had been threatened. The following comments from our interview with this parent illustrate the frustration she felt upon learning that the school failed to notify her of the cyberbullying. According to the mother, a student at her daughter's school posted a picture of the school on a social networking site with the word "hell" written on it and the student threatened to "go out with a bang". She reportedly included a list of female classmates who she did not like.

> *Interviewer:* What was your reaction when you learned of the cyberbullying targeting your daughter?
>
> *Parent:* Extreme anger that I wasn't notified by the school, because the parent who brought it to my attention had been there to see the principal earlier in the day, to bring it to her attention and [the principal's] initial reaction was that she couldn't believe she was being bothered by this "yet again" because there had been another incident regarding this particular Web site a few months prior. My second reaction was fear, that what did this mean for my daughter, having my daughter on this list? What do we do now, what are our rights as a parent, where do we turn – because we had never dealt with this before?

This parent filed a police report on her own, not knowing what else to do. It would have been much better if the school had notified all parents involved and helped them find appropriate resources to address the situation. The parents were unable to meet with the principal the next day, but they did meet with an assistant administrator, who was unaware of the details of the incident. They also took their concerns to the superintendent's office.

Interviewer: Did the assistant principal have any actions she could recommend?

Parent: Not initially. She brought in the school resource officer, who happened to be at the school at the time. He shed some light on it and said it had happened before, but since it didn't happen on school property using school equipment there was nothing they could do. [The assistant principal] indicated she would contact the district office, but she was just so blind sided [since the principal had given her few details] by it she didn't really know what to do. We didn't feel like there were going to be any actions or any action quick enough for the kids on the list, so I took it upon myself to take it to the superintendent's office. The superintendent for our area took it very seriously and got the legal team involved. It was only then that other parents from the school were notified.

Interviewer: Were there statements [on the Web site] that made you concerned for the students' safety?

Parent: Yes. She put a picture of the middle school on the Web site with the word "Hell!" written in red and said she was tired of these girls thinking they were all that, she would take care of it, she would go out with a bang ... The police thought it was threatening enough to pursue an investigation.

Put yourself in the place of this mother for a moment. It is extremely distressing for a parent to view threatening messages targeting one's son or daughter. In fact, some of our interviews indicated that the parents were more distraught over the cyberbullying and threats than their child who was being targeted. In any case, parents will likely be very concerned about threats and harassment toward their child, and they need to know that the school will assist and support them as they attempt to deal with the situation, even if the messages are posted at a home computer outside of the school day. When this parent felt that the school was not responsive, she went a step further to the school district office. Fortunately, the district superintendent for her area was concerned and notified the other parties involved. A great deal of fear, frustration, and anger on the part of the parents could have been alleviated if the principal at the school had been more proactive initially, by notifying the parents of the targeted students, and contacting law enforcement about the threatening statements.

Parents of students who engage in cyberbullying behavior also need to be informed by the school administration of their child's actions as soon as possible. While it is true that some parents may view cyberbullying as insignificant or normal teenage behavior, many parents will be distressed to learn that their son or daughter has engaged in such negative behavior and will appreciate being notified. Such notification allows them to take steps to monitor their child's online behavior more closely. The parents of students who engage in cyberbullying may need resources to help them talk with their child about appropriate online use, and suggestions of how to monitor their child's online presence. Schools can refer them to such Web sites as www.stopbullying.gov, www.connectsafely.org, www.wiredsafety.org, and our own Web site, www.cyberbullyhelp.com, to learn more about monitoring their child.

On occasion, threatening statements might be severe enough to warrant a referral to a therapist for a consultation. Students who post statements that express a desire to hurt themselves or others (cyber threats) should be referred for a psychological assessment to determine if they are suicidal or homicidal. The school counselor may work with the administration to make such referrals. This will be discussed further in our section on appropriate referrals to mental health resources.

School discipline for cyberbullying – a delicate issue

Parents of the victim of cyberbullying often want to know if there will be consequences for the students who bullied their child. If a student has violated the school's acceptable use of technology policy by using school-based technology to cyberbully another student, then the school should provide consequences for the cyberbullying behavior and advise the parents of the targeted student that the policy is being followed. If the student used his or her own technology (such as a cellular phone) but sent the messages while at school, the behavior may also warrant school-imposed consequences. This is why it is important to have evidence of the date and time that messages were sent. Many school districts ban the use of cellular phones during the school day, but then look the other way when students text message during the day. There is also a trend for more districts to allow cell phone use during prescribed periods of the day, and some schools are even incorporating their use into educational purposes. However setting a clear policy on the possession and use of mobile phones and the development of consequences for their misuse is critical if schools wish to limit their disruption to the learning environment.

It is especially challenging for school personnel, however, when the cyberbullying behavior occurs outside of the school day on home computers or cellular phones. While many administrators believe that they should be able to discipline students for cyberbullying behaviors that disrupt the school day, the standard for doing so is high. The cyberbullying must include severe or substantial threat of disruption to the learning environment, and "point of view" speech is usually protected under the First Amendment (Willard, 2007). Even if a student posts or electronically communicates outrageous comments about a classmate or teacher, if it occurs on a home computer it may be protected speech. Public school officials may be legally challenged if they impose consequences on students' right to free speech.

Private school officials have more leeway to discipline for such infractions because they do not represent a government entity. Public school officials *may* be able to discipline for cyberbullying if they have required students to sign a student behavior code that lists cyberbullying behaviors as inappropriate even if they occur outside of school. The best course of action for administrators is to consult with an attorney before disciplining students for cyberbullying behavior that has taken place outside of the school day, but still assist the family of the targeted student by providing support and referrals where appropriate. See Chapter 7 for a more detailed analysis of legal issues related to cyberbullying.

When counselors or administrators learn that one of their students has been a target of cyberbullying, they should look for evidence of traditional bullying that has occurred at school in addition to the cyberbullying behaviors. School officials who have implemented policies against bullying can impose consequences for bullying behavior occurring at school that has accompanied the cyberbullying outside of school. If this is the case, personnel should follow their district policy and guidelines for responding to the traditional bullying, but take sufficient time to determine the full extent of the bullying, both cyberbullying and traditional bullying. The perpetrator(s) and targeted student(s) should be interviewed individually, with a strong message against further retaliation on either side.

But keep in mind that the goal of discipline is to teach. Punitive consequences rarely take into account the complexities of the situation and may actually exacerbate bullying and cyberbullying. Without an opportunity to reflect on their actions, students who are suspended may be motivated to retaliate and may now have even more time to engage in online bullying while at home. That is why many educators find it useful to implement "restorative practices" when intervening in bullying behavior. These practices focus on "repairing the harm" that has been done to the relationships on campus and off campus. We include an example of an intervention that involved restorative practices at the end of this chapter.

If the target is a faculty member

Students have also been known to target faculty members through Web sites. A male high school student in one of our focus groups shared the following comments:

> "There is a teacher we didn't like ... so we kind of made fun of that teacher ... we made a facebook blog about them."

The steps that we discussed previously in terms of response options and removal of offensive material are still relevant when one or more students target a faculty member; however, the school administration may need to take time to carefully assess the motivation of the students. There are a variety of reasons why students may target a particular teacher. However, there is always a possibility that the students are retaliating against perceived bullying behavior on the part of the adult faculty member (Willard, 2007). If such motivation appears plausible, the administration may need to take steps to investigate and address the situation.

Develop a protocol for responding to sexting that involves a multidisciplinary team approach

While it is beyond the scope of this book to discuss all of the legal issues involved in intervening in sexting behaviors among youth, it is the authors' recommendation that educators work as a team with law enforcement to establish a protocol for responding to students' production or distribution of sexually explicit photographs via mobile phone or the Internet. The protocol should take into account the differences between experimental and aggravated sexting typologies as identified by Wolak and Finkelhor (2011). Aggravated sexting behaviors involve adults and youth or youth only and include criminal or abusive behavior such as extortion, threats, or sending an image maliciously after an interpersonal conflict. These behaviors extend beyond creating, possessing, or sending a sexual image. Experimental sexting behaviors are not criminal or abusive but occur between minors where there is a romantic attraction or attention seeking behaviors. They may also occur between pre-adolescents acting on impulse without sexual motivation. The protocol should also allow for a response that best meets the needs of the minor child in light of any legal requirements that are mandated by law enforcement statutes and the courts.

Threat assessment

A couple of years ago, a mother called the student assistance office of one of the authors to seek guidance about some statements her daughter had posted on her blog, which was on a social networking site. On this blog, her daughter asked others to comment on whether or not she should kill herself. The author recommended that the daughter see a therapist immediately and explained the process by which she could arrange for an assessment of her daughter. "Has anyone responded to what she wrote?" the author asked her mother. "No," her mother responded with anguish in her voice. The daughter was seen for an assessment and hospitalized the same day for being actively suicidal. The author realized at that time that school personnel were entering into a new era where adults would have avenues for much deeper glimpses into young people's private psyches – whether they liked it or not.

Many school districts utilize a suicide/homicide protocol to guide educators in intervening with a student who has made statements about hurting himself or others. It is recommended that school districts engage in threat analysis for any reports of cyberbullying that allude to suicide or homicide (Willard, 2007). The student assistance office mentioned previously has a staff member at a central office "on call" daily to assist the counselors in determining whether to send a student for an assessment for risky behavior. Several years ago, the on-call counselors began to notice that more and more students were coming to their attention as a result of threats that students had sent by e-mail, instant message, or online posting to a social networking site. It is recommended that educators respond to online threats just as they would to a spoken or written threat, by including online threats in their threat assessment procedures and taking the appropriate disciplinary, referral, or police report action as indicated. Many school districts have procedures in place to do so and increasingly make use of a multi-disciplinary approach (i.e. administrator, counselor, school psychologist, school resource officer) in their review.

Referrals to mental health resources

A student who has engaged in cyberbullying acts should be carefully assessed to determine what dynamics are occurring in his or her home and school life that may have influenced his or her actions. Willard (2006) suggests that counselors and administrators look at the cyberbullying content as well as the student's overall relationships to determine if they are dealing with "put down" material generated by a power oriented bully/wannabee, or at "get back" material generated by a frustrated victim. Preliminary data suggest that a fair percentage of students who engage in cyberbullying may be bully/victims or passive victims who are retaliating online (Kowalski & Limber, 2007). If the student has been bullied at school and is reacting to such actions by making cyber threats or cyberbullying others, he or she needs help and support in dealing with the bullying he or she has experienced. The administrator, school counselor, parent, and child should work together to develop a safety plan or other strategies for a bullied student that reduce the further bullying at school. The student's level of social skills should also be assessed and resources or referrals offered to a student who exhibits limited skills. Often the school counselor is the appropriate person to meet with the student and his or her parents to make recommendations of outside assistance. The cyberbullying incident may, in fact, be an opportunity to provide the student with much needed resources and referrals to deal with social and behavioral issues that are affecting the student's performance at school. It is imperative, however, that students who are bullied at school are given support to eliminate the school bullying, rather than imply they are to blame for the bullying.

Informal resolution/accountability circles

Mediation is typically discouraged in dealing with traditional bullying behaviors. The imbalance of power is such that calling together a victim and a perpetrator, and asking them to work together to solve the conflict can seem like a revictimization to the targeted student. A helpful analogy is to think about bringing a child abuser and his or her victim together and telling them both, "We are going to resolve this abuse through mediation." The child would not be powerful enough or safe enough in this environment when facing his or her tormentor and might go along with whatever the abuser (or person engaging in bullying) said. That is why the Olweus Bullying Prevention Program (and indeed most bullying prevention programs, as well as the HRSA's National Bullying Prevention Campaign) strongly recommends that children who bully and children who are bullied be interviewed individually and a safety plan be developed for students who are being bullied at school that includes increased supervision by adults, consequences for the student engaged in the bullying, and clear avenues for the victim to ask for help and report further victimization (Olweus et al., 2007). Scheduling changes may be necessary (preferably moving the child who bullies) to ensure that the targeted child is not further victimized.

Because schools are frequently limited in the consequences they can give in cases of cyberbullying, we are interested in positive alternatives to civil lawsuits or criminal prosecution that schools can recommend to parents. In some cases of bullying, there may be benefit in borrowing from a model of intervention developed by the legal system that is called "restorative justice," which has been defined as:

> a theory of criminal justice that focuses on crime as an act against another individual or community rather than the state. The victim plays a major role in the process and receives some type of restitution from the offender. Restorative justice takes many different forms, but all systems have some aspects in common. Victims have an opportunity to express the full impact of the crime upon their lives, to receive answers to any lingering questions about the incident, and to participate in holding the offender accountable for his or her actions. Offenders can tell their story of why the crime occurred and how it has affected their lives. They are given an opportunity to make things right with the victim to the degree possible through some form of compensation. (word IQ, 17 July, 2006)

This type of intervention involves bringing victims and *remorseful* perpetrators together *willingly*, with a scripted process where the victims are able to share the impact of the perpetrators' actions on their lives, and the perpetrators have an opportunity to apologize for their actions and repair the harm done. Much training is required to properly administer restorative justice programs in the legal system, and much preparation background work is necessary. Although a full restorative justice program may be too time consuming for most school administrators, one of the authors has successfully used what we call an "accountability circle" in the school setting after attending a training program on restorative justice. The accountability circle blends some of the principles of restorative justice with those of mediation and will be described in more detail below. We believe that school counselors and administrators (with training) can use these principles to intervene in more serious cases of cyberbullying (as well as other school incidents) when the parents of the parties involved are willing, when the targeted student is willing and emotionally prepared, and when the student who engaged in the cyberbullying behavior (and his or her parents) have demonstrated some remorse.

Burssens and Vettenburg (2006) write about a similar form of restorative justice called "restorative group conferencing" (also sometimes referred to as "family group conferencing"), that has been used successfully in a number of countries. They indicate that it should be reserved for more serious offenses at school owing to the time involved, and their research investigated the use of restorative school conferencing with incidents of serious theft, extortion, physical intimidation of a teacher, bullying among students, and a serious fight where students were injured. Their research suggested that the restorative group conferences were judged as very positive and that the process "eased or even eliminated tensions within a class or school" (p. 12). Before pursuing such strategies, school administrators need to understand that the focus of the accountability circle is on repairing the harm done, rather than on punitive consequences. School personnel who are interested in learning more about restorative justice practices may wish to visit: www. restorativejustice.org. Without this type of intervention, staff may be left giving parents the only options of pressing criminal charges or civil lawsuits as a response to the cyberbullying that occurs off school grounds.

Steps in setting up accountability circles
Typically the school counselor or other student assistance professional is the appropriate person to arrange for an accountability circle for the parties involved. The school counselor acts as the facilitator in such a scenario. He or she should contact the parents of the victim as well as the perpetrator to make sure that they seem willing to and capable of making the meeting a constructive experience. The victim should always have the right to refuse attendance at the meeting or to say that the meeting should not take place. It is possible to do an accountability circle with the victim's parents rather than the victim herself, as was done in the McClain case described in Chapter 5. While Mrs McClain's daughter, Brandy, did not wish to attend the meeting, she was agreeable to her parents attending. Her parents felt strongly that they wanted to meet with the perpetrator and her parents. All parties should be made aware that the meeting is voluntary and can end at any time if the agreed upon guidelines are not followed by the parties involved. The facilitator should explain to the victim (if participating) and

his or her parents that they will have an opportunity to explain how the incident impacted them individually and as a family, and what, if any, actions they would like to see to resolve the situation. The parents of the offender will also have an opportunity to share how the incident impacted them and to express remorse for their child's actions. The perpetrator will have the opportunity to share his or her remorse and any circumstances surrounding their behavior. After the facilitator summarizes the experiences

Box 6.1   Accountability script

Questions for student offender:

- What happened?
- What were you thinking at the time?
- What have you thought about since the incident?
- Who do you think has been affected by your actions?
- How have they been affected?

Questions for the student who was harmed:
  (*These questions can also be asked of the parents of the parties involved.*)

- What was your reaction when you first saw the Web site/messages/ etc.?
- How do you feel about what happened?
- What has been the hardest thing for you?
- How did your family and friends react when they heard about the incident?

Summarize and follow up with:

- What are the main issues?
- What do you want as a result of this meeting?

Resolution/signed agreement to include:

- Restitution and/or counseling
- Safety issues
- Retaliation issues
- Follow-up meetings if needed

of the parties involved, they agree on the steps necessary to repair the harm. The restitution steps are written down and signed by all the parties in attendance with targeted dates identified and responsibility for monitoring identified. A sample facilitator's script for use with an accountability circle is included in Box 6.1.

A successful accountability circle can provide a genuine learning experience for all of the parties involved and can help to heal the relationships that have been harmed as a result of the incident. The student who has been cyberbullied (and his or her parents) has the opportunity to fully describe his or her experience and make an assertive request for a remedy to the situation. The student who has engaged in cyberbullying behavior has the opportunity to become more empathetic, gain a new perspective on his or her behavior, and make amends for such behavior. The result is that the participants may gain new competencies and the school environment may become safer as students take responsibility for their actions.

Summary

As bullying over the Internet becomes more commonplace, educators must become equally prepared to address this new form of bullying. To avoid dealing with such instances is to ignore a significant form of social interaction among our students. Educators have always been in the business of instructing children to use appropriate behavior, and the appropriate use of technology should not be an exception. Because we live in an information society where students must have advanced skills in technology to compete, and where an increasing amount of socializing will take place using the tools of technology, educators must familiarize themselves with strategies for the prevention and intervention of cyberbullying behavior in order to ensure that civility is consistently taught in all forms of social interaction, be they face-to-face or online.

7

LAWS AND POLICIES

with Nancy Willard and Rebecca Alley

As we noted earlier, attention to bullying among students exploded in the American media in the wake of the tragic shootings at Columbine High School. After 1999, there also was a flurry of state legislation related to bullying, as 30 states passed laws addressing bullying within a span of less than 8 years (Alley & Limber, 2009). At the same time, several widely publicized lawsuits raised concerns among many educators about their legal options and responsibilities to prevent and address bullying in their schools.

With the advent of cyber technologies, there has been a whirlwind of media attention to cyberbullying and harassment, and a resulting uncertainty by many educators about how to meet ethical and legal duties to protect students from cyberbullying without infringing on their rights under the U.S. Constitution. In this chapter, we will discuss emerging state laws addressing cyberbullying. We also will summarize current case law, with an eye to answering three primary questions: (1) When may school personnel be held liable (under federal or state laws) for failing to address cyberbullying? (2) Under what circumstances can school personnel address cyberbullying without fear of violating students' First Amendment rights to freedom of speech and expression? (3) Under what circumstances can school personnel monitor or search student Internet records without fear of violating students' constitutional protections against illegal searches and seizures? Finally, we will address the development of school policies on cyberbullying, in light of emerging law.

Before addressing these issues, several words of caution are in order. First, this chapter is limited in its legal analysis to the American public

Cyberbullying: Bullying in the Digital Age, Second Edition. Robin M. Kowalski, Susan P. Limber, and Patricia W. Agatston.
Published 2012 by Blackwell Publishing Ltd.

school context. Second, although this chapter describes current state laws relating to cyberbullying and describes the likely application of existing case law to instances of cyberbullying within American public schools, it is not intended to substitute in any way for the advice of local counsel, who are in a position to assess local laws and policies and the rapidly changing legal landscape. We strongly advise school administrators to consult with their district's attorney on these issues.

State Laws and Their Relevance to Cyberbullying

One important first step in considering legal obligations to address cyberbullying is for school personnel to become familiar with relevant state laws addressing bullying. At the time of this writing (April 16, 2011), 46 states had laws related to bullying. These statutes vary quite a bit in their definitions of bullying and in their specific requirements, but almost all require state or local officials (typically school districts) to establish policies against bullying among students in public schools. (For a review of key elements of these policies, see Alley & Limber, 2009; U.S. Department of Education, 2010).

In 2007, only five state laws (Arkansas, Idaho, Iowa, South Carolina, and Washington) explicitly addressed bullying through electronic communications. Since that time, many other states have passed new legislation so that, as of the time of this writing, 30 states have laws explicitly addressing bullying by electronic means. Thirty states (see Table 7.1) include cyberbullying or electronic acts or communications in their laws addressing bullying among students at school. Tennessee does not explicitly include cyberbullying in its bullying law, but state law does hold that threatening by electronic communication by any person is a misdemeanor.

In 2010, the U.S. Department of Education identified key components of state laws on bullying. Among these key components was a "specific definition of bullying that includes a clear definition of cyberbullying" (p. 2). Of the 29 states (excluding Tennessee), six use and define the term cyberbullying in their laws. Nevada law (Nev. Rev. Stat. Ann § 388.122, 2010) simply notes that cyberbullying involves "bullying through the use of electronic communication." Similarly, Oregon law (ORS § 339.351, 2010) defines cyberbullying as "the use of any electronic communication device to harass, intimidate or bully." The remaining four states provide a bit more detail about the means through which cyberbullying may occur. New Hampshire law (RSA 193-F:2, 2010) defines cyberbullying as "[bullying] undertaken

Table 7.1 Summary of state laws on cyberbullying (current as of April 16, 2011).

State	Bullying law?	Does law explicitly address cyberbullying or bullying through electronic means?	Cyberbullying mentioned (C) or bullying through electronic means (E) only?	Does law apply only on school grounds or with school network? (U=unspecified)	Is a policy on bullying required?
Alabama	Y Ala. § 16-28B-1 (2010)	Y	E	Y	Y
Alaska	Y Alaska Stat. §14.33.200 (2010)	NO	–	Y	Y
Arizona	Y A.R.S. § 15-341 (2010)	NO	–	Y	Y
Arkansas	Y A.C.A. Tit. 6, Subtit. 2, Ch. 18, Subch. 5 Note (2010)	Y	E	NO	Y
California	Y Cal Ed Code § 32261 (2009)	Y	E	Y	Y
Colorado	Y C.R.S. 22-32-109.1 (2010)	NO[1]	–	Y	Y
Connecticut	Y Conn. Gen. Stat. § 10-222d (2010)	NO	–	Y	Y

(continued)

Table 7.1 (cont'd)

State	Bullying law?	Does law explicitly address cyberbullying or bullying through electronic means?	Cyberbullying mentioned (C) or bullying through electronic means (E) only?	Does law apply only on school grounds or with school network? (U = unspecified)	Is a policy on bullying required?
Delaware	Y 14 Del. C. § 4112D (2010)	Y	E	Y	Y
Florida	Y Fla. Stat § 1006.147 (2010)	Y	E	Y	Y
Georgia	Y O.C.G.A. § 20-2-751.4 (2010)	Y	E	Y	Y
Hawaii	NO	NO	–	–	–
Idaho	Y Idaho Code § 18-917A (2010)	Y	E	U	Y
Illinois	Y 105 ILCS 5/27-13.3 (2010)	Y	E	Y	Y
Indiana	Y Burns Ind. Code Ann. § 20-33-8-0.2 (2010)	NO	–	Y	Y

State	Statute				
Iowa	Iowa Code §280.28 (2010)	Y	E	Y	Y
Kansas	K.S.A. § 72-8256 (2009)	Y	C	Y	Y
Kentucky	KRS §158.155 (2010)	Y (criminal code)	–	–	NO
Louisiana	La. R.S. 17:416.13 (2010)	Y	C	NO	Y
Maine	20-A M.R.S. § 1001 (2010)	NO	–	U	Y
Maryland	Md. Education Code Ann. § 7-424 (2010)	Y	E	Y	NO
Massachusetts	ALM GL ch. 71, § 370 (2010)	Y	C	NO	Y
Michigan	NO	NO	–	–	–
Minnesota	Minn. Stat. § 121A.0695 (2009)	Y	E	U	Y

(continued)

Table 7.1 *(cont'd)*

State	Bullying law?	Does law explicitly address cyberbullying or bullying through electronic means?	Cyberbullying mentioned (C) or bullying through electronic means (E) only?	Does law apply only on school grounds or with school network? (U = unspecified)	Is a policy on bullying required?
Mississippi	Y Miss. Code Ann § 37-11-67 (2010)	Y	E	Y	Y
Missouri	Y § 160.775 R.S.Mo. (2010)	NO	–	U	Y
Montana	NO	NO	–	–	–
Nebraska	Y R.R.S. Neb. § 79-2,137 (2010)	Y	E	Y	Y
Nevada	Y Nev. Rev. Stat. Ann. § 388.122 (2010)	Y	C	U	Y
New Hampshire	Y RSA 193-F:2 (2010)	Y	C	NO	Y
New Jersey	Y N.J. Stat. § 18A:37-13 (2011)	Y	E	NO	Y
New Mexico	Y² 6.12.7 NMAC	Y	E	Y	Y

State	Citation				
New York	N.Y. Educ. Law Tit. 1, Art. 2 (2010)	NO[3]	—	Y	Y
North Carolina	N.C. Gen. Stat. § 14-458.1 (2010)	Y	E	Y	Y
North Dakota	HB 1465 (2011)	NO	E	Y	Y
Ohio	ORC Ann. 3301.22 (2010)	NO	—	U	Y
Oklahoma	70 Okl. St. § 24-100.2 (2010)	Y	E	NO	Y
Oregon	ORS § 339.351 (2010)	Y	C	Y	Y
Pennsylvania	24 P.S. § 13-1303.1-A (2010)	Y	E	Y	Y
Rhode Island	R.I. Gen. Laws § 16-21-24 (2010)	Y	E	Y	Y
South Carolina	S.C. Code Ann. § 59-63-120 (2009)	Y	E	Y	Y

(continued)

Table 7.1 (*cont'd*)

State	Bullying law?	Does law explicitly address cyberbullying or bullying through electronic means?	Cyberbullying mentioned (C) or bullying through electronic means (E) only?	Does Law apply only on school grounds or with school network? (U = unspecified)	Is a policy on bullying required?
South Dakota	NO	NO	–	–	–
Tennessee	Y Tenn. Code Ann. § 49-6-812 (2010)	NO	–	Y	Y
Texas	Y Tex. Educ. Code § 25.0342 (2010)	NO	–	U	Y[4]
Utah	Y Utah Code Ann. § 53A-11a-101 (2010)	NO	–	Y	Y
Vermont	Y 16 V.S.A. § 11 (2010)	NO	–	Y	Y
Virginia	Y Va. Code ann. § 8.01-220.1:2 (2010)	Y	E	U	Y[5]
Washington	Y Rev. Code Wash. (ARCW) § 28A.300.285 (2010)	Y	E	U	Y

State	Citation				
West Virginia	W.Va. Code § 18-2C-1 (2010)	Y	NO	–	Y
Wisconsin	Wis. Stat. §118.46 (2010)	Y	NO	–	Y
Wyoming	Wyo. Stat. § 21-4-312 (2010)	Y	Y	E	Y
TOTAL		46	31	44	44

[1] Not included explicitly in the definition of bullying but addresses cyberbullying in discussion of bullying prevention.

[2] The New Mexico Administrative Code, which has the force of law, addresses bullying.

[3] Not included explicitly in the definition of bullying but discussed in relation to education on internet safety.

[4] Requires student code of conduct to prohibit and address bullying.

[5] Requires student code of conduct to address bullying.

through the use of electronic devices [which] include, but are not limited to, telephones, cellular phones, computers, pagers, electronic mail, instant messaging, text messaging, and websites." Kansas law (K.S.A. § 72-8256, 2009) defines cyberbullying as "bullying by use of any electronic communication device through means including, but not limited to, e-mail, instant messaging, text messages, blogs, mobile phones, pagers, online games and websites." According to Louisiana law (R.S. 17:416.13, 2010), cyberbullying is:

> harassment, intimidation, or bullying of a student on school property by another student using a computer, mobile phone, or other interactive or digital technology or harassment, intimidation, or bullying of a student while off school property by another student using any such means when the action or actions are intended to have an effect on the student when the student is on school property.

Massachusetts law (ALM GL ch. 71, § 370, 2010) provides the most detailed definition of cyberbullying:

> ... bullying through the use of technology or any electronic communication, which shall include, but shall not be limited to, any transfer of signs, signals, writing, images, sounds, data or intelligence of any nature transmitted in whole or in part by a wire, radio, electromagnetic, photo electronic or photo optical system, including, but not limited to, electronic mail, internet communications, instant messages or facsimile communications. Cyber-bullying shall also include (i) the creation of a web page or blog in which the creator assumes the identity of another person or (ii) the knowing impersonation of another person as the author of posted content or messages ... Cyber-bullying shall also include the distribution by electronic means of a communication to more than one person or the posting of material on an electronic medium that may be accessed by one or more persons ...

Twenty-four state laws do not use the term cyberbullying, but instead explicitly note that bullying (or harassment) includes electronic acts or communications. For example, South Carolina law (S.C. Code Ann § 59-63-120, 2009) defines bullying as:

> a gesture, an electronic communication, or a written, verbal, physical, or sexual act that is reasonably perceived to have the effect of: (a) harming a student physically or emotionally or damaging a student's property, or placing a student in reasonable fear of personal harm or property damage; or (b) insulting

or demeaning a student or group of students causing substantial disruption in, or substantial interference with, the orderly operation of the school.

Among these 30 state laws that explicitly address cyberbullying, electronic bullying, or electronic harassment, most of them explicitly limit the scope of the law to require that districts have policies that address actions that take place on school grounds, during school activities, using school equipment, or using a school's computer system (see Table 7.1). For example, Pennsylvania law (24 P.S. § 13-1303. 1-A, 2010) defines bullying as "an intentional electronic, written, verbal or physical act, or a series of acts ... which occurs in a school setting." The law further clarifies that "'school setting' shall mean in the school, on school grounds, in school vehicles, at a designated bus stop or at any activity sponsored, supervised or sanctioned by the school." Other laws include acts that may take place off campus but through the use of school computer systems. Georgia's law notes that bullying "means an act which occurs on school property, on school vehicles, at designated school bus stops, or at school related functions or activities, *or by the use of data or software that is accessed through a computer, computer system computer network, or other electronic technology of a local school system ...*" (emphasis added). Several states (Arkansas, Louisiana, Massachusetts, New Hampshire, New Jersey and Oklahoma) explicitly state that districts should have policies that apply to cyberbullying that occurs *off of school property*. For example, the Arkansas law:

appl[ies] to an electronic act whether or not the electronic act originated on school property or with school equipment, if the electronic act is directed specifically at students or school personnel and maliciously intended for the purpose of disrupting school, and has a high likelihood of succeeding in that purpose ... (A.C.A. Tit. 6, Subtit. 2, Ch. 18, Subch. 5 Note (2010))

Massachusetts law similarly prohibits bullying:

at a location, activity, function or program that is not school-related, or through the use of technology or an electronic device that is not owned, leased or used by a school district or school, if the bullying creates a hostile environment at the school for the victim, infringes on the rights of the victim at school or materially and substantially disrupts the education process or the orderly operation of a school. (ALM GL ch. 71 § 370, 2010)

Under New Jersey law, school policies "shall include provisions for appropriate responses to harassment, intimidation, or bullying ... that occurs off school grounds, *in cases in which a school employee is made aware of such actions*" (emphasis added, N.J. Stat. § 18A:37-13, 2011). Several state laws that address cyberbullying or bullying through electronic means are silent about the location of the bullying behaviour.

Among those states that have bullying laws but do not specifically address cyberbullying (or bullying through the use of electronic acts or communications), most of them arguably cover at least some instances of cyberbullying. Several provide definitions of bullying, which may, to a greater or lesser extent, be interpreted to include various acts of cyberbullying. For example, according to Indiana law,

> "bullying" means overt, repeated acts or gestures, including (1) verbal or written communications transmitted; (2) physical acts committed; or (3) any other behaviors committed by a student or group of students against another student with the intent to harass, ridicule, humiliate, intimidate, or harm the other student.

Presumably, cyberbullying behaviour would be covered by this law under provision 1 ("written") or 3 ("other") behavior. Several other state laws address bullying but fail to define the term (e.g., Alaska, Arizona, Maine, Minnesota, Virginia).

A key issue that must be kept in mind with respect to these state statutes is that the statutes set forth the requirement that districts have a bullying prevention policy and the minimum requirements for that policy. The lack of a statutory reference to provisions that would address off-campus speech that has had a significant disruption at school reflects a lack of understanding about the legal standard. Many of these statutes have not been updated to reflect the emerging legal standard. These legal issues are addressed later in this chapter. Upon consultation with district legal counsel, districts can develop policies that comply with constitutional standards, as articulated by the courts, and allow the school to formally respond to cyberbullying situations regardless of the geographic origin of the student speech.

Litigation

Recent legal attention to bullying has not been limited to actions by state legislatures, however (Alley & Limber, 2009). There also has been speculation about an increased focus within the courts on bullying, perhaps most visibly in the form of lawsuits filed by parents against schools for harm caused to their bullied children (e.g., Seper, 2005). For example, in 2004 the Anchorage School District in Alaska paid $4.5 million to settle a lawsuit filed by the family of a middle school student who had tried to commit suicide after he was bullied at school (Pesznecker, 2004). The following year, a New Jersey appellate court upheld a jury award for $50,000 to a high school student who had been physically and verbally abused by his peers who thought he was gay (Mikle, 2005).

High-profile news accounts notwithstanding, it is extremely difficult to document whether and how much bullying-related litigation may have actually increased in recent years (Alley & Limber, 2009). Why? First, many, if not most, lawsuits that involve bullying are likely settled out of court, making court records of such litigation scarce and by no means representative. Second, there is no national system for counting and tracking the lawsuits related to incidents of school violence that do, in fact, make it to court. Third, the primary legal databases, on which lawyers and legal scholars rely, include only those court decisions that have been appealed. This means that cases that are decided at the trial court level and are not ultimately appealed are not represented in these databases. As a result, these databases may be skewed to over-represent the "close" cases and underrepresent the "easy" cases, which are more likely to be settled out of court or not reach appeal.

Added to these general difficulties of tracking trends in bullying-related litigation are challenges of tracing legal developments related to cyberbullying, in particular. Cyberbullying is a relatively new phenomenon, and published case law relevant to cyberbullying is scant and still somewhat unclear, particularly as it relates to behavior that occurs off school grounds, as is discussed below.

With these caveats in mind, we will turn to address several legal questions that are most relevant to school personnel concerned with cyberbullying, namely: (1) When might school personnel be liable for failing to address cyberbullying? (2) Under what circumstances can school personnel intervene to address cyberbullying without violating students' First Amendment rights to freedom of expression? and (3) Under what circumstances can school personnel monitor or search student Internet records without violating Fourth Amendment restrictions on illegal searches and seizures?

Under what circumstances may school personnel be held liable for
failing to address cyberbullying?

School personnel have a duty to protect students in their care and to ensure that there is no substantial interference with their rights to receive an education (Willard, 2006). School districts may be held liable for failing to stop bullying (and, specifically, cyberbullying) if personnel are found to have acted negligently or if they violate provisions of relevant federal or state statutes.

Statutory liability

Although there currently is no federal law against bullying per se, victims and their parents may, depending on the circumstances, sue for damages under a number of federal laws that prohibit harassment against protected classes of individuals (Alley & Limber, 2009). The federal laws that are most often implicated in such cases relate to sexual- or gender-based harassment, racial harassment, and disability harassment.

Claims of sexual harassment or gender discrimination usually rely on Title IX of the Education Amendments Act of 1972. Under this federal statute, "no person ... shall, on the basis of sex, be excluded from participation in, be denied the benefits of, or be subjected to discrimination under any education program or activity receiving Federal financial assistance" (Education Amendments Act of 1972, 2006). In the case of *Davis v. Monroe County Board of Education* (1999), the U.S. Supreme Court ruled that, under Title IX, schools and school districts (but not individual school personnel) may be liable for student-on-student sexual harassment when it can be shown that the school or district acted with "deliberate indifference" toward harassment that was "so severe, pervasive, and objectively offensive" (p. 650) that it denies victims equal access to education. In order to prove that a school acted with "deliberate indifference," a court must find that school personnel had actual knowledge of the harassment and that their response was clearly unreasonable in light of the known circumstances. In addition, the court must find that there has been a significant impact of the harassment on the student's access to education, as evidenced by more than "a mere decline in grades" (p. 652). Finally, the Supreme Court distinguished acts of harassment from common forms of bullying, noting that:

> It is not enough to show ... that a student has been "teased," or "called ... offensive names[.]" Comparisons to an "overweight child who skips gym class because the other children tease her about her size," the student "who refuses to wear glasses to avoid the taunts of 'four-eyes,'" and "the child who refuses to go to school because the school bully calls him a 'scardy-cat' at recess," are inapposite and misleading. (p. 652)

Subsequent lower court rulings have applied the *Davis* standard to other forms of peer harassment, in addition to sexual harassment. There are, for example, two other contexts, in addition to peer sexual harassment, in which victims may sue under Title IX (Alley & Limber, 2009). The first involves nonsexual harassment of female students based on their gender (e.g., gender-based name calling). The second involves harassment of students based on perceived sexual orientation or a "failure to meet gender stereotypes" (although many courts have not found that Title IX prohibits sexual orientation harassment; Alley & Limber, 2009).

The *Davis* standard has also been applied to claims of racial harassment. Under Title IV of the Civil Rights Act of 1964, "[n]o person ... shall, on the ground of race, color, or national origin, be excluded from participation in, be denied the benefits of, or be subjected to discrimination under any program or activity receiving Federal financial assistance." Students may sue a school or school district for peer racial harassment under Title IV. However, in order to be successful, they must show that the school or district acted with deliberate indifference toward harassment that is so severe, pervasive, and objectively offensive that it deprives the victim of access to educational opportunities.

Students or their parents also may bring claims against a school or school district for peer harassment that is based on the physical or mental disability of the victim (Alley & Limber, 2009). Typically, such claims are brought under Section 504 of the Rehabilitation Act of 1973 and Title II of the Americans with Disabilities Act of 1990 (ADA; 2006), which have similar provisions. Section 504 provides that "[n]o otherwise qualified individual with a disability ... shall, solely by reason of her or his disability, be excluded from the participation in, be denied the benefits of, or be subjected to discrimination under any program or activity receiving Federal financial assistance."

Similarly, Title II of the ADA states that: "[n]o qualified individual with a disability shall, by reason of such disability, be excluded from participation in or be denied the benefits of the services, programs or activities of a public entity, or be subjected to discrimination by any such entity." Courts that have considered claims based on Section 504 and Title II frequently rely on the *Davis* standard, reasoning that a school district or school may be liable for student harassment of another student based on the victim's disability when the school or district acted with deliberate indifference to harassment that was so severe, pervasive, and objectively offensive that it denied the victim equal access to educational resources and opportunities (Alley & Limber, 2009; see e.g., *K.M. v. Hyde Park Central School District*, 2005). Although courts have varied in their findings of what types of harassment (e.g., physical violence, name calling) are sufficient to meet the

Davis standard, at least some have found that nonphysical acts, such as verbal taunting or social isolation of developmentally disabled victims, may in fact be sufficiently severe to qualify under *Davis* (e.g., *K.M. v. Hyde Park Central School District*, 2005).

Lower courts appear to be increasingly paying attention to the effectiveness of the school response. In situations where the schools had a policy against bullying and did respond in some manner when situations were reported, but neither the policy nor the response were effective in stopping the ongoing harm, the courts have begun to question whether the failure to stop the harm, despite the actions taken, constitute deliberate indifference. For example, in a 2000 case, *Vance v. Spencer County Public School District*, the court stated:

> [W]here a school district has knowledge that its remedial action is inadequate and ineffective, it is required to take reasonable action in light of those circumstances to eliminate the behavior. Where a school district has actual knowledge that its efforts to remediate are ineffective, and it continues to use those same methods to no avail, such district has failed to act reasonably in light of the known circumstances.

It also appears that the U.S. Department of Education Office for Civil Rights is getting more active in this area. On October 26, 2010, the Office issued a Dear Colleague letter (DCL) addressing harassment and bullying. Discriminatory harassment may include harassment or bullying that is grounded in race, disabilities, and gender, including sexual orientation. This document specifically noted:

> ED is issuing the DCL to clarify the relationship between bullying and discriminatory harassment, and to remind schools that by limiting their responses to a specific application of an anti-bullying or other disciplinary policy, they may fail to properly consider whether the student misconduct also results in discrimination in violation of students' federal civil rights… What are a school's obligations under these anti-discrimination statutes?
>
> - Once a school knows or reasonably should know of possible student-on-student harassment, it must take immediate and appropriate action to investigate or otherwise determine what occurred.
> - If harassment has occurred, a school must take prompt and effective steps reasonably calculated to end the harassment, eliminate any hostile environment, and prevent its recurrence. These duties are a school's responsibility even if the misconduct also is covered by an anti-bullying

policy and regardless of whether the student makes a complaint, asks the school to take action, or identifies the harassment as a form of discrimination. (U.S. Department of Education Office for Civil Rights, 2010, p. 2)

Under what conditions may individuals (e.g., teachers, principals, or other school staff) be held liable under federal law in cases of student-on-student harassment? As mentioned earlier, only school districts or schools – and not individual staff members – may be held liable for sexual harassment under Title IX or racial harassment under Title IV. It is less clear whether individuals may be held liable for student-on-student disability harassment under Section 504 or Title II. Some jurisdictions have allowed these claims, whereas others have not (Alley & Limber, 2009).

There is at least one other federal statute that may allow students and their parents to bring claims against individual school personnel under federal law. Section 1983 of the Civil Rights Act is a federal law that allows citizens to bring lawsuits to collect damages against state officials, including school teachers, administrators, and other district employees, who deprived them of their rights under federal law. Although the federal rights that are involved vary, in litigation related to instances of harassment or bullying, the federal right in question is often the Fourteenth Amendment to the U.S. Constitution. There are two clauses of the Fourteenth Amendment that are relevant (Alley & Limber, 2009). The first, known as the Due Process Clause, states that "[n]o State shall ... deprive any person of life, liberty, or property, without due process of law." Courts have found that due process rights may be violated when state officials engage in conduct of such an egregious nature as to be conscious-shocking (*County of Sacramento v. Lewis*, 1998), but as Alley and Limber (2009) point out, "they have been reluctant to impose liability on state officials for failing to prevent a person, such as a school child, from being injured by a third party, such as another school child" (see *DeShaney v. Winnebago County Department of Social Services*, 1989). In cases involving school violence, some courts have set an even higher bar and have required deliberate indifference on the part of school personnel in order to find them liable for peer-on-peer harassment or attacks under Section 1983 (see e.g., *Stevenson v. Martin County Board of Education*, 2001).

The second clause of the Fourteenth Amendment, commonly referred to as the Equal Protection Clause, also is occasionally relied on in lawsuits related to harassment of students by other students. The equal protection clause states that "[n]o State shall ... deny to any person ... the equal protection of the laws." In order to be successful, a litigant must show that a defendant (e.g., a school teacher) discriminated against them as a member of an identifiable class and that the discrimination was intentional (see *Flores v. Morgan Hill Unified School District*, 2003). This discrimination may be based on a number of class characteristics, including gender, race, disability, and religion. In the case of student harassment at school, students (or parents on their behalf) bringing the suit must show that a school official treated them differently than other students, as would be the case if a principal failed to enforce a school's antiharassment policy to prevent students from harassing gay students, even though the principal enforced the policy to protect the rest of the student body (Alley & Limber, 2009).

As Alley and Limber (2009, p. 69) note, "there are numerous high hurdles for litigants bringing lawsuits in federal court" for injuries arising out of school bullying or peer-on-peer harassment. Some have succeeded, particularly where a victim has suffered severely and school officials knew of a pattern of harassment against the victim but took no action. However, many victims of bullying are unable to bring suit under federal law because they are not a member of a protected class.

In such cases, they may choose, instead, to file suit under any number of state laws that address concerns such as intentional infliction of emotional distress, negligence, and privacy violations, as well as under various provisions of state education codes. Perhaps the most common suits involve claims that school personnel acted negligently to prevent or address bullying.

Negligence
Negligence is "the failure to exercise the standard of care that a reasonably prudent person would have exercised in a similar situation" (*Black's Law Dictionary*, 2009, p. 1133). It may involve: (a) doing something that a reasonable person would not have done under similar circumstance, or (b) failing to do what a reasonable person would have done under similar circumstances.

Claims of negligence are based on state laws related to the conditions under which liability may be imposed on public officials. As Willard (2006) notes, some states have immunity laws that protect school officials against negligence claims, whereas others do not. As a result, there may be considerable variation from state to state in the manner in which negligence claims are decided.

Generally, an individual bringing a claim of negligence against school personnel must show: (a) a legal duty (e.g., a duty to anticipate foreseeable dangers for students in their care and a duty to take necessary precautions against these dangers), (b) a breach of that duty (failure to use reasonable care in the context of a foreseeable risk), (c) proximate cause (the breach of the duty was a substantial factor in leading to injury or harm), and (d) actual injuries, loss, or damages (Willard, 2006). Willard examined these elements within the context of school personnel's duty to protect students from possible harms caused by using cyber technologies at school.

Do school administrators have a duty to protect the safety of students who use the Internet at school through the district's system? Willard concludes, "Yes, clearly" (p. 69). School personnel have a general duty to provide safe schools and adequate supervision of students within their care. A more specific duty is outlined in The Children's Internet Protection Act (CIPA, 2007). CIPA is a federal law enacted to address concerns about access to offensive content over the Internet on school and library computers. The law imposes certain requirements on any school or library that receives funding support for Internet access or internal connections from the "E-rate" program, a program that makes certain technology more affordable for eligible schools and libraries. Among CIPA's requirements are that schools adopt and implement a policy addressing the safety and security of minors when using e-mail, chat rooms, and other forms of direct electronic communications.

Willard (2006) argues that not only do school personnel have a duty to protect the safety of students who use the Internet while at school, but they also have a similar duty in cases where districts provide students with the ability to access the school's Internet system while off campus, where schools allow students to take home district-owned computers, and where schools permit students to use cell phones or other mobile communication devices at school.

Not only do school officials have a *legal duty* to ensure the safety and security of students in such situations, but they also should be able to *foresee* that students may use cyber technologies to harm other students. Given the emerging evidence that students use such technologies to bully, threaten, and harass each other, and given the intense media attention to this issue, these behaviors should come as no surprise to school officials.

Provided that school officials have a legal duty to protect the safety and security of students and that they should be able to foresee misuse of cyber technologies to cause harm, a critical question in determining negligence becomes, "What is a *reasonable standard of care* that school personnel should be expected to provide in order to protect students?" Until courts address this issue directly, it will be difficult to answer this question. However, the standard is generally expressed as, "what a reasonably prudent person would do in similar circumstances" (Willard, 2006, p. 70).

We believe that reasonably prudent administrators should, at a minimum: (a) develop rules and policies that prohibit the use of district computers and other cyber technologies to bully or harass others, (b) establish policies and procedures that limit students' use of school Internet resources for nonacademic purposes, (c) educate students and staff about cyberbullying and the school's policies and procedures (see Chapter 5), (d) provide adequate supervision and monitoring of students (including their use of the Internet; see Chapter 6), (e) establish effective mechanisms for students and staff to report suspected cyberbullying or other misuse of cyber technologies (see Chapter 6), and (f) establish effective procedures to respond to reports (see Chapter 6; see also Willard, 2006, for similar recommendations for administrators). If they do so, we believe it would be much less likely that they would be successfully sued for negligence.

Under what circumstances can school personnel intervene
to address cyberbullying without fear of violating students'
First Amendment rights?

In their efforts to protect students from foreseeable harm, educators may, on occasion, have to balance their need to protect the right of other students to receive an education against students' rights under the U.S. Constitution, including First Amendment rights to freedom of speech. The U.S. Supreme Court has clearly held that "First Amendment rights ... are available to teachers and students" and that students do not "shed their constitutional rights of speech or expression at the schoolhouse gate" (*Tinker v. Des Moines Independent Community School District*, 1969, p. 506). Nevertheless, the Court has also placed a number of limitations on this speech. Student speech is not protected by the Constitution (and, therefore, may be suppressed or punished) if it: (1) constitutes a threat; (2) is lewd, vulgar, or profane; (3) is (or appears to be) sponsored by the school; or (4) otherwise materially disrupts the schools or invades the rights of others. Even though the U.S. Supreme Court has not directly addressed cases involving First Amendment questions raised by "cyber speech," several seminal decisions likely would apply to such cases and will be discussed briefly below.

The clearest guidance is provided in cases where student speech could be characterized as a threat. In *Watts v. United States* (1969), the Supreme

Court ruled that a true threat is not protected by the Constitution. Several years later, the Court clarified that, in order to constitute a threat, a statement must actually be threatening, and there also must be "proof that the speaker intended the statement to be taken as a threat" (*Rogers v. United States*, 1975, p. 48) even if there was no intent to carry it out. Presumably, based on these Supreme Court rulings, any student speech that is found to be a "true threat" (including messages sent through cyber space) may be regulated without fear of violating students' First Amendment rights.

United States federal courts have recognized that students have rights to free speech and free expression that must be balanced against schools' interest in maintaining an appropriate learning environment and protecting the rights of other students. There have been four Supreme Court cases addressing students' First Amendment speech rights. The cases are: *Tinker v. Des Moines Independent Community School District* (1969), *Bethel School District v. Fraser* (1986), *Hazelwood School District v. Kuhlmeier* (1988), and *Morse v. Frederick* (2007).

The landmark case involving student free speech rights is the case of *Tinker v. Des Moines Independent Community School District.* Tinker involved a group of high school students who decided to wear black armbands to school to protest the Vietnam War. The Court began its opinion by stating that students do not "shed their constitutional rights to freedom of speech or expression at the schoolhouse gate" (p. 506). However, the Court acknowledged "the special characteristics of the school environment" by permitting school officials to prohibit student speech if that speech "would substantially interfere with the work of the school or impinge upon the rights of other students," including the right "to be secure." The Court upheld the rights of the students to protest because their protest had not created a substantial disruption or interference. However, this standard has been applied at the lower court level supporting the authority of school officials to respond if student speech has, or if there are good reasons to believe it could, cause a substantial disruption or interference.

In *Fraser*, the Supreme Court found in favor of school officials who disciplined a student whose speech before a school assembly included sexual references. The Court distinguished between the purely political speech in *Tinker* and the student's vulgarity, and held that school officials had the authority "to prohibit the use of vulgar and offensive terms in public discourse" (p. 683). Justice Brennan's statement in his concurrence in *Fraser* is particularly relevant to the present discussion. Brennan noted that "if [the] respondent had given the same speech outside of the school environment, he could not have been penalized simply because government officials considered his language to be inappropriate" (p. 688). This last statement is very important from the perspective of school officials in terms of response to student off-campus speech merely on the basis that they find such speech to be vulgar and offensive.

The issue involved in *Hazelwood* was a principal's decision to remove several articles from publication in the school newspaper. The Court found that the school newspaper was not a public forum because the school did not intend to open the paper to indiscriminate use by the students. Therefore, the Court indicated it was appropriate for school officials to impose educationally related restrictions on student speech. This standard would apply to any material that students might post on a publicly accessible school Web site, because this material would be presented as if coming from the school.

Morse involved a cryptic, pro-drug use statement, "Bong hits 4 Jesus," on a banner raised by a student across the street from a school during a time when students had been released to watch a parade for the Olympic torch, which was considered to be a school activity. The Court ruled that public school officials may restrict student speech at a school activity when the speech is reasonably viewed as promoting illegal drug use. The Court specifically rejected the arguments of the school district and school leadership organizations that the First Amendment permits school officials to censor any speech that could be considered offensive. Instead, the focus of the Court was on the importance of allowing school officials to respond if the speech is related to student safety concerns.

The importance of the focus on student safety was strengthened by the comments made by Justice Alito in his concurring opinion:

> [A]ny argument for altering the usual free speech rules in the public schools cannot rest on a theory of delegation but must instead be based on some special characteristic of the school setting. The special characteristic that is relevant in this case is the threat to the physical safety of students ... But due to the special features of the school environment, school officials must have greater authority to intervene before speech leads to violence. And, in most cases, *Tinker's* "substantial disruption" standard permits school officials to step in before actual violence erupts. (p. 3)

Applying the above standards, it would appear that *Hazelwood, Fraser, Tinker,* and *Morse* would all apply to student speech conducted through the district Internet system or transmitted by students using their personal digital devices while on campus. However, when student speech originates off-campus, it appears that only *Tinker* and *Morse* would apply.

Numerous cases have held that the *Tinker* substantial disruption standard applies to student speech that originated off-campus. These cases have involved off-campus student newspapers, as well as cases related to student online speech. Further, intervention by school officials has been upheld in situations where there were reasons to predict the potential of school violence or significant disruption of the delivery of instruction or school operations. For example, schools can prevent students from wearing confederate symbols if there has been a history of racial violence (Mahling, 1996); or they can respond to student off-campus speech that provides directions for how to hack the school's computer (*Boucher v. School Board of the School District of Greenfield*, 1998).

All but one of the off-campus online speech cases involved student speech directed at a school staff member. In these cases, the courts have generally held that the school must demonstrate that this speech has or could lead to a substantial disruption in the delivery of instruction or school operations, not merely disruption of a staff member.

The most important case addressing the issue of speech that has been directed at a student who is now feeling unsafe or is unable to learn or participate in school activities is *Saxe v. State College Area School District* (2001) – a decision that was written by then-Judge Alito whose language from the Supreme Court decision on *Morse* was quoted above. The State College Area School District's anti-harassment policy had been challenged on the basis that it was overbroad and could impact speech that someone might find merely offensive. The Court did find some of the provisions were overbroad, but in discussing various provisions of the policy, the Court noted:

> "We agree that the Policy's first prong, which prohibits speech that would "substantially interfer[e] with a student's educational performance," may satisfy the Tinker standard. The primary function of a public school is to educate its students; conduct that substantially interferes with the mission is, almost by definition, disruptive to the school environment. (pp. 47–48)

Note specifically the use of the term "a" student – which leads to the presumption that school officials can respond to student speech that interferes with the rights of any individual student, not the school or school activities. Further, the court appeared to be drawing a close connection between the two prongs of *Tinker*, essentially stating that speech that substantially interferes with a student's education constitutes a substantial disruption. Further, the Court noted that to establish a significant interference with a student's education requires both the subjective perspective of the student and an objective perspective. This decision is very important from the perspective of cyberbullying, because most often student speech is being directed at one student and the disruption or interference is solely of that student's ability to feel safe at school and learn.

Thus, looking at all of this case law, it appears that school officials have the legal authority to respond to student off-campus online speech in situations where this speech has caused, or there are particular reasons to believe it will cause, a substantial disruption at school or interference with the rights of students to be secure. This might involve the threat of violent altercations between students, significant interference with the delivery or instruction, or a situation where, based on both a subjective and objective perspective, there has been a significant interference with the ability of any student to receive an education. However, school officials cannot respond to student off-campus speech merely because they find the speech offensive or contrary to the school's educational mission.

Let's consider this standard from a different perspective. If the off-campus online speech of a student or students has caused, or there are good reasons to believe it could cause, physical violence between students at school, a significant interference in the ability of teachers to teach and students to learn, or if it is preventing any other student from feeling safe at school and learning or participating in other school activities, would any rational individual argue that school officials should not respond?

From a school administrator perspective, the factors that must be considered include those shown in the following list. School administrators can use this list as a "checklist" when they are considering whether or not their response to a student's off-campus speech is warranted.

- *Notice.* It is prudent for districts to ensure that their disciplinary policy provides clear notice to students and their parents that the school can and will discipline students for off-campus speech that causes or threatens a substantial disruption at school or interference with rights of any other students to be secure and receive an education.
- *School "nexus" or impact.* If a school administrator intends to respond, there needs to be a nexus between the off-campus online

speech and the school community and an impact that has or is predicted to occur at school. In this context, "school" includes school-sponsored field trips, extracurricular activities, sporting events, and transit to and from school or such activities. Therefore, administrators could respond if student speech could lead to violence at a school football game.

- *Impact has occurred or is reasonably foreseeable.* School administrators must be able to point to a specific and particular reason why they believe a substantial disruption or interference will occur. Timing is an issue. Their formal response needs to be for the purpose of preventing a foreseeable substantial disruption or interference.
- *Material and substantial impact.* The impact must be (or it must be reasonably foreseeable that it will be) significant. This does not include school official anger or annoyance, disapproval of the expression of a controversial opinion, or speech that is contrary to the educational mission of the school. The impact must also be more than simply a situation that requires a school administrator to investigate.
- *Disruption of school or interference with rights of students.* The speech must have caused, or it must be reasonably foreseeable that it will cause: significant interference with instructional activities, school activities, or school operations; physical or verbal violent altercations; or significant interference with a student's ability to participate in educational programs or school activities. It is necessary to assess the interference with students' education based on the target's subjective response and a reasonable observer perspective. Thus, a school administrator should keep records regarding how the targeted student is responding, so that if there are any questions, an objective third party reviewing this would agree that the student's response was justified.
- *Causal relationship.* The speech has to be, or it must be reasonably foreseeable that it will, be the actual cause of the disruption.

Unfortunately, sometimes when parents contact school officials because their child is being harmed by other students in off-campus postings, the response of the administrator is "off-campus, not my job." The reason for this response is that the legal standards have not been made clear to many administrators. If the off-campus speech is clearly preventing a student from feeling safe at school and receiving an education, school officials must have the authority to respond to protect the right of that student to receive an education.

When can school personnel monitor or search
student Internet records?

It is important to determine whether and to what degree school personnel may monitor or search student Internet records for cyberbullying and other inappropriate speech. School personnel may attempt to address cyberbullying through monitoring and searching of students' Internet records on campus. Under what conditions are such actions permissible, and when may they violate Fourth Amendment prohibitions against unreasonable searches and seizures?

The Supreme Court, in the case of *New Jersey v. T.L.O.* (1985), considered whether school officials violated the rights of a high school girl when an assistant vice principal searched her purse and found marijuana and evidence of drug dealing. The Court ruled that teachers or other school officials may legitimately search a student if: (a) there are reasonable grounds for suspecting that the search will produce evidence that the student has violated (or is currently violating) a law or a school rule, and (b) the measures adopted in conducting the search are "reasonably related to the objectives of the search and not excessively intrusive in light of the age and sex of the student and the nature of the infraction" (p. 342).

In light of the Court's decision in *T.L.O.*, most schools have developed search and seizure policies for student desks and lockers. Typically, these policies note that students should expect limited privacy in the contents of their desks and lockers, and they stipulate that general inspections may occur on a regular basis (Willard, 2006). More specific searches of individual desks or lockers may be conducted where school personnel have reasonable suspicion of the presence of items that are illegal or that may provide evidence of activities that are illegal or against school rules. As Willard (2006) notes, "these same standards can be applied in the context of analysis of Internet usage records and computer files" (p. 61).

There is arguably a higher degree of expectation of privacy in students' records that are maintained on their personal digital devices, computers, or cell phones, as long as those records have not been publicly shared, even if the devices are used at school. The extent of privacy of these records is under some debate. However, there are federal and state laws that protect the privacy of electronic communications. The Electronic Communications Privacy Act (1986) provides protections at a federal level. States also have similar state statutes protecting the privacy of electronic communications.

In 2006, a federal court in Pennsylvania applied the *T.L.O.* reasonableness standard in the context of a search of cell phone records in the case of *Klump v. Nazareth Area School District* (2006). In *Klump*, a teacher had confiscated a student's cell phone because it was visible in class, which was a violation of a school policy that prohibited the display or use of cell phones during instructional time. An administrator then searched through the student's stored text messages, voicemail, and phone number directory. The student filed a suit, asserting that these actions constituted an unreasonable search.

The court determined that the district had reasonable suspicion that the display/use policy was violated, but it did not have reasonable suspicion that any other law or policy had been violated. Thus, the confiscation of the cell phone was justified, but the search of the phone records violated the student's Fourth Amendment rights.

Litigation is emerging in other situations of a similar nature. It appears that sometimes when school administrators confiscate a student's cell phone simply because it was used during a time that was inappropriate, they believe they have the right to look through all of the phone's records. Clearly, this is not the case. Administrators only have the right to search through the records if the circumstances that led to the seizure provide reasonable suspicion that a search of the records will review evidence that the student had violated the law or a policy. That a cell phone was simply used when it should not have been used provides no justification to search any records. Being used in class during a test would provide reasonable suspicion that would justify looking at the recent text messages to see if the student was cheating. A credible report that a student has been distributing a nude image would provide reasonable suspicion to justify looking at photos.

However, there are several additional complicating factors. One of these is the question of which standard applies when a law officer is called to the school in relation to an intention to search. This is most likely to occur in situations where the cyberbullying also involves the distribution of nude images. Does the reasonable suspicion standard apply, or must the officer establish probable cause and obtain a search warrant or obtain consent to search? Or can the officer search if there are exigent circumstances – an important need to search to protect the safety of someone whose image is being distributed? If a law officer does not have a search warrant, that officer must obtain consent. This consent must be knowing and voluntary – that is, the student must know that he or she has the ability to refuse consent. Can a school administrator search without consent? This is unclear. Should students and their parents be advised of their right to refuse consent to search by a law officer without a search warrant? The standards in this area are unclear, and vary based on interpretations in different states. Obviously, this is an issue that must be addressed with the district's legal counsel.

Because of the lack of clarity in this area, no school staff members, other than the school administrators, should make a decision about the appropriateness of a search. This is simply too complicated an area to seek to communicate these standards to other staff. Staff should only confiscate a device and then give it to the administrator.

School Policies Related to Cyberbullying

As mentioned earlier in this chapter, more than half of all states in the U.S. have passed bullying laws that encourage or require schools to develop policies addressing bullying among students. Many administrators have created such policies even when not legally required to do so. With the recent attention to cyberbullying among students, administrators are increasingly grappling with whether and how to address cyberbullying and related behaviors within the school's bullying policies and within policies that govern acceptable uses of technology by students. We will discuss trends in the development of these policies and provide examples of language from actual and sample policies in the field. In establishing any such policies, administrators are again encouraged to consult legal counsel and be mindful of the need to protect students' First Amendment rights (as established by the U.S. Supreme Court in its *Tinker, Fraser, Hazelwood,* and *Morse* decisions) and Fourth Amendment rights (consistent with the Supreme Court's decision in *T.L.O.*) that were outlined earlier.

Bullying policies

Although most bullying laws require school districts to develop policies on bulling, these policies vary dramatically from district to district, as do the sample/model policies on bullying that are developed by state departments of education or other state-level organizations (Swearer, Limber, & Alley, 2009). As Swearer and colleagues (2009) note, "well-written policies can lay the foundation for clear communication about expectations for appropriate behavior and consequences for bullying behaviors" (p. 39). Careful implementation of such policies also communicates to the entire school community (as well as broader community) the serious nature of bullying.

We recommend that school bullying policies include the following key elements (see also, Swearer, Espelage, & Napolitano, 2009; U.S. Department of Education, 2010)[1]:

1. A clear and appropriate definition of bullying and a non-exclusive list of behaviors that constitute bullying. In order to avoid possible inconsistency and confusion, the definition should be consistent with the definition provided in the state's statute. Where no state law exists or where a statute fails to define bullying, officials are encouraged to adopt a definition consistent with that used by researchers and practitioners in the field (see Chapter 2), which includes direct as well as indirect forms of bullying, including cyberbullying.

2. Clear prohibitions against bullying, which cover bullying that occurs on school campus, at school-sponsored activities or events, on school-provided transportation, through school-owned technology, or that otherwise creates a significant disruption to the school environment (see e.g., U.S. Department of Education, 2010). Language should be added to address off-campus bullying, such as the language in the Massachusetts statute:

   > Bullying shall be prohibited ... at a location, activity, function or program that is not school-related or through the use of technology or an electronic device that is not owned, leased or used by a school district or school, if the bullying creates a hostile environment at the school for the victim, infringes on the rights of the victim at school or materially and substantially disrupts the education process or the orderly operation of a school. (ALM GL ch. 71 § 370, 2010)

   Prohibitions should also cover behaviors that "perpetuat[e] bullying by spreading hurtful or demeaning material even if the material was created by another person (e.g., forwarding offensive e-mails or text messages)" (U.S. Department of Education, 2010, p. 3).

3. Procedures for students, family members, staff, and others to report bullying, including a process to report anonymously. The procedure also should clearly identify appropriate school personnel to receive

reports (U.S. Department of Education, 2010). For example, New
Jersey's model policy states:

> All board of education members, school employees, and volunteers and
> contracted service providers who have contact with students, are
> required to verbally report alleged violations of this policy to the prin-
> cipal or the principal's designee on the same day when the individual
> witnessed or received reliable information regarding any such incident.
> All board of education members, school employees, and volunteers and
> contracted service providers who have contact with students, also shall
> submit a report in writing to the school principal within two school
> days of the verbal report...Students, parents, and visitors are encour-
> aged to report alleged violations of this policy to the principal on the
> same day when the individual witnessed or received reliable informa-
> tion regarding any such incident. Students, parents, and visitors may
> report an act of harassment intimidation or bullying anonymously.
> (State of New Jersey, Department of Education, 2011, p. 18)

The New Jersey Department of Education further encourages school
district policy makers to take into account that:

> The goal of a reporting procedure is to facilitate the identification,
> investigation and response to alleged violations of this policy by mak-
> ing the reporting process prompt, simple and non-threatening. The
> district should consider every mechanism available to simplify report-
> ing, ... including standard reporting forms and Web-based reporting
> mechanisms. For anonymous reporting, schools should consider locked
> boxes located in areas of the school where reports can be submitted
> without fear of being observed. (State of New Jersey, Department of
> Education, 2011, p. 18)

Policies also should address retaliation against individuals who report
bullying. Delaware's Model Bully Prevention Policy suggests the
following language relevant to retaliation: "The District further prohibits reprisal, retaliation or false accusation against a target, witness
or one with reliable information about an act of bullying" (n.d., p. 1).

4. Prompt investigation of bullying reports. School policies should include
    procedures for prompt investigation of all reports of bullying and
    appropriate responses to these reports. These responses should include
    immediate intervention strategies to protect a bullied student, notifica-
    tion of his or her parents, and notification of the parents of the alleged
    perpetrator (U.S. Department of Education, 2010).

5. Consequences for bullying. Policies should identify appropriate conse-
    quences for bullying behavior and note that the particular action taken
    will depend on the characteristics of the student(s) involved and the
    situation (Swearer et al., 2009). For example, Michigan's model policy
    (Michigan State Board of Education Model Anti-Bullying Policy, n.d.)
    states:

> Consequences for a student who commits an act of bullying and harass-
> ment shall vary in method and severity according to the nature of the
> behavior, the developmental age of the student, and the student's history
> of problem behaviors and performance, and must be consistent with the
> board of education's approved code of students conduct. Remedial meas-
> ures shall be designed to: correct the problem behavior; prevent another
> occurrence of the behavior; and protect the victim of the act. (p. 4)

Similarly, Massachusetts' Model Bullying Prevention and Intervention
Plan (Massachusetts Department of Elementary and Secondary
Education, 2010) states:

> Upon the principal or designees determining that bullying or retaliation
> has occurred, the law requires that the school or district use a range of
> responses that balance the need for accountability with the need to teach
> appropriate behavior…If the principal or designees decides that discipli-
> nary action is appropriate, the disciplinary action will be determined on
> the basis of facts found by the principal or designee, including the nature
> of the conduct, the age of the student(s) involved, and the need to balance
> accountability with the teaching of appropriate behavior. (pp. 10–11)

New Jersey's Department of Education provides the following minimum model policy language for school districts:

> The district board of education authorizes the principal of each school to
> define the range of ways in which school staff will respond once an inci-
> dent of harassment, intimidation or bullying is confirmed…The district
> board of education recognizes that some acts of harassment, intimida-
> tion or bullying may be isolated incidents requiring that the school offi-
> cials respond appropriately to the individuals committing the acts. Other
> acts may be so serious or parts of a larger pattern of harassment, intimi-
> dation or bullying that they require a response either at the classroom,
> school building or school district levels or by law enforcement officials.
> (State of New Jersey, Department of Education, 2011, p. 22)

6. Support and referral services for students and families. Policies should include language that directs school staff to assess children who are bullied for possible problems that may have resulted from the bullying and provide support and referrals for these children and their families, as warranted. Similarly, policies should direct staff to provide support and referrals, as needed, for children who are involved in bullying, as well as their families.

7. Training and prevention. Policies should include a provision for school districts to provide training for all staff to prevent, identify, and appropriately respond to bullying, including cyberbullying. For example, in Iowa's Sample Anti-Bullying/Anti-Harassment Policy (n.d.), the following language is optional but strongly suggested:

> The superintendent ... is responsible for organizing training programs for students, school officials, faculty, staff, and volunteers who have direct contact with students. The training will include how to recognize harassment and what to do in case a student is harassed. It will also include proven effective harassment prevention strategies. The superintendent will also develop a process for evaluating the effectiveness of the policy in reducing bullying and harassment ...

Policies addressing use of technology by students

Most schools have developed policies that address acceptable uses of technology by students and Internet safety and security issues. (As noted earlier, all schools that receive funding from the "E-rate" program are required to do so under the Children's Internet Protection Act [2007].) Within these policies, administrators should provide clear prohibitions against cyberbullying and related behavior and clarify procedures for monitoring or searching students' Internet records.

Prohibitions against use of cyber technology to cyberbully

Many schools have expressly prohibited cyberbullying and related behavior in their acceptable use policies. For example, in its administrative rules, Cobb County (GA) School District (2008) prohibits:

1. Accessing, sending, creating or posting material or communication that is:
   a. Damaging;
   b. Abusive;
   c. Obscene, lewd, profane, offensive, indecent, sexually explicit, or pornographic;

d. Threatening or demeaning to another person; or
e. Contrary to the District's Rules on harassment and/or bullying.
2. Posting anonymous or forging electronic communications.

The U.S. Department of Justice (n.d.) provides a Model Acceptable Use Policy for Information Technology Resources in the Schools, which requires, in part, that students:

- Respect and practice the principles of community.
  - Communicate only in ways that are kind and respectful.
  - Report threatening or discomforting materials to a teacher.
  - Not intentionally access, transmit, copy, or create material that violates the school's code of conduct (such as messages that are pornographic, threatening, rude, discriminatory, or meant to harass).
  - Not intentionally access, transmit, copy, or create material that is illegal (such as obscenity, stolen materials, or illegal copies of copyrighted works).
  - Not use the resources to further other acts that are criminal or violate the school's code of conduct.
  - Not send spam, chain letters, or other mass unsolicited mailings.
  - Not buy, sell, advertise, or otherwise conduct business, unless approved as a school project.

In their acceptable use policies or behavior codes, some school districts also address use of technology off of school grounds. When doing so, they should be careful to be in compliance with the *Tinker* standard, which allows suppression of speech if there is material disruption to class work, substantial disorder, or invasion of others' rights. For example, the Prince William County, Maryland (2009) Acceptable Use and Internet Safety Policy states the following:

> PWCS reserves the right to discipline students or employees for actions taken off-campus, which would violate this Regulation if occurring on-site, if such actions adversely affect the safety, well-being, or performance of students while in school, on school buses, at school activities, or coming to and from school; if such actions threaten violence against another student or employee, if such actions violate local, state or federal law, or School Board policies or regulations or the Code of Behavior, or if such actions disrupt the learning environment, administration, or orderly conduct of the school.

Notification of students' privacy limits

In order to ensure that school policies do not violate students' Fourth Amendment rights (i.e., are in accordance with the *T.L.O.* standards) and to help deter improper use of school computers, administrators are advised to establish user policies that notify students about the limits of their privacy and the likelihood of routine monitoring of files. Willard (2006) recommends the following model policy language:

> Users have a limited expectation of privacy in the contents of their personal files, communication files, and record of web research activities on the district's Internet system. Routine maintenance and monitoring, utilizing both technical monitoring systems and staff monitoring, may lead to discovery that a user has violated district policy or the law. An individual search will be conducted if there is reasonable suspicion that a user has violated district policy or the law. Students' parents have the right to request to see the contents of their children's files and records. (p. 62)

Willard (2006) also recommends that administrators provide reminders on log-in screens and in school computer labs about students' limited expectations of privacy.

Conclusions

With the recent flurry of public interest in cyberbullying and the focus on the harms that it may cause, many school administrators are concerned about meeting their ethical and legal duties to protect students without infringing on their constitutionally protected rights. Some administrators are considering whether and how cyberbullying fits with their existing policies about bullying and/or the appropriate uses of school technology. Others, perhaps prompted by state laws that increasingly require district or school-wide policies on cyberbullying, are developing new policies that include attention to cyberbullying.

Whether developing new policies or refining existing policies about bullying, we encourage administrators to become well acquainted with current research on students' use of emerging technologies, the nature and prevalence of cyberbullying and other forms of bullying among children and youth, and best practices in preventing and addressing bullying; this research finds that bullying is best addressed through comprehensive school-wide efforts. As local policies will be most effective where they reflect unique assets and needs of the community, we encourage administrators to develop these policies through a process that involves input from all relevant stakeholders, including educators, parents, and students (see also Alley & Limber, 2009). Finally, administrators (and their legal counsel) should be aware of the variety of state and federal laws that may be relevant to these policies.

As is often the case in any rapidly changing legal landscape, there remains some uncertainty about how U.S. law may be applied to forms of cyber speech, particularly those that occur away from school grounds. However, it appears clear that schools may, under certain circumstances, be held liable under state or federal laws for failing to address cyberbullying or harassment. Under many state laws, students (or parents on their behalf) may bring claims of negligence against school personnel for failing to use reasonable care to protect students from foreseeable harms caused by cyberbullying. Under a variety of federal laws, students who are members of protected classes may bring lawsuits against schools or school districts for injuries arising out of peer-on-peer harassment based on race, gender, or disability.

In their efforts to protect students from harms caused by cyberbullying, it appears that administrators may legitimately suppress cyber speech that takes place on school grounds under certain conditions: (a) If the speech constitutes a threat; (b) if it is lewd, vulgar, or profane; (c) where the speech is (or appears to be) sponsored by the school; or (d) when it materially disrupts the school or the rights of others. In addition, following precedent set in cases involving searches of school lockers and desks, it appears that students should expect limited privacy in the contents of their computers at school and that administrators may make general inspections of school computers and Internet accounts on a regular basis. More specific searches of computers or accounts may be conducted where school personnel have reasonable suspicion of the presence of content that is illegal or that may provide evidence of activities that are illegal or against school rules.

Lest our legal review leave readers with the inaccurate impression that administrators' primary goals should be to avoid liability, we conclude this chapter with a reminder that, in developing and enforcing sound policies that focus on the prevention of bullying (including cyberbullying), administrators will not only decrease the chances that legal action will be brought against schools and school districts but they will, more importantly, decrease the likelihood that children will continue to suffer from being bullied.

Note

1. All such provisions should be carefully analyzed to ensure that they are consistent with state law. To the extent that provisions of state laws are viewed to be unclear or too narrow, administrators may want to seek legal guidance to expand or clarify provisions in their policies (Swearer et al., 2009).

8

CONCLUSION

Lauren, an 8th grade student, was startled when she was walking down the hall at school one morning and a male student said, "Hey Lauren, I saw your MySpace last night." Lauren was puzzled because she didn't have a "MySpace", and she wasn't really sure what one was. Fortunately, she had a close relationship with her school counselor and went to see her to get advice. The counselor contacted Lauren's mother to let her know about the incident, and shared with her a link to the MySpace page that allows an individual to report a false profile. The counselor and parent were unable to locate the actual profile and were unsure what screen name was used for the profile since a search under Lauren's first and last name did not show any profile evidence.

Fortunately, the school administrators did not let such a roadblock stop them in addressing the situation. The counselor spoke to the boy who had made the remark to Lauren and asked for his help in locating the name of the profile. In addition, she asked Lauren to see if any of her friends knew anything about the profile. In fact, a friend of Lauren's overheard two class-mates on the school bus admit to setting up the profile.

The administrator and counselor met with the classmates separately to explain the seriousness of impersonating another individual online, and to give them a warning that this was cyberbullying. They asked the students to remove the profile, and warned them against any retaliation toward Lauren. The counselor and administrator let the students know that they would be monitoring the situation with Lauren closely. They also contacted the parents of the students involved. While the students admitted that they had set up the profile, they initially were quick to blame each other. The admin-istration, however, emphasized the seriousness and cruelty of the incident,

Cyberbullying: Bullying in the Digital Age, Second Edition. Robin M. Kowalski,
Susan P. Limber, and Patricia W. Agatston.
© 2012 Robin M. Kowalski, Susan P. Limber, and Patricia W. Agatston.
Published 2012 by Blackwell Publishing Ltd.

and one of the students was so affected by their conversation that she remarked, "I am going to apologize to Lauren right now!"

We have attempted to present a thorough overview of what we currently know about cyberbullying; where it is similar to and dissimilar from traditional forms of bullying; what strategies educators, parents, and community members can take to prevent cyberbullying; and how adults can intervene effectively when it occurs. As highlighted in Chapter 4, there are still many areas where questions remain that require further research, and, as noted in Chapter 7, relevant laws and policies are still evolving. These limitations, however, should not keep parents, educators, and other adults from responding to and addressing cyberbullying. As demonstrated in the above incident, which occurred in a school where one of the authors consults, adults can be proactive in the face of limited information and limited school policies. A willingness on the part of adults to monitor online behavior, teach social skills, and protect youth who are harassed on or off campus, through traditional or cyberbullying, will enable adults to respond effectively to our children's desire to socialize online.

What We Know and What We Question

We have noted throughout this book that youth spend significant amounts of time online, and that the overwhelming majority (93%) of preteens and teens have Internet access (Lenhart, 2010). We also have discussed the many ways that young people bully others online, whether through instant messaging (the most common form of cyberbullying among American children), e-mail, or postings on social networking sites such as Facebook. Youth are assuming others' identities through stolen passwords to e-mail or instant message accounts, and entire Web sites have been created to target classmates or teachers. Cyberbullying through the use of cellular phones and smart phones is also common and is particularly challenging for parents and educators to monitor, because cellular phones are, by nature, more private, and are often readily accessible to the cyberbully. With Facebook and other social networking applications readily available on many cell phones, it seems reasonable to expect that cyberbullying via cellular phone will increase as students find it easier to target their peers through posting comments on Facebook or MySpace in addition to text messaging throughout the day.

As outlined in Chapters 3 and 4, our review of the research indicates that cyberbullying is a form of bullying behavior that is prevalent among adolescents and for which policies are needed (Kowalski & Limber, 2007;

Tokunaga, 2010; Ybarra et al., 2006). It is important to recognize that, as with traditional bullying, young people are more likely to engage in cyber-bullying if they believe that adults and bystanders are unlikely to intervene (Williams & Guerra, 2007). This same research indicates that students perceive adults to be less likely to intervene in bullying that occurs over the Internet, which may help explain the prevalence rates of cyberbullying behavior.

Recent research (Kowalski & Fedina, 2011) highlights the need to focus attention on the cyberbullying experiences of special needs populations. Although the prevalence rates of cyberbullying victimization obtained in this study were similar to those observed among children without disabili-ties, the significant online presence of children with disabilities as a means of lubricating their "social" interactions highlights the need to include these populations in prevention and intervention efforts.

The research also suggests that cyberbullying behavior is not limited to adolescents. Rather, college students (Kowalski et al., 2012) and working individuals (Giumetti et al., 2011) report considerable exposure to electronic bullying. Whatever the age of the targets and perpetrators, the consequences of exposure to cyberbullying may be significant and, in some cases, fatal (Hinduja & Patchin, 2010b).

Though still relatively early in its development, research on cyberbullying has spanned several countries. As discussed in Chapter 4, although the prev-alence rates and methods of cyberbullying vary slightly from one country to another, most, if not all, developed countries are being forced to deal with this phenomenon (see Shariff, 2008). As attention to cyberbullying contin-ues to increase, it will be important that researchers and policy-makers adopt an interdisciplinary and multicultural approach to the topic.

While we are learning more about cyberbullying, there is still much that is unknown about this new form of bullying. The research on traditional bullying presented in Chapter 2 provided a context for examining how cyberbullying is similar to and different from traditional bullying. The defi-nition of traditional bullying that is widespread involves behavior that is repeated, intentionally aggressive and based on an imbalance of power. Cyberbullying often meets the definition of intentionally aggressive behav-ior. Although cyberbullying shares these characteristics, questions may be raised about the repetitiveness of actions online. Might repeated viewings of a one-time posting of an aggressive message constitute cyberbullying? This issue needs further clarification and research. Similarly, the nature of an online power imbalance also warrants further attention. We suspect that the Internet is such a powerful (and often anonymous) tool that the ability to reach vast audiences with a single mouse click frequently tilts the balance of power in favor of the perpetrator of cyberbullying. Power also can result simply from technological expertise. Again, this is an issue that needs further exploration by researchers.

Chapter 2 also explained the myriad of harmful consequences that both perpetrators and victims of traditional bullying may experience. That these effects also follow from cyberbullying was discussed in Chapter 4. Research by two of the authors suggests that children who experience cyberbullying or are provocative victims have higher rates of anxiety than students who cyberbully others or those who are not involved at all (Kowalski & Limber, 2011). Youth who are cyber bully/victims report higher level of depression, anxiety, and school absences relative to individuals not involved with cyberbullying (Kowalski & Limber, 2011). Research has also confirmed that two out of five youths (particularly pre-adolescents) who are targets of Internet harassment experience emotional distress (Ybarra et al., 2006). Our individual and focus group interviews suggest that at least some students avoid school, have their academic performance affected, and experience damaged relationships after enduring cyberbullying, but other young people emerge relatively unscathed from such incidents. Additional research on possible effects of cyberbullying is needed, including studies that examine which forms of cyberbullying and what conditions surrounding the cyberbullying may be particularly harmful for youth.

We noted in Chapter 4 that there is even less research available regarding the perpetrators of cyberbullying; however, the Kowalski and Limber (2011) study suggests that students who cyberbully have slightly lower self-esteem than those not involved in cyberbullying at all (although cyber victims and bully/victims appear to have still lower self-esteem than cyberbullies). We also noted in Chapter 4 that the perpetrators of cyberbullying share feelings of enjoyment, power and/or revenge as motivations for their actions (Kowalski & Witte, 2006). Such motives are obvious cause for concern and are deserving of further study.

How Can We Use This Information to Prevent Cyberbullying?

As we have learned from the research on traditional bullying, when youth participate in activities with little or no adult supervision, bullying often thrives. Youths' use of technology is no exception, and we hope that this book will be a wakeup call to parents and educators that youth need more guidance, training, and supervision when utilizing the myriad of technologies that are both available to them and integral parts of their lives. Such guidance also needs to be offered in a developmentally appropriate manner, recognizing that supervision of a 10-year-old will be different than supervision of a 16-year-old. Just as parents and educators provide developmentally appropriate supervision in children's activities at home and school, adults need to provide such supervision and guidance in children's online activities as well. The following conversation that took place during one of our middle school girls' focus groups demonstrates the range of involvement of parents in their children's online lives. The comments were made by 13- and 14-year-old students in the group.

> "If you have a MySpace, let your parents check it."
>
> "My mom doesn't know that I have a MySpace."
>
> "Noooooo!"
>
> "I don't tell my mom what goes on at school … for my mom to see my MySpace, well she would have a lot of questions."
>
> "My mom wouldn't approve of a lot of my friends. She wouldn't want them at my house because some of my friends have very big potty mouths."
>
> "I don't have any dirty comments on my MySpace."

Keep in mind that these are not 17-year-olds discussing their MySpace; the majority of these girls were 13 years of age. This is clearly an age where it would be developmentally appropriate for parents to provide guidance to a child setting up a personal profile online. Yet, only two of the focus group participants suggested that their MySpace would meet parental approval.

We also recommend that parents educate themselves regarding each new piece of technology they consider purchasing for their children, and that they spend time discussing with their children acceptable and unacceptable uses of such technology and possible consequences for violations. Parents who learn to use the technology that their children operate will be better prepared to monitor its use. Staying in touch with popular youth technology will facilitate more communication between a parent and child about such devices. Parents can educate themselves about various technologies by talking to salespersons, computer experts, and searching for information online. In addition, school and community organizations can assist by hosting frequent parent workshops on the Internet as well as other popular youth technologies. Such workshops on "technology and youth" should include both positive uses and potential abuses and would greatly assist parents in navigating the rapidly evolving world of technology. It is recommended that a "teen expert" panel be present when possible to update adults on the current trends and uses of social media.

In addition to providing supervision, adults need to teach youth how to communicate effectively online. Adults can make use of some of the key research findings described in this book in order to help shape the developmentally appropriate messages they give youth about Internet behavior. Because of the higher prevalence rates of cyberbullying in middle school, prevention messages need to begin prior to middle school. Parents and educators should begin to provide messages about appropriate online behavior in primary school so that youth receive consistent messages beginning at early ages. As children increasingly use computers and cellular phones at ever younger ages, it is recommended that lessons on "digital citizenship" be infused throughout the curriculum.

As discussed in Chapter 4, because cyberbullying can be a form of online retaliation by victims of traditional bullying, we encourage educators to do everything possible to address traditional bullying at school to avoid bully–victim conflicts from escalating online. Incorporating research-based bullying prevention programs that also discuss cyberbullying is an important step in the prevention of cyberbullying in schools. While some schools may wish to incorporate curricula specific to cyberbullying, we recommend that such curricula tie into a comprehensive bullying prevention program that focuses on steps that bystanders can take to prevent or intervene in any form of bullying behavior among their peers. In addition to educating students about cyberbullying, teachers and administration need training regarding the seriousness of cyberbullying, and school districts should include cyberbullying in their acceptable use of technology polices and their bullying policies.

Youth who believe that cyberbullying is just a form of "online entertainment" need messages from their schools and communities that such behavior is, in fact, a form of bullying that is malicious and may have far-reaching consequences. Internet Service Providers, as well as Web sites popular among youth, often have acceptable use policies that provide guidelines for using their services, plus consequences for violation of the guidelines. Many of these youth-oriented Web sites include safety tips and guidelines for appropriate "netiquette" that parents can review with their children.

Young people also need to be aware that some forms of online bullying, including sexting, may be considered criminal acts. While laws differ across countries and states, cyberbullying may meet the definition of libel, harassment, stalking, or even sexual exploitation in a given community. The myth of online anonymity is another issue presented in Chapter 3 that needs to be addressed in our prevention efforts. Youth who falsely believe that posting under a screen name protects their true identities may be more likely to abstain from cyberbullying if they realize that comments can still be traced back to their accounts.

The media could also be a tool for prevention. Youth can create positive "social norming" campaigns that illustrate that most youth do not partici-pate in cyberbullying and do not think it is right to hurt others online. Youth are heavily influenced by their peers, and it can be very powerful for them to realize that they are part of the larger group who is making healthy choices online. Student-produced posters and video public service announcements can create a positive atmosphere and increase positive bystander behavior by "norming" appropriate and helpful behavior around bullying that occurs online or offline.

How Can We Use This Information to Intervene in Cyberbullying?

In Chapters 5 and 6, we have attempted to provide helpful tips for both parents and educators to respond to cyberbullying, and we outlined the legal obligations of educators in Chapter 7. While a variety of actions are possible when dealing with cyberbullying, many educators and parents are unfamiliar with how to intervene (or are unsure of their legal obligations or limits in doing so) and do not begin to educate themselves until a child or student has been victimized. In addition, adults cannot intervene if they do not know that abuses are occurring. As mentioned throughout this book, participants in our focus groups indicate that students are reluctant to report cyberbullying because they lack confidence in adults' ability to provide assistance or intervene effectively without making matters worse. Punishing the victim by banning his or her use of technology or telling students that educators are not able to intervene in cyberbullying situa-tions will decrease young people's trust in adults and further discourage them from reporting abuse. Adults need to encourage youth to report cyberbullying by frequently discussing cyberbullying, providing non-threatening and, in some cases anonymous, reporting mechanisms at school, and explaining and reassuring students that adults can be of assistance. Adults at home can respond proactively by reminding children that if they are bullied online they will be supported rather than punished for telling an adult. Adults who take time to familiarize themselves with the technologies that are popular with youth will be more likely to intervene quickly and calmly when cyberbullying occurs. In addition, school administrators should work closely with local law enforcement when cyberbullying and cyber threats become criminal in nature and take time to conduct a thorough investigation and craft an appropriate multidisciplinary response.

We noted in Chapter 5 that if the parents of a targeted student learn that the perpetrator of the cyberbullying is a student at their child's school, they may need to meet with school officials and request assistance to end the abuse. Parents should be prepared to share evidence of the cyberbullying and also request investigation of any traditional bullying that may occur on campus. Educators need to support the targeted students and their parents by investigating and, where appropriate, having serious talks with the students engaged in cyberbullying behavior. They should also notify the parents of the student engaged in cyberbullying behavior if they have evidence to support the targeted student's claim. Of course, parents may also be able to contact the parents of the student engaged in cyberbullying on their own when it is not a fellow student, or when they wish to first attempt to end the cyberbullying without the school's involvement. However, such interactions may be emotionally charged and difficult to handle. Finally, student assistance team staff (administrators, counselors, psychologists, and social workers) may find a restorative justice model, as outlined in Chapter 6, useful in attempting to resolve cyberbullying situations in a manner that is beneficial to all parties and reduces the risk of retaliatory aggression.

In Chapters 5 and 6, we discussed how to report abuse posted or sent via text messages, e-mail, instant messages, and social networking sites, noting that many youth-oriented Web sites have links to report cyberbullying, and ISPs and cell phone providers are generally responsive to reports of cyberbullying over their networks. However, we recognize that new technologies and sites will continue to emerge that provide new opportunities for abuse. That is why we also recommend that adults use youth as resources, not only to mentor their peers on appropriate Internet use, but also to advise adults on the online activities that youth frequent.

Where Do We Go from Here?

Our narrow focus on cyberbullying was necessary to bring attention to this form of online abuse that has erupted quickly on our landscape. Yet discussions of cyberbullying really must be part of a larger dialogue about media literacy that is occurring in the United States and in many countries globally. Much attention has been given to the role that television has played in shaping our culture over the past 50 years. The suggestions that experts in the field give to parents for helping their children to become media literate and to mitigate the negative messages viewed via the television are also applicable, to a degree, to the Internet. The challenge to date is that "surfing the Internet" is largely a solitary habit; however, making it more of a family or community experience will help parents, educators, and youth leaders deal with some of the current concerns we face. Consider these tips advocated by media literacy expert Ronald Slaby:

> Parents, teachers, and other adults can directly alter the effects of media violence on children and youth when they watch programs and movies with them while commenting critically on the depiction of violence and discussing nonviolent alternatives; they also can teach media literacy skills that permit young viewers to "see through" the falseness of particular media presentations. (Slaby, 2002, p. 329)

In addition to watching television programs and movies with our children, it is time to "surf the Internet" with our children and teach the skills that are necessary to ensure that the use of the Internet is an educational and social enhancer, rather than a negative force in our children's lives. The 11th Annual Media Wise Video Game Report Card points out that "every child who engages in playing video games is undertaking a powerful, developmental experiment – the results of which we don't understand" (Walsh, Gentile, Walsh, & Bennett, 2006). The same could be said of the children who spend vast amounts of time online, whether through social networking sites, online gaming, instant messaging, or text messaging. As multiple new ways to interact online become available, the challenge to adults in general and parents in particular is to become familiar with the myriad of new methods by which youth are engaged in online activities, and to actively participate in these new technologies. Parents and educators need to address the online experiences of children by communicating media guidelines and expectations for appropriate use, defining and explaining why certain activities are inappropriate, setting time limits, and using effective monitoring tools. As the Video Game Report Card suggests, adults also need to "watch what your kids watch, play what your kids play" (Walsh et al., 2006, p. 2). In the online world, Walsh's advice could be adapted to include, "Visit the sites your kids visit, use the technologies your kids use."

Rather than focusing on only the negative aspects of social media, parents and educators can find ways to engage youth to use popular technologies in meaningful ways. As we discussed in Chapter 5, an example involves teaching youth how to use a social networking site to promote themselves in a positive manner that would appeal to prospective admissions counselors, employers, and, of course, friends. Older teens can lead discussions with younger students about the importance of protecting their privacy online and share their favorite tips for doing so. Educators can develop lessons that show young people appropriately posting their opinions on Web sites using engaging topics, such as the environment, politics, and community service. There may be a few adults who could benefit from this type of training as well!

Engaging our youth in a variety of activities where they are "unplugged" will make it easier to limit their time online. Inviting children to participate in regular physical activity and creative outlets such as art and music will be more effective than simply nagging a child to turn off the computer.

Finally, through a concerted effort to engage in the media experience of our children, the lines of communication can be opened and greater understanding gained, not only of the harmful uses of technology, but the many benefits that await our children who use technology wisely.

REFERENCES

A.C.A. Tit. 6, Subtit. 2, Ch. 18, Subch 5 Note (2010).

Aftab, P. (2011). http://www.wiredsafety.net.

Agatston, P., & Carpenter, M. (2006). Electronic bullying survey. Unpublished manuscript.

Agatston, P., Kowalski, R. M., & Limber, S. P. (2011). Youth views on cyber bullying. In J. Patchin & S. Hinduja (Eds.), *Cyberbullying prevention and response: Expert perspectives*. New York: Routledge.

Ahmed, E., & Braithwaite, V. (2004). Bullying and victimization: Cause for concern for both families and schools. *Social Psychology of Education, 7*, 35–54.

Akwagyiram, A. (2005, May 12). *Does "happy slapping" exist?* Retrieved from http://news.bbc.co.uk/1/hi/uk/4539913.stm.

Ali, R. (2010, October 26). *Dear Colleague Letter: Harassment and bullying.* Retrieved from http://www2.ed.gov/about/offices/list/ocr/letters/colleague-201010.pdf.

Alley, R., & Limber, S. P. (2009). Legal issues for school personnel. In S. M. Swearer, D. L. Espelage, & S. A. Napolitano (Eds.), *Bullying prevention and intervention: Realistic strategies for schools* (pp. 53–73). New York: Guilford.

ALM GL ch. 71, § 370 (2010).

Alonzo, M., & Aiken, M. (2004). Flaming in electronic communication. *Decision Support Systems, 36*, 205–213.

American Psychological Association Zero Tolerance Task Force (2008). Are zero tolerance policies effective in the schools? An evidentiary review and recommendations. *American Psychologist, 63*, 852–862.

Americans with Disabilities Act of 1990, 42 U.S.C. § 12134 (2006).

Anderson, M., Kaufman, J., Simon, T. R., Barrios, L., Paulozzi, L., Ryan, G., Hammond, R., Modzeleski, W., Feucht, T., Potter, L., & the School-Associated Violent Deaths Study Group (2001). School-associated violent deaths in the United States, 1994–1999. *Journal of the American Medical Association, 286*, 2695–2702.

Anthony, B. J., Wessler, S. L., & Sebian, J. K. (2010). Commentary: Guiding a public health approach to bullying. *Journal of Pediatric Psychology, 35*, 1113–1115.

Archive of CRN home page topics for discussion: On the fatal stabbing of a sixth-grade girl (2004, June 11). Retrieved from http://www.childresearch.net/cgi-bin/topics/column.pl?no=00215&page=1.

Arseneault, L., Bowes, L., & Shakoor, S. (2010). Bullying victimization in youths and mental health problems: Much ado about nothing? *Psychological Medicine: A Journal of Research in Psychiatry and the Allied Sciences, 40*, 717–729.

Arseneault, L., Walsh, E., Trzesniewski, K., Newcombe, R., Caspi, A., & Moffitt, T. E. (2006). Bullying victimization uniquely contributes to adjustment problems in young children: A nationally representative cohort study. *Pediatrics, 118*, 130–138.

Atlas, R. S., & Pepler, D. J. (1998). Observations of bullying in the classroom. *Journal of Educational Research, 92*, 86–99.

Attorney General to review 'happy-slap' sentence. (2010, August 29). Retrieved from http://www.bbc.co.uk/news/uk-england-london-10808090.

Axon, S. (2010, June 3). The "Star Wars Kid": Where is he now? Retrieved from http://mashable.com/2010/06/03/star-wars-kid/.

Baldry, A. C. (2003). Bullying in schools and exposure to domestic violence. *Child Abuse & Neglect, 27*, 713–732.

Baldry, A. C. (2004). "What about bullying?" An experimental field study to understand students' attitudes towards bullying and victimization in Italian middle schools. *British Journal of Educational Psychology, 74*, 583–598.

Bargh, J. A., McKenna, K. Y. A., & Fitzsimons, G. M. (2002). Can you see the real me? Activation and expression of the "true self" on the Internet. *Journal of Social Issues, 58*, 33–48.

Bauer, N., Lozano, P., & Rivara, F. P. (2007). The effectiveness of the Olweus Bullying Prevention Program in public middle schools: A controlled trial. *Journal of Adolescent Health, 40*, 266–274.

Baumrind, D. (1967). Child care practices anteceding three patterns of preschool behavior. *Genetic Psychology Monographs, 75*, 43–88.

Becker, K., & Schmidt, M. H. (2005). When kids seek help on-line: Internet chat rooms and suicide. *Reclaiming Children and Youth, 13*, 229–230.

Beder, M. (2006, May 23). Free speech fight hits Kirkwood High. *St. Louis Post-Dispatch*. Retrieved from http://www.stltoday.com/stltoday/news/Stories.nsf/education/story/CD0CE6B1B78A488D.

Belluck, P. (2006, July 2). Web postings worry summer camp directors. *The New York Times*. Retrieved from http://news.zdnet.com/2100-9588_22-6087060. html.

Belsey, B. (2006). Cyber bullying: An emerging threat to the "always on" generation. Retrieved from http://www.cyberbullying.ca.

Beran, T., & Li, Q. (2005). Cyber-harassment: A study of a new method for an old behavior. *Journal of Educational Computing Research, 32*, 265–277.

Bethel School District v. Fraser, 478 U.S. 675 (1986).

Biersdorfer, J. D. (2006, August 21). How to digitally hide (somewhat) in plain sight. *The New York Times*, p. B–3.

Bjorkqvist, K., Lagerspetz, K. M. J., & Osterman, K. (1992). The development of direct and indirect aggressive strategies in males and females. In K. Bjorkqvist & P. Niemela (Eds.), *Of mice and women: Aspects of female aggression* (pp. 51–64). San Diego, CA: Academic Press.

Black, S. (2003). An ongoing evaluation of the bullying prevention program in Philadelphia schools: Student survey and student observation data. Paper presented at the Safety in Numbers Conference, Atlanta, GA.

Black, S. A., & Jackson, E. (2007). Using bullying incident density to evaluate the Olweus Bullying Prevention Programme. *School Psychology International, 28*, 623–638.

Black's Law Dictionary (2009). 9th ed., B. A. Garner (Ed.). St. Paul, MN: West Group.

Blair, A., & Norfolk, A. (2004, September 25). Modern bullies are seeking victims through cyber space. *The Times (London)*, Home News, 3.

Boucher v. School Board of the School District of Greenfield, 134 F.3d 821 (7th Cir. 1998).

Boulton, M. J. (1994). Understanding and preventing bullying in the junior school playground. In P. K. Smith & S. Sharp (Eds.), *School bullying* (pp. 132–59). London: Routledge.

Boulton, M. J., & Underwood, K. (1992). Bully victim problems among middle school children. *British Journal of Educational Psychology, 62*, 73–87.

Bowes, L., Arseneault, L., Maughan, B., Taylor, A., Caspi, A., & Moffitt, T. E. (2009). School, neighborhood, and family factors are associated with children's bullying involvement: A nationally representative longitudinal study. *Journal of the American Academy of Child and Adolescent Psychiatry, 48*, 545–553.

Boyd, D. (2009). Taken out of context: American teen sociality in networked publics. *Dissertation Abstracts International Section A: Humanities and Social Sciences, 70*(4–A), 1073.

Buhs, E. S., Ladd, G. W., & Herald, S. L. (2006). Peer exclusion and victimization: Processes that mediate the relation between peer group rejection and children's classroom engagement and achievement? *Journal of Educational Psychology, 98*, 1–13.

Buhs, E., S., Ladd, G. W., & Herald-Brown, S. L. (2010). Victimization and exclusion: Links to peer rejection, classroom engagement, and achievement. In S. R. Jimerson, S. M. Swearer, & D. L. Espelage (Eds.), *The handbook of school bullying: An international perspective* (pp. 163–172). New York: Routledge.

Bullycide memorial page: Cases of bullycide (n.d.). Retrieved from http://www.bullyonline.org/schoolbully/cases.htm.

Burssens, D., & Vettenburg, N. (2006). Restorative group conferencing at school: A constructive response to serious incidents. *Journal of School Violence, 5,* 5–16.

Byrne, B. J. (1994). Bullies and victims in school settings with reference to some Dublin schools. *Irish Journal of Psychology, 15,* 574–586.

Cairns, R. B., Cairns, B. D., Neckerman, H. J., Gest, S. D., & Gariépy, J. L. (1988). Social networks and aggressive behaviour: Peer support or peer rejection? *Developmental Psychology, 24,* 815–823.

Camodeca, M., & Goossens, F. A. (2005). Aggression, social cognitions, anger and sadness in bullies and victims. *Journal of Child Psychology and Psychiatry, 46,* 186–197.

Campos, B., Keltner, D., Beck, J. M., Gonzaga, G. C., & John, O. P. (2007). Culture and teasing: The relational benefits of reduced desire for positive self-differentiation. *Personality and Social Psychology Bulletin, 33,* 3–16.

Carpenter, M. (2003, May 25). "R U There? Wt R U Doing Aftr Scl?": (Or how the young are taking over the world through instant messaging). *Pennsylvania Post Gazette,* p. A–1.

Carrington, P. M. (2006, June 6). Internet increases cyberbullying. Retrieved from http://timesdispatch.com/servlet/Satellite?pagename=Common%2FMGArticle%2FPri.

Center for the Digital Future at the USC Annenberg School. (2005). *The 2005 Digital Future Report.* Retrieved from http://www.digitalcenter.org.

Center for the Digital Future at the USC Annenberg School. (2010). *The 2010 Digital Future Report.* Retrieved from http://www.digitalcenter.org.

Centers for Disease Control and Prevention. (2010). Youth risk behavior surveillance – United States, 2009. Surveillance summaries. *MMWR, 59* (No. SS–5).

Charach, A., Pepler, D. J., & Zieler, S. (1995). Bullying at school: A Canadian perspective. *Education Canada, 35,* 12–18.

Charny, B. (2003, December 2). Gymgoers wary of camera phones. Retrieved from http://news.com.com/2102-1037_3-5112823.html.

Cheng, Y., Newman, I. M., Qu, M., Chai, Y., Chen, Y., & Shell, D. F. (2010). Being bullied and psychosocial adjustment among middle school students in China. *Journal of School Health, 80,* 193–199.

Children's Internet Protection Act, 20 U.S.C. § 9134(f). (2007).

Civil Rights Act of 1964, 42 U.S.C. § 1983 (2006). ("Title IV").

Cluver, L., Bowes, L., & Gardner, F. (2010). Risk and protective factors for bullying victimization among AIDS-affected and vulnerable children in South Africa. *Child Abuse & Neglect, 34*, 793–803.

Cobb County School District Administrative Rules (2008). Retrieved from http://www.cobbk12.org/centraloffice/adminrules/I_Rules/rule%20IJNDB.htm.

Cohen, L. E., & Felson, M. (1979). Social change and crime rate trends: A routine activity approach. *American Sociological Review, 44*, 588–605.

Common Sense Media (October 6, 2010). *National poll: Three out of four parents say social networks aren't protecting kids' online privacy*. Retrieved from http://www.commonsensemedia.org/about-us/press-room/press-releases/online-privacy-poll.

Constine J. (March 10, 2011). Facebook's new social safety features lets users confront bullies, ask friends for help. Retrieved from http://www.insidefacebook.com/2011/03/10/social-safety-report-bullies/.

Cook, C. R., Williams, K. R., Guerra, N. G., Kim, T. E., & Sadek, S. (2010). Predictors of bullying and victimization in childhood and adolescence: A meta-analytic investigation. *School Psychology Quarterly, 25*, 65–83.

County of Sacramento v. Lewis, 523 U.S. 833 (1998).

Coyne, I., Chesney, T., Logan, B., & Madden, N. (2009). Griefing in a virtual community: An exploratory study of Second Life residents. *Journal of Psychology, 217*, 214–221.

Cox Communications Teen Internet Safety Survey, Wave II – in Partnership with the National Center for Missing and Exploited Children (NCMEC) and John Walsh. Retrieved from http://www.cox.com/takeCharge/includes/docs/survey_results_2007.pdf.

Cox Communications. (2009). Teen online & wireless safety survey: Cyberbullying, sexting, and parental controls. Retrieved from http://www.cox.com/takecharge/safe_teens_2009/media/2009_teen_survey_internet_and_wireless_safety.pdf.

Craig, W. M. (1998). The relationship among bullying, victimization, depression, anxiety, and aggression in elementary school children. *Personality & Individual Differences, 24*, 123–130.

Craig, W., & Pepler, D. J. (1997). Observations of bullying and victimization in the schoolyard. *Canadian Journal of School Psychology, 13*, 41–60.

Craig, W., Harel-Fisch, Y., Fogel-Grinvald, H., Dastaler, S., Hetland, J., Simons-Morton, B., et al. (2009). A cross-national profile of bullying and victimization among adolescents in 40 countries. *International Journal of Public Health, 54*, S216–S224.

Crisp, J. (2006, August 2). Fairytale ending for girl who defied yobs. *Macclesfield Express*. Retrieved from http://www.macclesfield-express.co.uk/news/s/215914.

Cunningham, P. B., Henggeler, S. W., Limber, S. P., Melton, G. B., & Nation, M. A. (2000). Patterns and correlates of gun ownership among nonmetropolitan and rural middle school students. *Journal of Clinical Child Psychology, 29*, 432–442.

Currie, C., Roberts, C., Morgan, A., Smith, R., Settertobulte, W., Sandal, O., & Barnekow Rasmussen, V. (2004). *Young people's health in context. Health behaviour in school-aged children (HBSC) study: International report from the 2001/2002 survey.* Retrieved from http://www.hbsc.org/downloads/IntReport04/HBSCFullReport0102.pdf.

Cyber bullies target girl (2006, July 5). *BBC News.* Retrieved from http://newsvote.bbc.Co.uk/mpapps/pagetools/print/news.bbc.co.uk/1/hi/England/nottinghams.

Cyber bullying (n.d.). Retrieved from http://www.loveourchildusa.org/parent_cyberbullying.php.

Dale, M. (2011, January 19). 'The stupidity of sexting.' Retrieved from http://www.pretorianews.co.za/the-stupidity-of-sexting-1.1013907.

Davis v. Monroe County Bd. of Educ., 526 U.S. 629 (1999).

Dawkins, J. L. (1996). Bullying, physical disability, and the pediatric patient. *Developmental Medicine and Child Neurology, 38*, 603–612.

Delaware's model bully prevention policy. (n.d.). Retrieved from http://www.doe.k12.de.us/infosuites/students_family/climate/files/bully%20prevention%20policy%20template.pdf.

Dempsey, A. G., Sulkowski, M. L., Nichols, R., & Storch, E. A. (2009). Differences between peer victimization in cyber and physical settings and associated psychosocial adjustments in early adolescence. *Psychology in the Schools, 46*(10), 962–972.

DeShaney v. Winnebago County Dep't of Soc. Servs., 489 U.S. 189, 197 (1989).

DesRochers, R. (2006, June 27). Don't feed the trolls. Dealing with cyber harassment. Retrieved from http://ezinearticles.com/?Dont-Feed-The-Trolls—Dealing-with-Cyber-harassment-&id=230627.

DeVoe, J. F., Peter, K., Noonan, M., Snyder, T. D., & Baum, K. (2005). *Indicators of School Crime and Safety: 2005* (NCES 2006–001/NCJ 210697). U.S. Departments of Education and Justice. Washington, DC: U.S. Government Printing Office.

Didden, R., Scholte, R., Korzilius, H., DeMoor, J., Vermeulen, A., O'Reilly, M., et al. (2009). Cyber bullying among students with intellectual and developmental disability in special education settings. *Developmental Neurorehabilitation, 12*, 146–151.

Dilmac, B. (2009). Psychological needs as a predictor of cyber bullying: A preliminary report on college students. *Educational Sciences: Theory & Practice, 9*, 1307–1325.

Dinkes, R., Kemp, J., & Baum, K. (2009). *Indicators of School Crime and Safety: 2009* (NCES 2010–012/NCJ 228478). National Center for Education Statistics,

Institute of Education Sciences, U.S. Department of Education, and Bureau of Justice Statistics, Office of Justice Programs, U.S. Department of Justice. Washington, DC.

Dodge, K. A, Coie, J. D., & Lynam, D. (2006). Aggression and antisocial behavior in youth. In W. Damon, R. Lerner, & N. Eisenberg (Eds.), *Handbook of child psychology:* Vol. 3. *Social, emotional, and personality development* (6th ed., pp. 719–788). New York: John Wiley & Sons, Inc.

Dooley, J. J., Pyzalski, J., & Cross, D. (2009). Cyberbullying versus face-to-face bullying: A theoretical and conceptual review. *Zeitschrift für Psychologie/Journal of Psychology, 217,* 182–188.

Dreikurs, R., & Stoltz, V. (1991). *Children: The challenge.* New York: Plume.

Duncan, R. D. (1999). Peer and sibling aggression: An investigation of intra-and extra-familial bullying. *Journal of Interpersonal Violence, 14,* 871–886.

Duncan, R. D. (2004). The impact of family relationships on school bullies and victims. In D.L. Espelage, & S. M. Swearer (Eds.), *Bullying in American schools: A social-ecological perspective on prevention and intervention* (pp. 227–244). Mahwah, NJ: Erlbaum.

Dybwad, B. (2005, April 26). Happy slapping increasingly slap-happy? Retrieved from http://www.engadget.com/2005/04/26/happy-slapping-increasingly-slap-happy/.

Dyrli, O. E. (2005, September). Cyber bullying: Online bullying affects every school district. Retrieved from http://www.DistrictAdministration.com.

Eagan, S. K., & Perry, D. G. (1998). Does low self-regard invite victimization? *Developmental Psychology, 34,* 299–309.

Education Amendments Act of 1972, Title IX, 20 U.S.C. § 1681(a). (2006).

Eisenberg, M. E., & Aalsma, M. C. (2005). Bullying and peer victimization: A position paper of the Society of Adolescent Medicine. *Journal of Adolescent Health, 36,* 88–91.

Eisenberg, M. E., Neumark-Sztainer, D., & Perry, C. (2003). Peer harassment, school connectedness, and academic achievement. *Journal of School Health, 73,* 311–316.

Eisenberg, M. E., Neumark-Sztainer, D., Story, M., & Perry, C. (2005). The role of social norms and friends' influences on unhealthy weight-control behaviors among adolescent girls. *Social Science & Medicine, 60,* 1165–1173.

Electronic Communications Privacy Act, 18 U.S.C. § 2510. ECPA Pub. L. 99-508. 100 Stat. 1848 (1986).

Espelage, D. L., & Swearer, S. M. (2003). Research on school bullying and victimization: What have we learned and where do we go from here? *School Psychology Review, 32,* 365–383.

Espelage, D. L., & Swearer, S. M. (Eds.). (2004). *Bullying in American schools: A social-ecological perspective on prevention and intervention.* Mahwah, NJ: Erlbaum.

Facebook statistics (2011). Retrieved October 5, 2011, from http://www.facebook.com/press/info.php?statistics.

Falkner, N. H. Neumark-Sztainer, D., Story, M., Jeffery, R. W., Beuhring, T., & Resnick, M.D. (2001). Social, educational and psychological correlates of weight status in adolescents. *Obesity Research, 9,* 32–42.

Famiglietti, C. (2011, January 21). Cyber-trolls vandalize facebook page for Isabella Grasso. Retrieved from http://glencove.patch.com/articles/cyber-trolls-vandalize-facebook-page-for-isabella-grasso.

Fandrem, H., Strohmeier, D., & Roland, E. (2009). Bullying and victimization among native and immigrant adolescents in Norway: The role of proactive and reactive aggressiveness. *The Journal of Early Adolescence, 29,* 898–923.

FAQ-MySpace.com. (2006). Retrieved from http://www.myspace.com/Modules/Help/Pages/HelpCenter.aspx?

Faris, R., & Felmlee, D. (2011). Status struggles: Network centrality and gender segregation in same- and cross-gender aggression. *American Sociological Review, 76,* 48–73.

FBI. Blogging can be dangerous (2005, October 30). Retrieved from http://www.bloggersblog.com/familyblogs.

Fein, R., Vossekuil, B., Pollack, W., Borum, R., Modzeleski, W., & Reddy, M. (2002). *Threat assessment in schools: A guide to managing threatening situations and to creating safe school climates.* Washington. DC: U.S. Department of Education, Office of Elementary and Secondary Education, Safe and Drug-Free Schools Program and U.S. Secret Service, National Threat Assessment Center.

Fekkes, M., Pijpers, F. I. M., Fredriks, A. M., Vogels, T., & Verloove-VanHorick, S. P. (2006). Do bullied children get ill, or do ill children get bullied? A prospective cohort study on the relationship between bullying and health-related symptoms. *Pediatrics, 117,* 1568–1574.

Fekkes, M., Pijpers, F. I. M., & Verloove-VanHorick, S. P. (2004). Bullying behavior and associations with psychosomatic complaints and depression in victims. *Journal of Pediatrics, 144,* 17–22.

Feyerick, D., & Steffen, S. (2009, April 9). "Sexting" lands teen on sex offender list. Retrieved from http://www.cnn.com/2009/CRIME/04/07/sexting.busts/index.html.

Fight Crime: Invest In Kids. (2006, August 17). Communications. Retrieved from http://www.fightcrime.org/releases/php?id=231.

Fight Crime sponsored studies: Opinion research corporation. (2006). *Cyber Bully Preteen.* Retrieved from http://www.fightcrime.org/cyberbullying/cyberbullyingpreteen.pdf.

Fight Crime sponsored studies: Opinion research corporation. (2006). *Cyber Bully Teen.* Retrieved from http://www.fightcrime.org/cyberbullying/cyberbullyingteen.pdf.

Finkelhor, D., Mitchell, K., & Wolak, J. (2000). Online victimization: A report on the nation's youth. National Center for Missing & Exploited Children.

Retrieved from http://www.unh.edu/ccrc/Youth_Internet_info_page. html.

Finkelhor, D., Ormrod, R., Turner, H., & Hamby, S. L. (2005). The victimization of children and youth: A comprehensive, national survey. *Child Maltreatment, 10*, 5–25.

Finkelhor, D., Turner, H., Ormrod, R., & Hamby, S.L. (2010). Trends in childhood violence and abuse exposure: Evidence from two national surveys. *Archives of Pediatrics & Adolescent Medicine, 164*, 238–242.

Flores v. Morgan Hill Unified Sch. Dist., 324 F. 3d 1130, 1134 (9th Cir. 2003).

Focus: Brave new world. (2006, July 9). Retrieved from http://www.timesonline. co.uk/article/0,2095-2261684,00.html.

Fonzi, A., Genta, M. L., Menesini, E., Bacchini, D., Bonino, S., & Costabile, A. (1999). Italy. In P. K. Smith, Y. Morita, J. Junger-Tasl, D. Olweus, R. Catalano, & P. Slee (Eds.), *The nature of school bullying: A cross-national perspective* (pp. 140–156). London: Routledge.

Fosse, G. K. (2006). *Mental health of psychiatric outpatients bullied in childhood.* Doctoral thesis, Department of Neuroscience, Faculty of Medicine, Norwegian University of Science and Technology, Trondheim.

Fox, C. L., & Boulton, M. J. (2005). The social skills problems of victims of bullying: Self, peer, and teacher perceptions. *British Journal of Educational Psychology, 75*, 313–328.

Fox, C. L., & Farrow, C. V. (2009). Global and physical self-esteem and body dissatisfaction as mediators of the relationship between weight status and being a victim of bullying. *Journal of Adolescence, 32*, 1287–1301.

Franek, M. (2005/2006). Foiling cyber bullies in the new wild west. *Educational Leadership, 63*, 39–43.

Garofalo, R., Wolf, R. C., Kessel, S., Palfrey, S. J., & DuRant, R. H. (1998). The association between health risk behaviors and sexual orientation among a school-based sample of adolescents. *Pediatrics, 101*, 895–902.

Gehrke, R. (2006, August 19). Shurtleff joins child advocate group's campaign against cyber bullying. *The Salt Lake Tribune.* Retrieved from http://www.sltrib.com.

Gini, G., & Pozzoli, T. (2009). Association between bullying and psychosomatic problems: A meta-analysis. *Pediatrics, 123*, 1059–1065.

Gini, G., Pozzoli, T., Borghi, F., & Franzoni, L. (2008). The role of bystanders in students' perception of bullying and sense of safety. *Journal of School Psychology, 46*, 617–638.

Girl tormented by phone bullies (2001, January 16). Retrieved from http://news.bbc.co.uk/1/ht/uk_news/education/1120597.stm.

Giumetti, G., Schroeder, A., Hatfield, A., McKibben, E., & Kowalski, R. M. (2011). Cyber-incivility @ work: The new age of interpersonal deviance. (in press). *Cyberpsychology, Behavior & Social Networking.*

Gonzales, A. L., & Hancock, J. T. (2011). Mirror, mirror on my Facebook wall: Effects of exposure to Facebook on self-esteem. *CyberPsychology, Behavior, & Social Networking, 14(1/2)*, 79–83.

Graham, S., & Juvonen, J. (2002). Ethnicity, peer harassment, and adjustment in middle school: An exploratory study. *Journal of Early Adolescence, 22*, 173–199.

Granneman, S. (2006, July 3). MySpace, a place without MyParents. Retrieved from http://www.securityfocus.com/print/columnists/408.

Gray, K. (2006, September 14). How mean can teens be? Retrieved from http://abclocal.go.com/kgo/story?section=bizarre&id=4560512&ft=print.

Gray, W. N., Kahhan, N. A., & Janicke, D. M. (2009). Peer victimization and pediatric obesity: A review of the literature. *Psychology in the Schools, 46*, 720–727.

Griffiths, L. J., Wolke, D., Page, A. S., & Horwood, J. P. (2005). Obesity and bullying: Different effects for boys and girls. *Archives of Disease in Childhood, 91*, 121–125.

Gross, E. F., Juvonen, J., & Gable, S. L. (2002). Internet use and well-being in adolescence. *Journal of Social Issues, 58*, 75–90.

Grossman, L. (2006, December 13). *Time*'s person of the year: You [Electronic version]. *Time, 168*.

Hamiwka, L. D., Yu, C. G., Hamiwka, L. A., Sherman, E. M. S., Anderson, B., & Wirrell, E. (2009). Are children with epilepsy at greater risk for bullying than their peers? *Epilepsy & Behavior, 15*, 500–505.

Harachi, T. W., Catalano, R. F., & Hawkins, D. (1999). Canada. In P. K. Smith, Y. Morita, J. Junger-Tasl, D. Olweus, R. Catalano, & P. Slee (Eds.), *The nature of school bullying: A cross-national perspective* (pp. 296–306). London: Routledge.

Harris Interactive and GLSEN. (2005). *From teasing to torment: School climate in America, A survey of students and teachers*. New York: GLSEN.

Harris, S., Petrie, G., & Willoughby, W. (2002). Bullying among 9th graders: An exploratory study. *NASSP Bulletin, 86*, 630.

Hass, N. (2006, January 8). In your Facebook.com. *The New York Times*, Section 4-A, pp. 30–31.

Hawker, D. S. J., & Boulton, M. J. (2000). Twenty years' research on peer victimization and psychosocial maladjustment: A meta-analytic review of cross-sectional studies. *Journal of Child Psychology and Psychiatry, 41*, 441–455.

Hawkins, D. L., Pepler, D. J., & Craig, W. M. (2001). Naturalistic observations of peer interventions in bullying. *Social Development, 10*, 512–527.

Haynie, D. L., Nansel, T., Eitel, P., Crump, A. D., Saylor, K., Yu, K., & Simons-Morton, B. (2001). Bullies, victims and bully/victims: Distinct groups of at-risk youth. *Journal of Early Adolescence, 21*, 29–49.

Hazelwood School District v. Kuhlmeier, 484 U. S. 269 (1988).

Health Resources and Services Administration. (2006). Take a stand, lend a hand: Stop bullying now. Retrieved from http://stopbullyingnow.hrsa.gov/adult/indexAdult.asp?Area=cyberbullying.

Health Resources and Services Administration. (2011). Retrieved from http://www.stopbullyingnow.hrsa.gov.

Helft, M. (2010, December 15). Facebook wrestles with free speech and civility. Retrieved from http://www.nytimes.com/2010/12/13/technology/13facebook.html?_r=1.

Hermann, M. A., & Finn, A. (2002). An ethical and legal perspective on the role of school counselors in preventing violence in schools. *Professional School Counseling, 6*, 46–54.

Hinduja, S., & Patchin, J. W. (2007). Offline consequences of online victimization: School violence and delinquency. *Journal of School Violence, 6*, 89–112.

Hinduja, S., & Patchin, J. W. (2008). Cyberbullying: An exploratory analysis of factors related to offending and victimization. *Deviant Behavior, 29*, 129–156.

Hinduja, S., & Patchin, J. W. (2010a). Bullying, cyberbullying, and suicide. *Archives of Suicide Research, 14*, 206–221.

Hinduja, S., & Patchin, J. W. (2010b). Sexting: A brief guide for educators and parents. Cyberbullying Research Center (http://www.cyberbullying.us).

Hinduja, S., & Patchin, J. W. (2011). High-tech cruelty. *Educational Leadership, 68*, 48–52.

Hodges, E. V. E., & Perry, D. G. (1996). Victims of peer abuse: An overview. *Journal of Emotional and Behavioural Problems, 5*, 23–28.

Hoff, D. L., & Mitchell, S. N. (2009). Cyberbullying: Causes, effects, and remedies. *Journal of Educational Administration, 47*, 652–665.

Hokoda, A., Lu, H. A., & Angeles, M. (2006). School bullying in Taiwanese adolescents. *Journal of Emotional Abuse, 6*, 69–90.

Holt, M. K., Kaufman Kantor, G., & Finkelhor, D. (2009). Parent/child concordance about bullying involvement and family characteristics related to bullying and peer victimization. *Journal of School Violence, 8*, 42–63.

Honigsbaum, M. (2005, April 26). Concern over rise of "happy slapping" craze. *The Guardian*. Retrieved from http://www.guardian.co.uk/mobile/article/0,2763,1470214,00.html.

Hoover, J. H., Oliver, R., & Hazler, R. J. (1992). Bullying: Perceptions of adolescent victims in the Midwestern USA. *School Psychology International, 13*, 5–16.

Imamura, A., Nishida, A., Nakazawa, N., Shimodera, S., Tanaka, G., Kinoshita, H., Ozawa, H., & Okazaki, Y. (2009). Effects of cellular phone email use on the mental health of junior high school students in Japan. *Psychiatry and Clinical Neurosciences, 63*, 701–703.

Internet bullies: The growing problem of internet bullying and "flaming." (2006, August). Retrieved from http://www.safesurfers.org/chat_room_flaming.htm.

Iowa Department of Education. (n.d.). Sample anti-bullying/anti-harassment policy. Retrieved from http://www.iowa.gov/educate/index.php?option=com_content&task=view&id=1030&Itemid=1293.

i-SAFE. (2004–2005). National assessment report: The effectiveness and measurable results of Internet safety education.

i-SAFE. (2005–2006). At risk online: National assessment of youth on the Internet and the effectiveness of i-SAFE Internet safety education.

i-SAFE. (2006–2007). National Assessment Center database: Query of pre-assessment questions for 5th through 8th grades nationwide for 06–07 academic year.

Ivester, M. (2009, February 4). A juicy shutdown. Retrieved from http://juicycampus.blogspot.com.

Janssen, I., Craig, W. M., Boyce, W. F., & Pickett, W. (2004). Associations between overweight and obesity within bullying behaviors in school-aged children. *Pediatrics, 113*, 1187–1194.

Jenkins, H. (2006). Discussion: MySpace and Deleting Online Predators Act (DOPA). Retrieved from http://www.digitaldivide.net/articles/view.php?ArticleID=592.html.

Jennings, R. (2010, October 26). Firesheep firefox extension opens fire on sheep-browsers. Retrieved from http://blogs.computerworld.com/17228/firesheep_firefox_extension_opens_fire_on_sheep_browsers.

Juvonen, J., Graham, S., & Schuster, M. A. (2003). Bullying among young adolescents: The strong, the weak, and the troubled. *Pediatrics, 112*, 1231–1237.

Juvonen, J., & Gross, E. F. (2008). Extending the school grounds? Bullying experiences in cyberspace. *Journal of School Health, 78*, 496–505.

Juvonen, J., Wang, Y., & Espinoza, G. (2011). Bullying experiences and compromised academic performance across middle school grades. *The Journal of Early Adolescence, 31*, 152–173.

Kärnä, A., Voeten, M., Poskiparta, E., & Salmivalli, C. (2010). Vulnerable children in varying classroom contexts: Bystanders' behaviors moderate the effects of risk factors on victimization. *Merrill-Palmer Quarterly, 56*, 261–282.

Keith, S., & Martin, M. E. (2005). Cyber bullying: Creating a culture of respect in a cyber world. *Reclaiming Children and Youth, 13*, 224–228.

Kennedy, K. (2006, April 23). Not-so-MySpace anymore. *The Ledger.com*. Retrieved from http://www.theledger.com/apps/pbcs.dll/articleID=/20060423/News/.

Kennedy, L. (2011, April 21). Girl who beat cancer is cyberbullied by best friend. Retrieved from http://www.parentdish.com/2011/04/21/cyber-bully/.

Kenny, J. (2011, January 17). Cyberbullying teens in Florida receive home confinement punishment. Retrieved from http://dns.tmcnet.com/topics/internet-security/articles/135478-cyberbullying-teens-florida-receive-home-confinement-punishment.htm.

Khalil, L. (2010, November 16). Cyber wolves in (fire) sheep clothing. QUEST Community Science Blog. Retrieved from http://www.kqed.org/quest/blog/2010/11/16/dont-get-hacked-by-firesheep-over-open-wi-fi/print/.

Kim, Y. S., Koh, Y., & Leventhal, B. (2005). School bullying and suicidal risk in Korean middle school students. *Pediatrics, 115,* 357–363.

King, L. (2006, August 15). No hiding from online bullies. Retrieved from http://www.news-leader.com/apps/pbcs.dll/article?Date=20060815.

Klomek, A. B., Marrocco, F., Kleinman, M., Schonfeld, I. S., & Gould, M. S. (2008). Peer victimization, depression, and suicidality in adolescents. *Suicide and Life-Threatening Behavior, 38,* 166–180.

Klump v. Nazareth Area School District 425 F. Supp. 2d 622 (E.D. Pa. 2006).

K.M. v. Hyde Park Cent. Sch. Dist., 381 F. Supp. 2d 343 (S.D.N.Y. 2005).

Kochenderfer, B. J., & Ladd, G. W. (1996). Peer victimization: Cause or consequence of school maladjustment? *Child Development, 67,* 1305–1317.

Kohler, C. (2007, January 23). Teen tube terrors. Retrieved from http://www.cablevisioneditorials.com/content/LI/2007/LI_2007-01-23.html.

Kosciw, J. G., Diaz, E. M., & Greytak, E. A. (2008). *The 2007 National School Climate Survey: The experiences of lesbian, gay, bisexual and transgender youth in our nation's schools.* New York: Gay, Lesbian, & Straight Education Network. Retrieved from http://www.glsen.org/binary-data/GLSEN_ATTACHMENTS/file/000/001/1290-1.pdf.

Kowalski, R. M. (2000). "I was only kidding!": Victims' and perpetrators' perceptions of teasing. *Personality and Social Psychology Bulletin, 26,* 231–241.

Kowalski, R. M. (2011). Cyber bullying intervention. Unpublished manuscript, Clemson University.

Kowalski, R. M., & Fedina, C. (2011). Cyber bullying in ADHD and Asperger Syndrome populations. *Research in Autism Spectrum Disorders, 5,* 1202–8.

Kowalski, R. M., Giumetti, G. W., Schroeder, A. W., & Reese, H. H. (2012). Cyber bullying among college students: Evidence from multiple domains of college life. In C. Wankel & L. Wankel (Eds.), *Misbehavior online in higher education.* Bingley, UK: Emerald Publishing Group.

Kowalski, R. M., & Limber, S. E. (2007). Electronic bullying among middle school students. *Journal of Adolescent Health, 41,* S22–S30.

Kowalski, R. M., & Limber, S. P. (2011). Physical and psychological consequences of traditional bullying and cyber bullying. Unpublished manuscript, Clemson University.

Kowalski, R. M., & Witte, J. (2006). Youth Internet survey. Retrieved from http://www.camss.clemson.edu/KowalskiSurvey/servelet/Page1.

Kraft, E. (2006). Cyber bullying: A worldwide trend of misusing technology to harass others. *The Internet Society II: Advances in Education, Commerce, & Governance, 36,* 155–166.

Kraut, R., Patterson, M., Lundmark, V., Kiesler, S., Mukopadhyay, T., & Scherlis. W. (1998). Internet paradox: A social technology that reduces social involvement and psychological well-being? *American Psychologist, 53,* 1017–1031.

Krug, E. G. (2002). *World report on violence and health,* Volume 1. World Health Organization.

Kruger, J., Epley, N., Parker, J., & Ng, Z. (2005). Egocentrism over e-mail: Can we communicate as well as we think? *Journal of Personality and Social Psychology, 89,* 925–936.

K.S.A. § 72-8256 (2009).

Kumpulainen, K., & Raasnen, E. (2000). Children involved in bullying at elementary school age: Their psychiatric symptoms and deviance in adolescence. *Child Abuse & Neglect, 24,* 1567–1577.

Kumpulainen, K., Raasnen, E., & Puura, K. (2001). Psychiatric disorders and the use of mental health services among children involved in bullying. *Aggressive Behavior, 27,* 102–110.

La. R.S. 17:416.13 (2010).

Lackner, C. (2006, September 15). Blog reveals "poster boy" for school shooters. *Ottawa Citizen.* Retrieved from http://www.canada.com/ottawacitizen/news/story.html?id=341f18cd-af34-412c-91f6-7e87aa30382c.

Lagerspetz, K. M. J., Bjorkqvist, K., & Peltonen, T. (1988). Is indirect aggression typical of females? Gender differences in aggressiveness in 11- to 12-year-old children. *Aggressive Behavior, 14,* 403–414.

Lampert, A. (2006, April 8). Star wars kid settles lawsuit. *The Gazette (Montreal),* p. A8.

Langdon, S. W., & Preble, W. (2008). The relationship between levels of perceived respect and bullying in 5th through 12th graders. *Adolescence, 43,* 485–503.

Larochette, A. C., Murphy, A. N., & Craig, W. M. (2010). Racial bullying and victimization in Canadian school-aged children. *School Psychology International, 31,* 389–408.

Leary, M. R. (1983). Social anxiousness: The construct and its measurement. *Journal of Personality Assessment, 47,* 66–75.

Leary, M. R., Kowalski, R. M., Smith, L., & Phillips, S. (2003). Violence and rejection: Case studies of the school shootings. *Aggressive Behavior, 29,* 202–214.

Leith, S. (2006, December 18). Cingular hooks up with MySpace.com. *The Atlanta Journal-Constitution,* p. A14.

Lenhart, A. (2009, December 15). Teens and sexting. Retrieved from http://www.pewinternet.org.

Lenhart, A. (2010, May 6). Cyberbullying: What the research is telling us. Retrieved from http://www.pewinternet.org/Presentations/2010/May/Cyberbullying-2010.aspx.

Lenhart, A., & Madden, M. (2007, January 7). Social networking websites and teens: An overview. Retrieved from http://www.pewinternet.org.

Lenhart, A., Madden, M., & Hitlin, P. (2005, July 27). Teens and technology: Youth are leading the transition to a fully wired and mobile nation. Retrieved from http://www.pewinternet.org.

Lenhart, A., Purcell, K., Smith, A., & Zickuhr, K. (2010). Social media and mobile internet use among teens and young adults. Retrieved from http://www.pewinternet.org/~/media//Files/Reports/2010/PIP_Social_Media_and_Young_Adults_Report_Final_with_toplines.pdf.

Lenhart, A., Rainie, L., & Lewis, O. (2001). Teenage life online: Pew Internet & American Life Project. Retrieved from http://www.pewinternet.org.

Levine, B. (2006). Taking on the cyber bullies. Retrieved from http://www.newsfactor.com/story.xhtml?story_id=43130.

Li, Q. (2006). Cyber bullying in schools: A research of gender differences. *School Psychology International, 27*, 157–170.

Limber, S. P. (2002). *Addressing youth bullying behaviors.* Proceeding from the American Medical Association Educational Forum on Adolescent Health: Youth Bullying. Chicago: American Medical Association.

Limber, S. P. (2003). Efforts to address bullying in U.S. Schools. *Journal of Health Education, 34*, S-23–S-29.

Limber, S. P. (2004). Implementation of the Olweus Bullying Prevention Program: Lessons learned from the field. In D. Espelage & S. Swearer (Eds.), *Bullying in American schools: A social-ecological perspective on prevention and intervention* (pp. 351–363). Mahwah, NJ: Erlbaum.

Limber, S. P. (2006a). The Olweus Bullying Prevention Program: An overview of its implementation and research basis. In S. Jimerson, & M. Furlong (Eds.), *Handbook of school violence and school safety: From research to practice* (pp. 293–307). Mahwah, NJ: Erlbaum.

Limber, S. P. (2006b). Peer victimization: The nature and prevalence of bullying among children and youth. In N. E. Dowd, D. G. Singer, & R. F. Wilson (Eds.), *Handbook of children, culture, and violence* (pp. 331–332). Thousand Oaks, CA: Sage.

Limber, S. P. (2011a). Development, evaluation, and future directions of the Olweus Bullying Prevention Program. *Journal of School Violence, 10*, 71–87.

Limber, S. P. (2011b). Implementation of the Olweus Bullying Prevention Program in American schools: Lessons learned from the field. In D. L. Espelage & S. M. Swearer (Eds.), *Bullying in North American schools* (2nd ed., pp. 291–306). New York: Routledge.

Limber, S. P., Nation, M., Tracy, A. J., Melton, G. B., & Flerx, V. (2004). Implementation of the Olweus Bullying Prevention Program in the Southeastern United States. In P. K. Smith, D. Pepler, & K. Rigby (Eds.), *Bullying in schools: How successful can interventions be?* (pp. 55–79). Cambridge, UK: Cambridge University Press.

Lisson, M. (2008). Out-of-control gossip on juicy campus website. Retrieved from http://abcnews.go.com/OnCampus/story?id=5919608.

Livingstone, S., & Brake, D. R. (2009). On the rapid rise of social networking sites: New findings and policy implications. *Children & Society, 24,* 75–83.

Loeber, R., & Stouthamer-Loeber, M. (1986). Family factors as correlates and predictors of juvenile conduct problems and delinquency. In M. Tonry & N. Morris (Eds.), *Crime and justice. An annual review of research, 7* (pp. 29–149). Chicago: University of Chicago Press.

Machlis, S. (2010, October 30). How to hijack Facebook using firesheep. *PCWorld.* Retrieved from http://www.pcworld.com/printable/article/id,209333/printable.html.

Magid, L., & Collier, A. (2007). *MySpace unraveled.* Berkeley, CA: Peachpit Press.

Magin, P., Adams, J., Heading, G., Pond, D., & Smith, W. (2008). Experiences of appearance-related teasing and bullying in skin diseases and their psychological sequelae: Results of a qualitative study. *Scandinavian Journal of Caring Sciences, 22,* 430–436.

Mahling, W. (1996). Second hand codes: An analysis of the constitutionality of dress codes in the public schools. *Minnesota Law Review, 80,* 715.

Maine School Management Association Sample Policy (2006). Retrieved from http://mainegov-images.informe.org/cabinet/Bullying_000.pdf.

Mandell, N. (2011, January 14). Florida girls in trouble with police after creating lewd fake Facebook profile for classmate. NYDailyNews.com. Retrieved from http://www.nydailynews.com/news/national/2011/01/14/2011-01-14_florida_girls_in_trouble_with_police_after_creating_lewd_fake_facebook_profile_f.html.

Marshall, J., & Stanfield, A. (2011). The realities of sexting (you can't unsend!). Retrieved from http://www.learningseed.com.

Martlew, M., & Hodson, J. (1991). Children with mild learning difficulties in an integrated and in a special school: Comparisons of behaviour, teasing and teachers' attitudes. *British Journal of Educational Psychology, 61,* 355–372.

Maryland State Department of Education. (2005). Harassment or intimidation (bullying) reporting form. Retrieved from http://www.marylandpublicschools.org/nr/rdonlyres/0700b064-c2b3-41fc-a6cf-d3dae4969707/7243/harassmentorintimidationbullyingreportingform.pdf.

Masiello, M., Good, K., Messina, A., Saylor, J., Schroeder, D. Limber, S., et al. (2009). *Bullying prevention: A statewide collaborative that works. A report to stakeholders.* Pittsburgh, PA: Highmark Foundation.

Mason, K. L. (2008). Cyberbullying: A preliminary assessment for school personnel. *Psychology in the Schools, 45,* 323–348.

Massachusetts Department of Elementary and Secondary Education. (2010). Model bullying prevention and intervention plan. Retrieved from: http://www.doe.mass.edu/bullying/ModelPlan.pdf.

Mazalin, D., & Klein, B. (2008). Social anxiety and the Internet: Positive and negative effects. *E-Journal of Applied Psychology, 4,* 43–50.

McKenna, K. Y. A., & Bargh, J. A. (2000). Plan 9 from cyberspace: The implications of the Internet for personality and social psychology. *Personality and Social Psychology Bulletin, 4,* 57–75.

Meadows, B., Bergal, J., Helling, S., Odell, J., Piligian, E., Howard, C., Lopez, M., Atlas, D., & Hochberg, L. (2005). The web: The bully's new playground. *People, 63,* 152–156.

Mehdizadeh, S. (2010). Self-presentation 2.0: Narcissism and self-esteem on Facebook. *CyberPsychology, Behavior, and Social Networking, 13,* 357–364.

Meland, E., Rydning, J. H., Lobben, S., Breidablik, H.J., & Ekeland, T.J. (2010). Emotional, self-conceptual, and relational characteristics of bullies and the bullied. *Scandinavian Journal of Public Health, 38,* 359–367.

Melton, G. B., Limber, S. P., Cunningham, P., Osgood, D. W., Chambers, J., Flerx, V., Henggeler, S., & Nation, M. (1998). *Violence among rural youth. Final report.* Washington, DC: U.S. Department of Justice, Office of Justice Programs, Office of Juvenile Justice and Delinquency Prevention.

Mepham, S. (2010). Disabled children: The right to feel safe. *Child Care in Practice, 16,* 19–34.

Merritt, M. (2009, May). New trend in cyberbullying: Griefing. *Norton.* Retrieved from: http://us.norton.com/familyresources/resources.jsp?title=ar_good_grief_for_online_games.

Mesch, G. S. (2009). Parental mediation, online activities, and cyberbullying. *Cyberpsychology & Behavior, 12,* 387–393.

Michigan State Board of Education. (n.d.). *Model anti-bullying policy.* Retrieved from http://www.michigan.gov/documents/mde/Model_Anti-Bullying_Policy_with_Revisions_338592_7.pdf.

Mikle, J. (2005, December 8). Harassed student's court win upheld. Asbury Park Press.

Miller, N.C., Thompson, N.L., & Franz, D.P. (2009, September). Proactive strategies to safeguard young adolescents in the cyberage. *Middle School Journal,* 28–34.

Mishna, F. (2003). Learning disabilities and bullying: Double jeopardy. *Journal of Learning Disabilities, 36,* 336–347.

Mishna, F., Cook, C., Gadalla, T., Daciuk, J., & Solomon, S. (2010). Cyber bullying behaviors among middle and high school students. *American Journal of Orthopsychiatry, 80,* 362–374.

Mishna, F., Saini, M., & Solomon, S. (2009). Ongoing and online: Children and youths' perceptions of cyber bullying. *Children and Youth Services Review, 31*, 1222–1228.

Moody, E. (2001). Internet use and its relationship to loneliness. *CyberPsychology & Behavior, 4*, 393–401.

Molcho, M., Craig, W., Due, P., Pickett, W., Harel-Fisch, Y., Overpeck, M., & the HBSC Bullying Writing Group (2009). Cross-national time trends in bullying behaviour 1994–2006: Findings from Europe and North America. *International Journal of Public Health, 54*, S225–234.

Morita, Y., Soeda, H., Soeda, K., & Taki, M. (1999). Japan. In P. K. Smith, Y. Morita, J. Junger-Tas, D. Olweus, R. Catalano, & P. Slee. (Eds.), *The nature of school bullying: A cross-national perspective* (pp. 309–323). New York: Routledge.

Morse v. Frederick, 127 2618 (S. Ct. 2007).

MTV/Associated Press Poll. (Sept. 23, 2009). *Digital Abuse Survey*. Retrieved from http://www.athinline.org/MTV-AP_Digital_Abuse_Study_Full.pdf.

Mulvaney, K. (2011, January 19). Smithfield high student charged in cyber bullying. Retrieved from http://www.projo.com/news/content/ SMITHFIELD_ FACEBOOK_01_10_11.

Mulvey, E., & Cauffman, E. (2001). The inherent limits of predicting school violence. *American Psychologist, 56*, 797–802.

Nabuzoka, D., & Smith, P.K. (1993). Sociometric status and social behaviour of children with and without learning difficulties. *Journal of Child Psychology and Psychiatry, 34*, 1435–1448.

Nakamoto, J., & Schwartz, D. (2010). Is peer victimization associated with academic achievement? A meta-analytic review. *Social Development, 19*, 221–242.

Nansel, T. R., Overpeck, M. D., Pilla, R. S., Ruan, W. J., Simons-Morton, B., & Scheidt, P. (2001). Bullying behavior among U.S. youth: Prevalence and association with psychosocial adjustment. *Journal of the American Medical Association, 285*, 2094–2100.

National Children's Home. (NCH; 2002). 1 in 4 children are victims of "on-line bullying." Retrieved from http://www.nch.org.uk/information/index. php?i=77&r=125.

Naylor, P., Cowie, H., & del Rey, R. (2001). Coping strategies of secondary school children in response to being bullied. *Child Psychology and Psychiatry Review, 6*, 114–120.

www.netlingo.com.

Nev. Rev. Stat. Ann. § 388.122 (2010).

New Jersey v. T.L.O., 469 U.S. 325 (1985).

N.J. Stat. § 18A:37-13 (2010).

O.C.G.A. § 20-2-751.4 (2006).

ORS § 339.351 (2010).

O'Connell, P., Pepler, D. J., & Craig, W. (1999). Peer involvement in bullying: Insights and challenges for intervention. *Journal of Adolescence, 22,* 86–97.

Ohio girls sentenced for MySpace threats (2006, June 28). Retrieved from http://mycrimespace.thetrenchcoat.com.

Ohio Resource Network for Safe and Drug Free Schools and Communities. (n.d.). Retrieved from http://www.ebasedprevention.org/uploadedFiles/robbs/Sample_District_Policy2(1). doc.70 Okl. St. § 24-100.3 (2006).

Olsen, S. (2006a, April 11). MySpace reaching out to parents. Retrieved from http://news.com.com/MySpace+reaching+out+to+parents/2009-1041-3-6059679.html?tag=nl.

Olsen, S. (2006b). Wi-fi gives kids access to unchaperoned Net. Retrieved from http://news.com.com/Wi-i+gives+access+to+unchaperoned+Net/2009-1025_3-6114522.html.

Olweus, D. (1973). *Hackkycklingar och översittare: Forskning om skolmobbning.* Stockholm, Sweden: Almqvist & Wiksell.

Olweus, D. (1978). *Aggression in the schools: Bullies and whipping boys.* Washington, DC: John Wiley & Sons, Inc.

Olweus, D. (1979). Stability of aggressive reaction patterns in males: A review. *Psychological Bulletin, 86,* 852–875.

Olweus, D. (1980). Familial and temperamental determinants of aggressive behavior in adolescent boys: A causal analysis. *Developmental Psychology, 16,* 644–660.

Olweus, D. (1993a). *Bullying at school: What we know and what we can do.* New York: Blackwell.

Olweus, D. (1993b). Victimization by peers: Antecedents and long-term outcomes. In K. H. Rubin & J. H. B. Asendort (Eds.), *Social withdrawal, inhibition, and shyness* (pp. 315–41). Hillsdale, NJ: Erlbaum.

Olweus, D. (1994). Annotation: Bullying at school: Basic facts and effects of a school-based intervention program. *Journal of Child Psychology and Psychiatry, 35,* 1171–1190.

Olweus, D. (2001). *Olweus' Core Program Against Bullying and Antisocial Behavior: a teacher handbook.* Bergen, Norway: Author.

Olweus, D. (2004a). The Olweus Bullying Prevention Programme: Design and implementation issues and a new national initiative in Norway. In P. K. Smith, D. Pepler, & K. Rigby (Eds.), *Bullying in schools: How successful can interventions be?* (pp. 13–36). Cambridge, UK: Cambridge University Press.

Olweus, D. (2004b). Bullying at school: Prevalence estimation, a useful evaluation design, and a new national initiative in Norway. *Association for Child Psychology and Psychiatry Occasional Papers No. 23,* 5–17.

Olweus, D. (2005). A useful evaluation design, and effects of the Olweus Bullying Prevention Program. *Psychology, Crime & Law, 11,* 389–402.

Olweus, D. (2010). Understanding and researching bullying: Some critical issues. In S.R. Jimerson, S. M. Swearer, & D. L. Espelage (Eds.), *The handbook of school bullying: An international perspective* (pp. 9–33). New York: Routledge.

Olweus, D., & Kallestad, J. H. (2010). The Olweus Bullying Prevention Program: Effects of classroom components at different grade levels. In K. Osterman (Ed.), *Indirect and direct aggression.* New York, NY: Peter Lang.

Olweus, D., & Limber, S. P. (2010a). Bullying in school: Evaluation and dissemination of the Olweus Bullying Prevention Program. *American Journal of Orthopsychiatry, 80,* 124–134.

Olweus, D., & Limber, S. P. (2010b). The Olweus Bullying Prevention Program: Implementation and evaluation over two decades. In S. R. Jimerson, S. M. Swearer, & D. L. Espelage (Eds.), *The handbook of school bullying: An international perspective* (pp. 377–402). New York: Routledge.

Olweus, D., & Limber, S. P. (2010c, November). *What do we know about bullying: Information from the Olweus Bullying Questionnaire.* Paper presented at the annual meeting of the International Bullying Prevention Association. Seattle, Washington.

Olweus, D. Limber, S. P., Flerx, V. C., Mullin, N., Riese, J., & Snyder, M. (2007). *Olweus Bullying Prevention Program: Schoolwide guide.* Center City, MN: Hazelden.

Olweus, D., Limber, S., & Mihalic, S. (1999). *Blueprints for Violence Prevention: Vol. 9. The Bullying Prevention Program.* Boulder, CO: Institute of Behavioral Science, University of Colorado.

Ong, C., Chang, S., & Wang, C. (2011). Comparative loneliness of users versus non-users of online chatting. *CyberPsychology, Behavior, and Social Networking, 14,* 35–40.

Opinion Research Corporation. (2006). Cyber bully teen. Retrieved from http://www.fightcrime.org/cyberbullying/cyberbullyingteen.pdf.

Ortega, R., & Mora-Merchan, J.A. (1999). Spain. In P. K. Smith, Y. Morita, J. Junger-Tas, D. Olweus, R. Catalano, & P. Slee (Eds.), *The nature of school bullying: A cross-national perspective* (pp. 157–173). London: Routledge.

Osmond, N. (2006, August 8). Cyber bullying is a faceless crime. *The Gulf News.* Retrieved from http://www.gulfnews.ca/index.cfm?iid=1684&sid=12668.

Owens, L., Shute, R., & Slee, P. (2000). "I'm in and you're out …": Explanations for teenage girls' indirect aggression. *Psychology, Evolution, & Gender, 2*(1), 19–46.

Pagliocca P. M., Limber, S. P., & Hashima, P. (2007). Evaluation report for the Chula Vista Olweus Bullying Prevention Program. Final report prepared for the Chula Vista Police Department.

Pardington, S. (2005, November 27). Is your little angel raising hell online? *The Sunday Oregonian,* p. A01.

Patchin, J. W., & Hinduja, S. (2006). Bullies move beyond the schoolyard: A preliminary look at cyber bullying. *Youth Violence and Juvenile Justice, 4,* 148–169.

Patchin, J. W., & Hinduja, S. (2010a). Changes in adolescent online social networking behaviors from 2006 to 2009. *Computers in Human Behavior, 26,* 1818–1821.

Patchin, J. W., & Hinduja, S. (2010b). Cyber bullying and self-esteem. *Journal of School Health, 80,* 614–621.

Patchin, J. W., & Hinduja, S. (2010c). Trends in online social networking: Adolescent use of MySpace over time. *New Media & Society, 12,* 197–216.

Paulson, A. (2003, December 30). Internet bullying. *The Christian Science Monitor.* Retrieved from csmonitor.com/2003/1230/p11s01-legn.html.

Pearce, M. J., Boergers, J., & Prinstein, M. J. (2002). Adolescent obesity, overt and relational peer victimization, and romantic relationships. *Obesity Research, 10,* 386–393.

Pellegrini, A. D. (2001). A longitudinal study of heterosexual relationships, aggression, and sexual harassment during the transition from primary school through middle school. *Journal of Applied Developmental Psychology, 22,* 1–15.

Pellegrini, A. D., & Bartini, M. (2000). An empirical comparison of methods of sampling aggression and victimization in school settings. *Journal of Educational Psychology, 92,* 360–366.

Perkins, H. W., Craig, D., & Perkins, J. (2011). Using social norms to reduce bullying: A research intervention among adolescents in five middle schools. Open access article retrieved http://gpi.sagepub.com/content/early/2011/04/08/136 8430210398004.

Peskin, M. F., Tortolero, S. R., & Markham, C. M. (2006). Bullying and victimization among black and Hispanic adolescents. *Adolescence, 41,* 467–484.

Pesznecker, K. (2004, July 1). District settled suit for millions. *Anchorage Daily News.*

Pham, A. (2002, September 9). Enter the "griefers." *Chicago Tribune.* Retrieved from http://www.gamegirladvance.com/archives/2002/09/09/enter_the_griefers. html.

Poulsen, K. (2006, February 27). Scenes from the MySpace backlash. Retrieved from http://www.wired.com/news/politics/1,70254-0.html.

Prince William County Schools. (2009). Computer systems and network services: PWCS acceptable use and internet safety policy. Retrieved from http://itech. departments.pwcs.edu/modules/groups/homepagefiles/cms/980798/File/ PWCS%20Acceptable%20Use%20Policy.pdf?sessionid=26cc615de64c079173 9a04d81991880b.

Privitera, C., & Campbell, M. A. (2009). Cyberbullying: The new face of workplace bullying? *CyberPsychology & Behavior, 12,* 395–400.

Promoting civil rights and prohibiting harassment, bullying, discrimination, and hate crimes: Sample policy for Massachusetts School Districts (2005). Boston: Office of the Massachusetts Attorney General.

P.S. Tit. 24, § 13-1303.1A (2010).

Pupils not the only victims of cyber bullies, says NAS/UWT (2006, July 28). *Education Parliamentary Monitor, 231,* 4.

Putting U in the picture – Mobile bullying survey 2005. Retrieved from http://www. stoptextbullying.com.

Queally, J. (2011, February 13). Newark teen's online identity stolen and used to destroy her reputation. Retrieved from http://www.nj.com/news/index. ssf/2011/02/someone_had_stolen_a_network_te.html.

Raskauskas, J., & Stoltz, A.D. (2007). Involvement in traditional and electronic bullying among adolescents. *Developmental Psychology, 43,* 564–575.

Redeker, B. (2006, September 15). Town tells white separatist singers "no hate here." Retrieved from http://articles.news.aol.com/news/_a/town-tells-white-separatist-singers-no/.

Reeckman, B., & Cannard, L. (2009). Cyberbullying: A TAFE perspective. *Youth Studies Australia, 28,* 41–49.

Reese, T. (2006). Teens help teens stay safe online. Retrieved from http://www. connectforkids.org/node/4045.html.

Rehabilitation Act of 1973, 29 U.S.C. § 794 (2006). ("Section 504 of the Rehabilitation Act").

Rigby, K. (1993). School children's perceptions of their families and parents as a function of peer relations. *The Journal of Genetic Psychology, 154,* 501–513.

Rigby, K. (1994). Psychosocial functioning in families of Australian adolescent schoolchildren involved in bully/victim problems. *Journal of Family Therapy, 16,* 173–187.

Rigby, K. (1996). *Bullying in schools: And what to do about it.* Briston, PA: Jessica Kingsley Publishers.

Rigby, K. (2002). *New perspectives on bullying.* London: Jessica Kingsley Publishers.

Rigby, K., & Slee, P. T. (1993). Dimensions of interpersonal relations among Australian school children and their implications for psychological well-being. *Journal of Social Psychology, 133,* 33–42.

Rigby, K., & Slee, P. T. (1999). Australia. In P. K. Smith, Y. Morita, J. Junger-Tasl, D. Olweus, R. Catalano, & P. Slee (Eds.), *The nature of school bullying: A cross-national perspective* (pp. 324–339). London: Routledge.

Rivers, I., & Smith, P. K. (1994). Types of bullying behaviour and their correlates. *Aggressive Behavior, 20,* 359–368.

Robers, S., Zhang, J., Truman, J., & Snyder, T. D. (2010). *Indicators of school crime and safety: 2010* (NCES 2011-002/NCJ 230812). U.S. Department of Education, U.S. Department of Justice Office of Justice Programs. Retrieved from http:// nces.ed.gov/pubs2011/2011002.pdf.

Roberts, L. D., Smith, L. M., & Pollock, C. M. (2000). "U r a lot bolder on the net": Shyness and Internet use. In W. R. Crozier (Ed.), *Shyness: Development, consolidation, and change* (pp. 121–138). New York: Routledge.

Rodkin, P. C., & Hodges, E V. E. (2003). Bullies and victims in the peer ecology: Four questions for psychologists and school professionals. *School Psychology Review, 32,* 384–400.

Rogers v. United States, 422 U.S. 35 (1975).

Rosenberg, M. (1965). *Society and the adolescent self-image.* Princeton, NJ: Princeton University Press.

Ross, S. (Executive Producer). (2006, September 12). *Primetime* [television broadcast]. New York: American Broadcasting Company.

Roth, D. A., Coles, M. E., & Heimberg, R. G. (2002). The relationship between memories for childhood teasing and anxiety and depression in adulthood. *Journal of Anxiety Disorders, 16,* 149–164.

RSA 193-F:2 (2010).

Rubin, K. H., Cheah, C., & Menzer, M. M. (2010). Peers. In M. H. Bornstein (Ed.), *Handbook of cultural developmental science* (pp. 223–237). New York: Psychology Press.

Russell, D. W., Flom, E. K., Gardner, K. A., Cutrona, C. E., & Hessling, R. S. (2003). Who makes friends over the Internet?: Loneliness and the "virtual" community. *The International Scope Review,* 10. Retrieved from http://www.socialcapital-foundation.org/PUBLICATIONS/TISR_journal1/volume%202003/issue%2010/Presentation%20Russell%20&%20al.htm.

www.ryanpatrickhalligan.org.

Salmivalli, C. (1995). Bullies, victims, and those others: Bullying as a groups process. *Psylzologia, 30,* 364–372.

Salmivalli, C. (2010). Bullying and the peer group: A review. *Aggression and Violent Behavior, 15,* 112–120.

Saxe v. State College Area School District, 240 F.3d. 200 (3d. Cir. 2001).

S.C. Code Ann. § 59-63-120 (2009).

Schools face new cyber bullying menace (2006, May 28). *The New Zealand Herald.*

7-year-old's pic exploited on MySpace (2006, June 29). Retrieved from http://mycrimespace.Thetrenchcoat.com/.

Seper, C. (2005, February 14). School bullies can land in court. *The Plain Dealer.*

Sex and tech. (2008). Retrieved from http://www.thenationalcampaign.org/sextech/PDF/SexTech_Summary.pdf.

Shah, D. (2008, February 22). JuicyCampus gushes gossip. *The Daily Princetonian.* Retrieved from http://www.dailyprincetonian.com/2008/02/22/20117/.

Shariff, S. (2008). *Cyber-bullying: Issues and solutions for the school, the classroom, and the home.* New York: Taylor and Francis.

Shariff, S., & Gouin, R. (2005). Cyber dilemmas: Gendered hierarchies, free expression, and cyber-safety in schools. Retrieved from http://www.oii.ox.ac.uk/research/cybersafety/extensions/pdfs/papers/shaheen_shariff.pdf.

Shayne, B. (2011, February 18). CMPD investigates cyberbullying from "burn page." Retrieved from http://www.wcnc.com/news/local/CMPD-investigating-cyberbullying-from-burn-page-116504028.html.

Shields, A., & Cicchetti, D. (2001). Parental maltreatment and emotion dysregulation as risk factors for bullying and victimization in middle childhood. *Journal of Clinical Child Psychology, 30*, 349–363.

Slaby, R. G. (2002). Media violence: Effects and potential remedies. In J. Katzmann (Ed.), *Securing our children's future: New approaches to juvenile justice and youth violence* (pp. 305–337). Washington, DC: The Brookings Institution.

Slonje, R., & Smith, P. K. (2008). Cyberbullying: Another main type of bullying? *Scandanavian Journal of Psychology, 49*, 147–154.

Smith, A. (2007, January 19). Cyber bullying affecting 17% of teachers, poll finds. *The Guardian.* Retrieved from www.education.guardian.co.uk.

Smith, P., Mahdavi, J., Carvalho, M., & Tippett, N. (2006). An investigation into cyber bullying, its forms, awareness and impact, and the relationship between age and gender in cyber bullying. A report to the Anti-Bullying Alliance. Retrieved from http://www.dfes.gov.uk/research/data/uploadfiles/RBX03-06.pdf.

Smith, P. K., Mahdavi, J., Carvalho, M., Fisher, S., Russell, S., & Tippett, N. (2008). Cyber bullying: Its nature and impact in secondary school pupils. *Journal of Child Psychology and Psychiatry, 49*, 376–385.

Smith, P. K., & Sharp, S. (1994). *Bullying at school.* London: Routledge.

Smith, P. K., Talamelli, L., Cowie, H., Naylor, P., & Chauhan, P. (2004). Profiles of non-victims, escaped victims, continuing victims and new victims of school bullying. *British Journal of Educational Psychology, 74*, 565–581.

Smokowski, P. R., & Kopasz, K. H. (2005). Bullying in school: An overview of types, effects, family characteristics, and intervention strategies. *Children and Schools, 27*, 101–110.

Sobotka, V. (2011, January 18). Chicago student circulates degrading list of girls on Facebook. Retrieved from http://www.digitaljournal.com/article/302687.

Social networking sites confound schools (2007, January). *E-School News, 10(1)*, p. 1.

Social networking sites: Online friendships can mean offline peril (2006, April 3). Retrieved from http://www.fbi.gov/page2/april06/socialnetworking040306.htm.

Solis, B. (2011, March 20). Interview: Technorati's Richard Jalichandra on the state and future of social media. Retrieved from http://www. technorati.com/blogging/article/interview-technoratis-richard-jalichandra-on-the/.

Sourander, A., Klomek, A. B., Ikonen, M., Lindroos, J., Luntamo, T., Koskelainen, M., Ristkari, T., & Henenius, H. (2010). Psychosocial risk factors associated with cyber bullying among adolescents. *Archives of General Psychiatry, 67,* 720–728.

Spriggs, A. L., Iannotti, R. J., Nansel, T. R., & Haynie. D. L. (2007). Adolescent bullying involvement and perceived family, peer and school relations: Commonalities and differences across race/ethnicity. *Journal of Adolescent Health, 41,* 283–293.

Stamoulis, K. (2011, March 16). SMUT list: Another case of online slut bashing. *Psychology Today.* Retrieved from http://www.psychologytoday.com/blog/the-new-teen-age/201103/smut-list.

State of New Jersey, Department of Education. (2011). Model policy and guidance for prohibiting harassment, intimidation and bullying on school property, at school-sponsored functions and on school buses. Retrieved from: http://www.state.nj.us/education/parents/bully.htm.

Statistics summary for youtube.com. (2011). Retrieved from www.alexa.com/siteinfo/youtube.com.

Stevenson v. Martin County Board of Education, 3 Fed. Appx. 25 (4th Cir. 2001).

Stiles, B. (2009, January 13). Teens face porn charges in 'sexting.' Retrieved from http://www.pittsburghlive.com/x/pittsburghtrib/news/westmoreland/s_606854.html.

Storch, E. A., Lewin, A. B., Silverstein, J. H., Heidgerken, A. D., Strawser, M. S., Baumeister, A., & Geffken, G. R. (2004a). Peer victimization and psychosocial adjustment in children with type 1 diabetes. *Clinical Pediatrics, 43,* 467–471.

Storch, E. A., Lewin, A. B., Silverstein, J. H., Heidgerken, A. D., Strawser, M. S., Baumeister, A., & Geffken, G. R. (2004b). Social-psychological correlates of peer victimization in children with endocrine disorders. *Journal of Pediatrics, 145,* 784–789.

Sudnow, D. (1967). *Passing on: The social organization of dying.* Englewood Cliffs, NJ: Prentice-Hall.

Suler, J. (2004). The online disinhibition effect. *Cyberpsychology and Behavior, 7,* 321–326.

Sullivan, B. (2006, August 9). Cyber bullying newest threat to kids. Retrieved from http://www.msnbc.msn.com/id/14272228/.

Sum, S., Mathews, R. M., Hughes, I., & Campbell, A. (2008). Internet use and loneliness in older adults. *CyberPsychology & Behavior, 11,* 208–211.

Sutton, J., Smith, P. K., & Swettenham, J. (1999a). Bullying and "theory of mind": A critique of the "social skills deficit" view of anti-social behaviour. *Social Development, 8,* 117–127.

Sutton, J., Smith, P. K., & Swettenham, J. (1999b). Social cognition and bullying: Social inadequacy or skilled manipulation? *British Journal of Developmental Psychology, 17,* 435–450.

Swartz, J. (2005, March 7). Schoolyard bullies get nastier online. *USA Today,* p. 01a.

Swearer, S. M., Espelage, D. L., & Napolitano, S. A. (2009). *Bullying prevention & intervention: Realistic strategies for schools.* New York: Guilford.

Swearer, S. M., Grills, A. E., Haye, K. M., & Cary, P. T. (2004). Internalizing problems in students involved in bullying and victimization: Implications for intervention. In D. L. Espelage & S. M. Swearer (Eds.), *Bullying in American schools: A social-ecological perspective on prevention and intervention* (pp. 63–83). Mahwah, NJ: Erlbaum.

Swinford, S. (2006, June 4). Focus: The school bully is moving into cyberspace. Retrieved from http://www.timesonline.co.uk/article/o,2087-2209828,00.html.

Take charge: Teen survey results. Retrieved from http://www.cox.com/takecharge/survey_results.asp.

Teen online & wireless safety survey: Cyberbullying, sexting, and parental controls. Retrieved from http://www.cox.com/takeCharge/includes/docs/2009_teen_survey_internet_and_wireless_safety.pdf.

Tenn. Code Ann. § 49-6-1015 (2006).

Tex. Educ. Code § 25.0341 (2006).

Thibaut, J. W., & Kelley, H. H. (1959). *The social psychology of groups.* Oxford, England: Wiley.

Thompson, D., Whitney, I., & Smith, P. (1994). Bullying of children with special needs in mainstream schools. *Support for Learning, 9*, 103–106.

Thompson, P. (2011, March 24). Teen 'mean girl' charged with cyber-bullying after creating Facebook page calling classmates 'hoes.' Retrieved from www.dailymail.co.uk/news/article-1369299/Facebook-Mean-Girl-charged-cyber-bullying-calling-classmates-hoes.html.

Tinker v. Des Moines Independent Community School District, 383 U.S. 503 (1969).

Tokunaga, R.S. (2010). Following you home from school: A critical review and synthesis of research on cyber bullying victimization. *Computers in Human Behavior, 26,* 277–287.

Trach, J., Hymel, S., Waterhouse, T., & Neale, K. (2010). Bystander responses to school bullying: A cross-sectional investigation of grade and sex differences. *Canadian Journal of School Psychology, 25,* 114–130.

Ttofi, M. M., & Farrington, D. P. (2009). What works in preventing bullying: Effective elements of anti-bullying programs. *Journal of Aggression, Conflict and Peace Research, 1,* 13–24.

Ttofi, M. M., Farrington, D. P., & Baldry, A. C. (2008). *Effectiveness of programmes to reduce bullying.* Stockholm, Sweden: Swedish National Council for Crime.

Tweens and internet safety. Retrieved from http://www.cox.com/takecharge/safe_teens/research.html.

Twemlow, S. W., Sacco, F. C., & Williams, P. (1996). A clinical and interactionist perspective on the bully-victim-bystander relationship. *Bulletin of Menninger Clinic, 60,* 296–313.

Twyman, K. A., Saylor, C. F., Saia, D., Macias, M. M.,Taylor, L. A., & Spratt, E. (2010). Bullying and ostracism experiences in children with special health care needs. *Journal of Developmental & Behavioral Pediatrics, 31*, 1–8.

Undheim, A. M, & Sund, A. M. (2010). Prevalence of bullying and aggressive behavior and their relationship to mental health problems among 12- to 15-year-old Norwegian adolescents. *European Child & Adolescent Psychiatry, 19*, 803–811.

Unnever, J. (2001). *Roanoke City Project On Bullying*. Final report of the Roanoke school-based partnership bullying study. Unpublished manuscript.

Unnever, J., & Cornell, D. G. (2003a). Bullying, self control, and ADHD. *Journal of Interpersonal Violence, 18*, 129–147.

Unnever, J. D., & Cornell, D. G. (2003b). The culture of bullying in middle school. *Journal of School Violence, 2(2)*, 5–27.

U.S. Const., Amend. XIV.

U.S. Department of Education. (2010). *Anti-bullying policies: Examples of provisions in state laws*. Retrieved from: http://www2.ed.gov/print/policy/gen/guid/secletter/101215.html.

U.S. Department of Education Office for Civil Rights. (2010). Dear colleague letter harassment and bullying (October 26, 2010): Background, summary, and fast facts. Retrieved from: http://www2.ed.gov/about/offices/list/ocr/docs/dcl-factsheet-201010.pdf.

U.S. Department of Justice. (n.d.). Model acceptable use policy for information technology resources in the schools. Retrieved from: http://www.justice.gov/criminal/cybercrime/rules/acceptableUsePolicy.htm.

Van der Wal, M. F., de Wit, C. A. M., & Hirasing, R. A. (2003). Psychosocial health among young victims and offenders of direct and indirect bullying. *Pediatrics, 111*, 1312–1317.

Vandebosch, H., & Van Cleemput, K. (2009). Cyberbullying among youngsters: Profiles of bullies and victims. *New Media and Society, 11*, 1349–1371.

Varjas, K., Henrich, C. C., & Meyers, J. (2007). Urban middle school students' perceptions of bullying, cyberbullying, and school safety. *Journal of School Violence, 8*, 159–176.

Vervoort, M. H. M., & Scholte, R. H. J. (2010). Bullying and victimization among adolescents: The role of ethnicity and ethnic composition of school class. *Journal of Youth Adolescence, 39*, 1–11.

16 V.S.A. § 11 (2006).

Walsh, D. (2004). *Why do they act that way?: A survival guide to the adolescent brain for you and your teen*. New York: Free Press.

Walsh, D., Gentile, D., Walsh, E., & Bennett, N. (2006). 11th annual Mediawise video game report card. Retrieved from http://www.media-family.org/research/report_vgrc_2006.html.

Wang, J., Iannotti, R. J., & Luk, J. W. (2010). Bullying victimization among underweight and overweight U.S. youth: Differential associations for boys and girls. *Journal of Adolescent Health, 47*, 99–101.

Wang, J., Iannotti, R. J., & Nansel, T. R. (2009). School bullying among adolescents in the United States: Physical, verbal, relational, and cyber. *Journal of Adolescent Health, 45*, 368–375.

Watt, N. (2006, May 17). "Happy slapping" spreads in London: Random victims get videotaped while being assaulted on streets. Retrieved from http://abcnews.go.com/Nightline/print?id=1972548.

Watts v. United States, 394 U.S. 705 (1969).

www.webopedia.com.

What is Bebo?: Best uses, features, and statistics about Bebo. Retrieved from http://www.finelinemultimedia.com/blog/web-marketing/bebo-features-statistics-bebo/.

Whitney, I., Rivers, I., Smith, P., & Sharp, S. (1994). The Sheffield project: Methodology and findings. In P. Smith, & S. Sharp (Eds.), *School bullying: Insights and perspectives* (pp. 20–56). London: Routledge.

Whitney, I., & Smith, P. K. (1993). A survey of the nature and extent of bullying in junior/middle and secondary schools. *Educational Research, 35*, 3–25.

Wiener, J., & Mak, M. (2009). Peer victimization in children with Attention-Deficit/Hyperactivity Disorder. *Psychology in the Schools, 46*, 116–131.

Willard, N. (2006). *Cyber bullying and cyberthreats: Responding to the challenge of online social cruelty, threats, and distress.* Eugene, OR: Center for Safe and Responsible Internet Use.

Willard, N. (2007). *An educator's guide to cyberbullying.* Center for Safe and Responsible Internet Use. Retrieved from http://www.cyberbully.org/docs/cpct.educators.pdf.

Williams, K., Chambers, M., Logan, S., & Robinson, D. (1996). Association of common health symptoms with bullying in primary school children. *British Medical Journal, 313*, 17–19.

Williams, K., Cheung, C. K. T., & Choi, W. (2000). Cyberostracism: Effects of being ignored over the Internet. *Journal of Personality and Social Psychology, 79*, 748–762.

Williams, K., Harkins, S., & Latané, B. (1981). Identifiability as a deterrent to social loafing: Two cheering experiments. *Journal of Personality and Social Psychology, 40*, 303–311.

Williams, K. R., & Guerra, N. G. (2007). Prevalence and predictors of Internet bullying. *Journal of Adolescent Health, 41*, S14–21.

Williams, T., Connolly, J., Pepler, D., & Craig, W. (2003). Questioning and sexual minority adolescents: High school experiences of bullying, sexual harassment and physical abuse. *Canadian Journal of Community Mental Health, 22*, 47–58.

Wing, C. (2005, November). Young Canadians in a wired world. Retrieved from http://www.media-awareness.ca.

Wolak, J., & Finkelhor, D. (March, 2011). Sexting: A typology. *Bulletin Produced by the University of New Hampshire Crimes Against Children Research Center.* Retrieved from http://www.unh.edu/ccrc/pdf/CV231_Sexting%20 Typology%20Bulletin_4-6-11_revised.pdf.

Wolak, J., Mitchell, K., & Finkelhor, D. (2006). Online victimization of youth: Five years later. Retrieved from http://www.unh.edu/ccrc/pdf/CV138.pdf.

Wong-Lo, M., & Bullock, L. M. (2011). Digital aggression: Cyberworld meets school bullies. *Preventing School Failure, 55,* 64–70.

Word IQ. (2006). Retrieved from http://www.wordiq.com/definition/ Restorative_justice.

World of Warcraft subscriber base reaches 12 million worldwide. (2010, October 7). Retrieved from http://us.blizzard.com/en-us/company/press/pressreleases. html?101007.

Ybarra, M., Diener-West, M., & Leaf, P. (2007). Examining the overlap in Internet harassment and school bullying: Implications for school intervention. *Journal of Adolescent Health, 41,* 542–550.

Ybarra, M. L., & Mitchell, K. J. (2004). Online aggressor/targets, aggressors, and targets: A comparison of associated youth characteristics. *Journal of Child Psychology and Psychiatry, 45,* 1308–1316.

Ybarra, M. L., Mitchell, K. J., Wolak J., & Finkelhor, D. (2006). Examining characteristics and associated distress related to Internet harassment: Findings from the second youth internet safety survey. *Pediatrics, 118,* 1169–1177.

YouTube. (2006, August 30). In *Wikipedia, the free encyclopedia.* Retrieved from http://en.wikipedia.org/w/index.php?title=YouTube&oldid=72890340.

Yuan, L. (2006, April 30). Social networking goes mobile. *The Kansas City Star,* H16.

Yude, C., Goodman, R., & McConachie, H. (1998). Peer problems of children with hemiplegia in mainstream primary schools. *Journal of Child Psychology and Psychiatry, 39,* 533–541.

Žaborskis, A., Cirtautienė, L., & Žemaitienė, N. (2005). Bullying in Lituanian schools in 1994–2004. *Medicina (Kaunas), 41,* 614–620.

Zayas, A. (2006, August 28). Do online deaths prompt teens to suicide? *St. Petersburg Times.* Retrieved from http://www.sptimes.com/2006/08/28/Tampabay/ Do_online_death_dialo_shtml.

AUTHOR INDEX

Cyberbullying: Bullying in the Digital Age, Second Edition. Robin M. Kowalski, Susan P. Limber, and Patricia W. Agatston.
© 2012 Robin M. Kowalski, Susan P. Limber, and Patricia W. Agatston.
Published 2012 by Blackwell Publishing Ltd.

Author Index 269

Shields, A. 39, 256
Shimodera, S. 243
Shute, R. 104, 252
Silverstein, J. H. 32, 257
Simon, T. R. 234
Simons-Morton, B. 21, 237
Slaby, R. G. 231, 256
Slee, P. T. 22, 33, 36, 43, 104, 241–2,
    250, 252, 254
Slonje, R. 106, 256
Smith, A. 59, 247, 256
Smith, L. 80, 246
Smith, L. M. 8, 255
Smith, P. K. 36, 39, 46, 57, 83,
    99, 103, 105–6, 121, 250,
    254, 256–8, 260
Smith, R. 238
Smith, W. 32, 248
Smokowski, P. R. 31, 256
Snyder, M. 252
Snyder, T. D. 21, 24, 238, 254
Sobotka, V. 14, 256
Soeda, H. 22, 250
Soeda, K. 22, 250
Solis, B. 76, 256
Solomon, S. 113, 249–50
Sourander, A. 83, 86, 257
Spratt, E. 31, 259
Spriggs, A. L. 27–8, 257
Stamoulis, K. 12, 257
Stanfield, A. 69, 248
Steffen, S. 70, 240
Stiles, B. 257
Stoltz, A. D. 99, 101, 107, 254
Stoltz, V. 239
Storch, E. A. 32, 110, 238, 257
Story, M. 32, 239–40
Stouthamer-Loeber, M. 53, 248
Strawser, M. S. 32, 257
Strohmeier, D. 28, 240
Sudnow, D. 66, 257
Suler, J. 86, 257

Sulkowski, M. L. 110, 238
Sullivan, B. 2, 257
Sum, S. 10, 257
Sund, A. M. 33, 259
Sutton, J. 39, 257
Swartz, J. 63, 257
Swearer, S. M. 26, 30, 214–15,
    217, 222, 233, 236, 239,
    247, 252, 258
Swettenham, J. 39, 257
Swinford, S. 72–3, 258

Taki, M. 22, 250
Talamelli, L. 34, 256
Tanaka, G. 243
Taylor, A. 31, 235
Taylor, L. A. 31, 259
Thibaut, J. W. 8, 258
Thompson, D. 31, 258
Thompson, N. L. 74, 249
Thompson, P. 14, 258
Tippett, N. 99, 256
Tokunaga, R. S. 98, 103, 105,
    225, 258
Tortolero, S. R. 29, 253
Trach, J. 43–4, 258
Tracy, A. J. 20, 248
Truman, J. 21, 97, 254
Ttofi, M. M. 52, 258
Turner, H. 24–5, 241
Twemlow, S. W. 43, 258
Twyman, K. A. 31–2, 259

Underwood, K. 36, 235
Undheim, A. M. 33, 259
Unnever, J. 31, 43, 259

Van Cleemput, K. 82, 259
Van der Wal, M. F. 34, 259
Vandebosch, H. 82, 259
Varjas, K. 83, 259
Verloove-VanHorick, S. P. 30, 33, 240

SUBJECT INDEX

ABC News 57
absenteeism 34, 226
academic performance 34–5, 123–4,
    158–9, 226
acceptable use policies 163–4, 178,
    218, 219
accessibility 11, 83–4
accountability circles 136, 182–6
adolescents see children; students
adults
    reporting bullying to 35, 121–2,
        139–40, 164–5
    supervision by 50–1, 227
    see also educators; parents; staff (in
        schools); teachers
age factors
    bullying (traditional) and
        25–6, 103
    cyberbullying and 59, 103–4, 225
    use of cyber technology and 6–7
aggression 19, 79, 82, 89, 104, 108
    direct/indirect 104
    proactive 38, 78
    reactive 38, 78
    of victims 41, 42
    see also bullying

Alabama 189
Alaska 189, 198
Alexa 74
Allen, Ernie 6
American Online (AOL) 60, 85, 90,
    152
American Psychological
    Association 23, 47
Americans with Disabilities Act
    (1990) 201, 203
anonymity 6, 9, 11, 16, 79, 82, 83, 86,
    148, 229
antisocial behavior 40, 47, 54
anxiety 30–1, 33, 35, 37, 38, 41, 226
    Interaction Anxiousness Scale 110
    social 8, 16, 78–9, 110–12, 113,
        114, 117
apologies 141
Arizona 189, 198
Arkansas 188, 189, 197
assessment 50, 161–2
Associated Press 69
Association of Teachers and
    Lecturers 59
Attention Deficit Hyperactivity
    Disorder (ADHD) 31